Hospitality Marketing

Neil Wearne was the marketing specialist and lecturer at the Regency Hotel School in South Australia from 1989. In that time he developed marketing courses and lectured students in the Diploma of Business (Hospitality). He combined his extensive experience in marketing management with his flair for communication to write a number of texts for students of hospitality marketing. Neil's talents in the areas of human behaviour, communication, illustration and writing produced a focus on the practical aspects of marketing which students understood. He maintained involvement with the hospitality industry and was able to inspire students with reference to current hospitality business practices. He maintained a dynamic marketing perspective, and is remembered by colleagues and students for his vital energy and innovative approaches to learning.

Sadly, Neil Wearne died suddenly on 4 June 1993.

Grahame Latham
Head, Regency Hotel School

Hospitality Marketing

Neil Wearne

Revised by Alison J. Morrison

Butterworth-Heinemann
Linacre House, Jordan Hill, Oxford OX2 8DP
225 Wildwood Avenue, Woburn, MA 01801-2041
A division of Reed Educational and Professional Publishing Ltd

A member of the Reed Elsevier plc group

OXFORD   BOSTON   JOHANNESBURG
MELBOURNE   NEW DELHI   SINGAPORE

First published by Hospitality Press Lty Ltd 1994
First published in Great Britain 1996
Reprinted 1998

British Library Cataloguing in Publication Data
Wearne, Neil
 Hospitality Marketing
 I. Title II. Morrison, Alison
 647.940688

ISBN 0 7506 2688 7

Printed and bound in Great Britain by Bath Press, Bath

Contents

Foreword

There is so little written in the field of hospitality marketing that when something definitive comes along, it's overwhelming. Neil Wearne has been laying a foundation for practical hospitality marketing for years and now *Hospitality Marketing* is the capstone on a masterpiece – 'must reading' for those in the industry as for those who would be in the industry. Today's competitive marketplace demands hospitality marketing skills and focus – a most important book at the right time.

Michael E. Hurst
15th Street Fisheries
Fort Lauderdale, Florida

Preface

This book is for students of hospitality, which means it is not only a textbook for people seeking a tertiary qualification in the subject of hospitality marketing but also for those wanting to add to their knowledge of the business.

There are thirty-three chapters, each one covering a topic of marketing. This enables a course to be structured around this work by creating either two terms of sixteen lessons (plus a bonus lesson) or three terms of eleven lessons.

Every endeavour has been made to make it an easy book to read with a minimal requirement for referral to a lecturer or other sources of information.

Operators and executives will discover that in many areas of marketing fresh insights are put forward that will materially assist them in the management of their establishments.

The teaching approach taken in this book is to direct the decisions concerning marketing strategies towards what happens to and for the customers. The objective is to build a customer base by constantly improving the customers' experiences at the point of sale. This approach is fundamentally different from the operators of establishments who consider marketing as primarily concerned with sales and advertising. This book shifts the major emphasis of hospitality marketing onto building a business from the inside by word-of-mouth rather than relying mostly on the endeavours of outside promotion.

Marketing is not like mathematics. There are very few true absolutes. Whereas in mathematics a hundred people can add up the same set of figures and should all arrive at the same answer, a hundred marketing people could be given a mass of data and arrive at a hundred separate marketing plans. Each plan may appear to be as workable as the other. In practice, though, the chances are that twenty will be successful, another thirty will provide a mediocre result, and the remaining fifty will fail with various degrees of haste.

There is a limited certainty in the implementation of a marketing strategy because its success or otherwise is reliant upon the reactions of people, singly and in large numbers, who form a market. The unpredictability of human behaviour means no one can be sure what people will do in a given set of circumstances. One can only assess what is most likely to happen based on how the market has reacted before. Upon this history of behaviour are the theories of marketing based.

Marketing is a series of decisions, and it is referred to as a process because in practice it is better to follow a step-by-step discipline to arrive at the best means of capitalizing on an opportunity or overcoming a difficulty. Without this discipline, one can overlook or fail to consider some aspect of the process.

The subject is learned by an examination of common practice and a study of the theories which have evolved from the experiences of others over time. To assist the student and the practitioner of hospitality marketing, in this book there are lists and procedures which can be referred to or memorized to help in deciding what to do when planning customer outcomes.

Throughout this book the subject of marketing is taught by stating the theory behind the topic, or defining its meaning, explaining how the theory is applied, giving examples and providing lists of options for application of the theory.

Acknowledgements

I would like to thank Jacquie Shanahan for this first (of what I hope is many) publication opportunity. A special mention goes to Jean Finlayson for her expert assistance in the production of the text. I doubt if Jean will ever forget the day a slip of her little finger wiped the computer disk of a third of this book! However, the most sincere of acknowledgements must go to the late Neil Wearne, the originator of this book. He brought a fresh, no nonsense, highly practical approach to the marketing of hospitality. As he said, hospitality is all about people and for people. It should be exciting and fun for all concerned as, in effect, that is the *raison d'être* of hospitality.

1   *The marketing function*

Aims of this chapter

1   To familiarize the reader with the subject of marketing by explaining its main functions and its role in society.
2   To explain the terms market, market demand, marketing, product and marketing planning.
3   To show how hospitality establishments make money.
4   To introduce the first steps of the marketing planning process.

Let's put marketing into perspective

Marketing should be an easy subject to understand because everywhere one looks there is evidence of marketing activity. There are media advertising, advertising signs, delivery vans, shops and retailers of all descriptions, factories, personal services and of course hotels and restaurants in profusion, and they are all visible indications of people busily marketing their businesses and their products for money and profit.

Fundamentally, marketing is about attracting customers and selling them products. The complexities of the subject arise from endeavouring to build or expand a market, and from the necessity in an open market to compete against others for the available business. This requires the owner of a business to have merchandise which has maximum sales appeal, prices which offer value, and additional services such as a central reservations office and credit facilities which make it easier for customers to make their purchases.

For the operator of a hospitality establishment, marketing is the means by which they can turn the basics of food, beverages and accommodation into desirable products by adding value through service and presentation. Being a good marketer is arguably the most important skill to have in business. It is an over-simplification to say this, but if there are no sales there is no business requiring other skills.

In the minor sense, selling a hot dog from a mobile stand involves a marketing function. Marketing a range of brands, such as those promoted by the Forte organization nationally and internationally through a computerized distribution network, is an example of marketing in the major sense.

Marketing can be more correctly defined as the process of creating, or making available, products and services which satisfy market needs and wants. The marketing process involves careful planning by management to allow for a large number of market variables. All of these market variables are caused by the separate requirements and preferences of people who, when grouped together, comprise a market.

The starting point in marketing planning is always people and their needs and wants. Other variables which management must consider include the financial and human resources at their disposal and the external influences which may not be within their ability to control, such as government actions and economic change.

Among the many important factors which have to be considered by management in the marketing process are the actions of competitors. Other establishments in a given market are constantly endeavouring to increase their share of available business. Financial loss or profit for a business owner depends on the success or otherwise of the moves and counter-moves used in a competitive marketing environment.

In the hospitality industry in particular, marketing is a term often used when referring to selling and advertising. However, marketing is not just selling and advertising. Yes, they are important marketing activities, but they are not the communication components of marketing. Effective marketing requires planning from the initial conception of a product right through to its delivery to the customer and thereafter to the retention of the customer. So, whereas selling and advertising are the noticeable aspects of marketing, they are only part of a total planning process.

A historical perspective

Marketing is as old as civilization. It is the origin of business. It started with simple bartering and then evolved into the centralized exchange process of a town market. Before long, trade – the exchange of goods and services for money – began between cities and countries. This resulted in large numbers of merchants venturing to distant places, across oceans and continents in search of new markets and opportunities for trade. Towns, roads, sea routes, train lines and air routes have resulted from trade requiring the movement of goods to markets and for buyers to get to the markets. Empire building and many wars have been brought about by nations and corporations greedy for bigger markets and/or access to markets denied to them by trading nations protecting their own markets.

The growth of hospitality has always been tied to the expansion of business, tourism and travel, and is arguably the oldest professional activity. Providing travellers with a place to stay and eat is mentioned in the earliest writings of people, and the concept of a hotel (public house or inn) pre-dates the Bible. In fact, the Egyptians, Greeks and Romans built pleasure and tourist resorts which rivalled today's massive complexes in style and grandeur, if not in modern appliances.

Civilization mainly functions as a consequence of trade and marketing. The successors to the traders or merchants of the past who searched for and found solutions to people's needs and wants are now called marketers. In the last 150 years, the process of either providing services or developing goods that can be manufactured and sold for profit has become a sophisticated business practice referred to as 'marketing'. Most markets don't just happen, they are brought into being by those who understand how people think. Good marketers have an appreciation of the fact that most people want to improve their way of life, and create products and services which help them to achieve that.

Hospitality means kindness in welcoming strangers or guests. The word comes from the Latin *hospes*, meaning guest, and developed into *hospice*, a place of shelter for travellers. These days, the services (or products) offered to the modern traveller by hospitality establishments can cater for every human comfort. The hospitality business is a massive industry encompassing all forms of transport, tourism, accommodation, eating, drinking, entertainment, recreation and activities. It is the world's largest employer of people and a vast consumer of physical resources. Some countries depend almost entirely on tourism and business travel and the consequent use that visitors make of the country's hospitality facilities. Even in a wealthy country such as the United States, tourism and hospitality is one of the three biggest income-earning industries.

The impact of hospitality marketing on society

A new project, factory or real estate development can be a huge boost to the prosperity of a city or region, involving finance, the production of a wide range of materials and the employment of large numbers of people. The influx of work extends to the increased sale of food, cars and consumer goods, etc., as the wage earners spend their earnings. This is called the multiplier effect.

An increase in tourism has the same multiplier effect, which is why it is so important. The provision of tourist facilities and hospitality establishments for a city or region is called its infrastructure. The market demand for hospitality in a city or region will determine the extent of its infrastructure and therefore how many hotels, budget lodges, tourist resorts, restaurants, special interest parks, etc. are required.

The demand for hospitality may change for reasons of government action, weather, business booms and busts, tourism fashions, special events, festivals, building projects or simply increased money and availability. Economic, political and environmental change can quickly affect this volatile industry. Suddenly, there can be either an under-supply or over-supply of facilities. The challenge for marketers is to meet each development and maintain a viable customer base.

With the exception of 1991 and 1986, the total number of overseas visitors to the UK rose steadily between 1980 and 1990. The overall decline in visitors in 1986 was largely attributable to a 25 per cent fall in numbers from North America, who feared Arab reprisals due to the Libyan bombing. In addition, the nuclear disaster at Chernobyl raised fears of a nuclear fallout in Europe. A similar decline occurred in 1991 when the Gulf War and the recession in the

Figure 1.1

USA caused the number of American visitors to the UK to fall by 22 per cent. As a result, 1986 and 1991 were times when there was an extreme over-supply of facilities. During 1991 the average room occupancy achieved by UK hotels was 54 per cent.

While the recession was a disaster for most of the hospitality industry, it created a golden opportunity for budget hotels. The limited facilities they offered were of less concern to travellers than the very attractive price which stood, in 1995, at £30–£35 for room only. As a result, in less than a decade the budget market has become the fastest-growing hotel sector in the UK. From virtually no purpose-built budget accommodation in the mid-1980s, the UK now boasts nearly 300, with a further 160 units expected by 1997. Regular, average room occupancy levels are approximately 80 per cent.

These two examples show that investment planning should be selective to growth areas in tourism and that the hospitality industry must be realistic about the sudden swings in demand which can and do occur. It is a very dynamic business and every decade witnesses a shift in market demand for varying types of accommodation and products.

In the 1950s and 1960s formal dining was provided mostly by the grander, traditional hotels and restaurants. It was expensive and consequently only accessible to a wealthy minority. In the last thirty years, lifestyles have changed from eating out being an exception to being the norm, embracing the widest range of restaurants and cuisines. Nowadays, the majority of the population have learned to enjoy the pleasures of dining out. Currently, nearly every nationality's food is represented in major cities. Even rural and coastal towns can usually boast a range of regional and ethnic restaurant outlets, serving quality food and offering a fair selection of wines.

There has been a steady shift in preference from formal to casual and lower priced eating out for several decades. This trend accelerated with the 1990s recession. As a consequence, during the 1990s new trends in travel, tourism and accommodation requirements have emerged. As the changes continue, the study of the hospitality industry, as always, has to be based on the reasons why people travel, why certain destinations are preferred and why certain types of accommodation and hospitality will be in demand.

Markets, market demand and other definitions

Some of the main terms used in marketing require definition. A market is a place of trade, or a group of people who have common needs and wants. Needs are basic human requirements such as food, shelter, transport, money, security and sex. Wants are the individual ways in which people prefer to satisfy their needs. For example, someone may need a vehicle to get to work and use for recreation, but they will prefer or want a particular type and brand of car. Some may want a bicycle or a motor bike.

For a hospitality business, a market is a group of people who require a place to stay, eat or drink. Because not everyone wants the same solution to their need for a product, there are many sub-markets, and products are developed which satisfy the requirements of each of these sub-markets. These sub-markets are termed market segments.

The size of a market is measured by the total number of people who want a particular type of product or service to satisfy their needs. This is called market demand. A coffee shop in a remote village, for example, would find that its market would be small and therefore there would be limited demand for its services.

The differences in the wants and needs of each market segment may be the result of where people live, their age, how they live, the size of their families, how much money they have to spend, their lifestyle preferences, what they want to achieve in life, peer group pressure or their attitudes towards the way a product performs or functions. The understanding of these differences is part of the planning process called market analysis, and the process of measuring the differences is covered by demographics (the science of population statistics) and psychodynamics or psychographics (the study of mental processes and forces).

What is a product? Services are products. Ideas are products. Countries and cities are products. People can be products. Anything that can be marketed is a product. (In not all instances is there a profit motive.) A hotel refers to everything it markets as a product or an outlet, such as a bedroom, bar, restaurant, room service, leisure facilities or a valet service.

How do they make their money?

The hospitality industry consists of a large number of different types of business, with each one having its own means of producing income. The main types of businesses in the category of hospitality are hotels, self-catering accommodation, guest houses, restaurants, pubs and bars and tourist resorts. Each style of establishment has one thing in common – they all add value to their business activity by providing a place for guests and giving service in exchange for a fee. The difference between what it costs the hospitality establishment to provide the place and the service, and the fee received in return, is called profit. Bedrooms, bars, restaurants, room service, leisure facilities and valet service, etc. are called 'products' or 'outlets' by the industry. Each product or outlet is expected to contribute to the hotel's income, which is why they can also be referred to as 'profit-earning centres'.

A hotel and other tourist accommodation receives most of its income from its main product, which is room hire or accommodation, representing around 45 per cent of its total revenue. This is why a hotel's occupancy rate (the number of customers occupying beds) is of continuing concern to the management of a property. Currently, annual average room occupancy varies between around 60 per cent and 70 per cent depending on geographic location. That means, on average throughout the year, between 60 per cent and 70 per cent of available rooms should be occupied. Obviously, some months the percentage will be lower and other months it will be higher than the average. For those hotels which are dependent on the business traveller, fewer rooms will be occupied on weekends than on working days. One of the management's marketing jobs therefore is to fill the down periods with customers to maintain the desired occupancy percentage average. They do this by offering special-value packages, weekend rates and holiday package rates. They also seek accommodation business from conventions, seminars, conferences and groups.

Providing rooms for guests requires a considerable investment by the owners of a property in the building, its facilities and fittings. This money is recovered over a period of time by including a fixed amount (called capital recovery) into the room rate. As well as providing a comfortable, often stylish property for guests to stay in, the hotel has to employ staff for cleaning, maintenance, reception, guest services and sales. In addition, it has to have people to manage and administrate. There are many sundry costs involved in the running of a hotel. These expenses, largely involving labour, are termed 'general overheads', and they too are incorporated as a percentage of the room rate.

The amount which is charged for room rate, the end price to the guest, depends on three factors: (1) the perceived value to guests provided by the hotel's property and services; (2) the market demand for hotel facilities and services prevailing at the time; and (3) the intensity of competition offered by other hotel operators.

After room hire, the next highest income earner for hotels is food and beverage sales – that is, their restaurants, bars, coffee shops, room service and the food and beverage required for functions, conferences, etc. Industry figures indicate that food sales account for around 34 per cent and beverages for 14 per cent of most UK hotel incomes. Minor operating departments, including telephone calls made by guests, provide a further 5 per cent of income. Rentals for shops owned by a property, such as a hairdresser, florist, newsagent, clothes shop, etc., contribute 1 per cent. These businesses are often independent operators who gain customers from the hotel's guests. The remaining 1 per cent of a hotel's income is contributed by services paid by guests for such things as laundry, valet, leisure facilities, health club, etc., depending on the type of operation.

Apart from the establishments which provide accommodation only, nearly every other type of hospitality business makes money from food and beverage sales. They buy raw materials, such as food produce and beverages, and add value by using labour to turn them into some form of value added product or service for sale to customers.

As a general rule for food and beverage types of outlets, the cost of materials amounts to about a third of the sale price; the labour required to make and service the products amounts to another third; and the remaining third is gross profit. The gross profit has to allow for a percentage to cover either capital recovery or rent (if the premises are leased) and the general overheads. What is left is net profit before tax. Owners and managers of establishments endeavour to minimize the running costs of materials, labour, overheads, interest paid on capital and rent so that they can maximize the amount of profit. This requires a careful balance between what the customers are prepared to pay and how much it costs to provide the products.

The marketing function has to take this balance into consideration. Its purpose is to find customers and meet their demands by providing products and services which have sufficient value to attract them to buy at the right price. If the marketing job is done well, the establishment will make money.

Marketing planning

Marketing is like a journey. One has to plan for it. This is called the marketing plan, and there are many factors to consider in marketing planning. The principles involved are universal and can be adapted to almost any business or organizational activity. To continue with the analogy of marketing and a journey, there has to be a destination and a reason for going there. These are called marketing objectives. One has to prepare for the journey and find out as much as possible about what can be seen and enjoyed at the ultimate destination. It is wise to be prepared for any likely happening. This is market analysis. The means of getting there, the route to be taken and how the problems of travel can be overcome are called strategies. Strategies are designed to achieve objectives. Marketing planning is a series of steps which make use of procedures and disciplines to direct one's thinking so that all the available information is examined before making a decision on the best strategies to implement.

The acronym ORGANISATION is an easy way of remembering the steps involved in the strategic planning process of marketing.

O: *Orientation*. What is the business about? What is its mission? A motive of making money. If it doesn't make money it won't survive, so making money is simply saying 'surviving'. A mission statement must describe the areas of activity in which it intends to operate, which services or products it intends to provide and which needs and wants of the market it proposes to satisfy. It should also express a sound philosophy upon which to base attitudes to customer service, management and staff policies.

R: *Research*. Who needs or wants the business and its products? One can never have enough information about the market in which the business intends to operate. A study of the people who comprise the market and its segments is mandatory.

G: *Gather data*. It is essential to know what is happening in the market place. Much of this information can be obtained from sales figures, market share, customer preferences, competition, etc.

A: *Analyse the data*. Assess the market. When all the available information is sorted, a big picture of the market should emerge. Decisions can now be made.

N: *Narrow* the total market to target markets and select the most viable ones.

I: *Identify* what you want to achieve. Set marketing objectives, the engine or driving force for the entire marketing planning process.

S: *Strategies*. Decide the marketing mix strategies, the methods to be employed which will achieve the marketing objectives. The marketing mix strategies are People, Product, Positioning, Price, Place and Promotion.

A: *Arrange* distribution. Decide where and how you will sell the establishment and its products.

T: *Tactics*. Decide which tactics you will use to implement the strategies. Tactics are short-term strategies, the communication tools of marketing, which usually embrace the promotion functions of selling, advertising, sales promotion, direct mail, publicity, etc.

I: *Implement* the plan. Inform the market through promotions or tactical communications.

O: *Observe* the results. What changed as a result of the plan? More customers? A larger market share? Greater awareness?

N: *Next.* What changes, improvements or modifications to the plan are now necessary to make the marketing more effective?

These are the basics of marketing. Each of these steps will be explained in full in the forthcoming chapters, but as can already be seen, marketing is really common sense.

Questions for discussion or revision

1   Provide some examples of the 'multiplier effect' of recent changes to the economy as a result of government actions.
2   What would be the multiplier effect of building a new hotel in your home town? How many people, products or services can you identify that would be involved or affected in some way?
3   We tend to think of a 'thing' when we use the term 'product'. Can you name some products which are not things?
4   By applying the definition of marketing to a hotel, and associating that definition with the dictionary definition of 'hospitality', what should be a hotel's main marketing concern?
5   A first stage of the strategic planning process in marketing is orientation. Orientate your college or university department as if your job was to market it.

Further reading

Medlik, S. (1994). *The Business of Hotels*. Oxford: Butterworth-Heinemann.

2 The marketing environment

Aims of this chapter

1 To show the importance of having a mission statement which describes the intentions of a business for the benefit of the owners, its staff, its customers and its suppliers.
2 To explain the environmental factors which have to be considered by management when establishing a marketing programme for a hospitality establishment.

The importance of the mission statement

If you don't understand the environment you are in you won't know where you are. If you don't have a mission you won't know what you are doing or why you are doing it. Every business has a purpose. Sure, its main purpose is profit, but that is like saying that the purpose of life is survival. A business has to provide a benefit to customers which is seen by them as a perceptible reason for its existence. There has to be a mission for the business which is not its existence and which is not merely oriented to profit. A mission describes how the business will achieve a profitable outcome. It has to nominate its purpose for being and stipulate the benefits it intends to provide to its customers and staff and, in the broadest sense these days, the contributions it intends to make to the greater good of society.

In the words of Peter F. Drucker, one of America's doyens of marketing and management, 'What the customer thinks he is buying, what he considers "value", is decisive – it determines what a business is, what it produces and whether it will prosper'. Therefore, before corporate goals are finalized and marketing planning can commence, management has to make a careful scrutiny of the market environment before deciding in which areas of the market it intends the business will operate. There may be many options, but not all options will be viable. Some markets may be overcrowded, others too difficult to be worthwhile. In addition, management has to assess the financial and human resources at its disposal. It should not attempt to compete in a market against competitors who can out-gun the establishment with money, size and superior experience.

The corporate goals and the corporate philosophies give an operation its purpose, style, image and policies, and they need to be written down in the form of a mission statement. A mission statement isn't something which gets stuffed in a drawer and forgotten about. It should be a living document which is meant to keep the business on track.

It is usually easier for a licensed club to prepare a mission statement because in most cases the club is created mainly for the benefits of its members or the needs of a local community, and such needs are known at the time of inception. For example, the mission statement for a golf club which is in a provincial town may read like this:

> Our aim is to provide membership to the local community which will enhance its quality of life. Such membership will give access to a challenging course. Furthermore, members will have exclusive club rooms providing a choice of either relaxing in a quiet, convivial lounge equipped with satellite TV, or the use of a fully stocked bar and accompanying restaurant. It is also the aim of the club to provide accommodation for a limited number of members' guests or honoured visitors who will be invited at the behest of the Club's board of management.

The message conveyed by this mission statement example provides little doubt about its intentions, and one gets the picture of an ageing membership with very settled, traditional views of life.

The business decisions required in the formulation of the mission statement, or the re-formulation when conditions change, depend on the environmental factors of the market in which it operates. The areas of specialization or emphasis will depend on the needs of the market to be targeted and the knowledge and experience of the operators to satisfy those needs adequately.

The aim of large hotels, for example, is to produce a quality guest experience. A hotel is a product in itself but which has many diversified sub-products forming a product mix. Its products may include accommodation, bars, off-sales, restaurant, laundry and, in many cases, a variety of recreational facilities such as leisure club, golf course, tennis courts, equestrian centre and more. Which of these products should be offered to customers and in what form? Whatever management decides, the reputation or image of the hotel will impact on all its products.

A small hotel has to fit as a whole entity into the physical and social ambience of a city or local community. A large four or five-star hotel has to meet the needs of a much larger clientele – domestic and international business people and tourists as well as the local market – but it still has to fit in with the environment of the region.

All of these considerations should be incorporated into a 'mission statement' so that there can be no doubt about what type of operation it is in the minds of its customers, its suppliers, its employees and every other individual or company associated with it in some way.

Here is a case situation where an establishment did not make it clear what it was.

Imagine a city hotel which is supposedly competing with Sheraton, Hilton, Marriot and Forte hotels among others. Imagine now a businesswoman who has decided to stay over because she hasn't quite finished some important negotiations with a customer. The place looks nice and the rates are attractive so she decides to book in.

'What time does the restaurant open?' she enquires casually as she is signing. 'We don't have a restaurant, madam,' says the receptionist. 'There are plenty of very good restaurants in the vicinity. However, breakfast is brought to you in the room at the time you nominate,' he adds, with a reassuring smile.

Somewhat taken aback, she pauses. 'Well, can I get a drink before I set forth on a voyage of discovery to find a restaurant? You know, sort of one for the road? Where's the bar?' The receptionist smiles apologetically. 'We don't have a bar either. Again, there are plenty of places to drink nearby.' 'How about having a drink in the room, then? No good?' she asks a little acidly. The receptionist grimaces, shamefaced. 'Sorry, we don't have room service, or a bar facility in the room. It is residential only. That's how we can maintain our low rates, you see,' he explains, with a dismissive shrug. He adds hopefully: 'We have a pool, sauna, gymnasium, squash court, half-court tennis.' 'Sorry, I wasn't actually looking for a place to have a work-out,' she responds, and hands the pen back to the receptionist. 'Look, I'm tired, hungry and thirsty. Can you tell me where I'll find a real hotel?'

The receptionist looks hurt and half-heartedly recommends some names. The woman listens impatiently and then picks up her bag. 'You're against alcohol, aren't you!' It is an accusation more than a question. 'As a matter of fact, we don't encourage drinking, madam.' He waves a hand indicating the whole building. 'I think you'll find what we offer, though, is appreciated by a large number of people. It is quiet, there is privacy, and we don't charge as much as others. You will always get a good night's sleep here.'

The woman stops. What she needs is a good night's sleep. Does she really need to drink in her room? She can get a meal and a glass or two of wine virtually next door and then retire to her quiet room, glance through her papers in preparation for the next day and face it refreshed. She puts down her bag and asks for the pen back.

The point of the case situation is that the hotel wasn't making its 'residential only' feature obvious from the beginning. The benefit being offered was a good night's sleep in a quiet, undisturbed atmosphere. It is arguable whether an alcohol-free policy could guarantee peace and quiet; however, the hotel was offering a marketable difference from the high-profile places in the same market.

The mission statement for an establishment like the example may read like this:

Our aim is to provide an alcohol-free environment for guests so that there is an alternative for those people who prefer to abstain. Around 30 per cent of people seldom or never drink alcohol, and it is our intention to cater for their needs. This should give our establishment a unique advantage and a strong competitive position, surrounded as we are by many licensed hotels with few differences between them other than price and standards of accommodation and service. It is also our aim to be residential only, which will limit costs involved, as opposed to a multi-outlet style of operation. This again will benefit our non-drinking guests by offering them low-cost accommodation.

The hotel's problem is that it has not communicated this mission to its market, resulting in customer confusion, unrealistic expectations in guests and probably missed opportunities.

The environmental factors

Building a business or changing it requires an understanding of the environment in which the place is going to operate. Environmental factors are either internal (controllable) or external (uncontrollable). The external, uncontrollable factors (also called macro-environmental factors) are market demographics, economics, competition, changing social needs and lifestyle values, new technology and governmental and legal forces. The internal, controllable factors (also called micro-environment factors) are the financial capabilities of the establishment, its human resources, its location, its suppliers, its agents or distributors, and its knowledge and ability to produce a product which matches the requirements of the market and an image or position in the market which is competitive.

It can be argued that location is 'uncontrollable' in that moving a property is not possible. However, the choice of location was controllable at the time of inception, and in any case the business can be relocated separately from the building. For example, a fast food outlet located in a business park which is about to close can successfully relocate the business in a building in the heart of the city.

Each of the environmental factors is subject to change, and clever management has to be alert to both short-term and long-term changes and make adjustments to the product mix and allocation of human and financial resources to cater for the change. Adjustments to social change, for instance, have become necessary on several occasions in recent years. The preference for more casual dining, for example, has caused many hotels to change their restaurants to become less formal. The strong interest in health and fitness has led numerous hotels to add leisure centres to the range of sub-products. Growing awareness of the consequences of cigarette smoking has led to the growth in demand for non-smoking areas in restaurants.

The potential customers

A hospitality establishment has to be mindful of its total customer potential and the degree of competition it will meet when attracting custom. A hotel cannot position itself to appeal to everyone. It must decide which segment of

Figure 2.1   *The social, political and economic environments in which an establishment operates will greatly affect the marketing decision*

the market it intends to try and capture, which requirements of that segment of the market it intends to satisfy and whether it has the resources to do it.

The large hotel groups set out to dominate a market with a tried and proven formula which has worked in most other markets. Even so, each hotel's product mix is adapted to the environment in which it operates. Theirs is not an inflexible formula.

The demographics of the potential customer base

Demography is the statistical study of human population and distribution. Every hospitality establishment needs to consider its customer potential in terms of numbers, age, gender and income and whether it will draw its custom from local, regional, national or international sources. For example, a theme restaurant which offers Scottish regional food would have limited potential for success in Glasgow where there are already several competitors offering the same type of fare. There would not be the population numbers to justify another restaurant of the same type. Its only hope would be to invest considerable time and effort into taking the available business away from the existing players. That would be expensive, and its success doubtful for many reasons.

Similarly, there is always a restaurateur who fondly believes that there is room for a really good restaurant which is the pinnacle of gourmet food and immaculate service. In a depressed economy and in an area which is mostly populated by middle to low income earners there are seldom the numbers to justify such a conclusion. There are more financial casualties at the top end of the restaurant market than there are at the far larger lower end where price and value are the major considerations.

The market's social needs and lifestyle values

In a small town, the community's needs for entertainment, celebrations, dining and various meetings will usually revolve around the local hotel if it is marketed properly. The environment dictates the type of operation management needs to run. A city establishment has a far greater market potential, certainly more diverse, but it has to decide which of the many social and lifestyle markets to target. That is not always easy.

Lifestyles change with each generation or every decade. When the children of the 'baby-boomers' of the post-Second World War era grew up and started spending, they had a quite different set of values and sought more conservative experiences than their parents who were 'raised in a bubble of affluence'. They were far more individualistic, avoided the aspirational cultures of their parents and had little style with which marketers could accurately identify. As it is usually lifestyle and aspirational values which direct much of the marketing effort, the post-war generation posed a problem for the marketers since they were not motivated by former lifestyle values. The result for hospitality marketing has been a splintered market environment requiring careful observation and research.

Cultural considerations

People's views of the world and the society in which they find themselves are conditioned by the country of their origin and the society which shaped their beliefs and values. Knowing this, many of the large and successful Asian hotels, for example, have developed their facilities to meet the demands of the Western cultures while still retaining some of the charm and mystery of their own environments. Although hotels are anxious to obtain their business, sometimes less consideration is waiting for Asians visiting establishments in Europe.

The hospitality industry is one which has to be multi-cultural in everything that it does. When preparing their menus, for example, food and beverage managers are affected in their choice of dishes by a wide variety of food and beverage preferences. In its accommodation arrangements managers have to be tolerant of racial differences. As a consequence, there is a sameness about hotels wherever one travels in the world. A traveller drugged and dropped into a hotel in most large cities wouldn't have a clue where he or she was for quite some time! However, this devolution of the hotel industry now offers opportunities for specialization in the products on offer and thereby attracting specific markets to certain establishments.

Various publics

When one is in business, one cannot operate in a self-controlled vacuum. As well as appealing to customers there are other groups in the environment to be considered, which can be termed 'publics'. A public is a group of people or organizations which can impact on the business's ability to achieve its objectives. There is the financial public, the banks, insurance companies, credit-checking companies, credit-card services and so on, all of whom can affect the financial standing of one's establishment. There is the media public, and in its many forms the media can singularly influence the public for or against an establishment. There is the public of 'concerned citizens', which are action groups of consumers or single issue political bodies which set themselves up as community 'watch-dogs' and concern themselves with physical and social issues. Consumerism has been a strong influence on all business in the past twenty years. It has grown in strength to the point where most governments will bow to the pressures of consumer groups, or at least drastically modify their legislation in consideration of their ability to affect voting intentions. For instance, consumer pressure has led to the hospitality industry being forced to go 'green' by the EC packaging directive which demands more recycling and less waste. There is the industry public, comprising associations and government agencies which are meant to monitor the industry and cause changes or controls supposedly for the benefit of industry members.

Most of these publics are handled by various specialists for the larger hotel groups, but for smaller hospitality establishments the job usually falls onto the owners' shoulders. The publics in any environment should never be ignored as they have a habit of impinging on the industry's operations both generally and singly, often for its benefit, but more often to its detriment.

Economic conditions prevailing

In times of recession, people seek greater value from their expenditure. The numbers travelling and wanting accommodation fall. The size of an operation affects the economies of scale necessary to meet boom, recession and recovery times, and needs to be understood in advance of their happening. Different markets are often sought under different economic conditions. There are also those who remain committed to delivering the 'top of the range' style of service for those guests who are less affected by economic change.

Often it is more hazardous to plan for an improvement in the economic environment. Optimism frequently leads to an over-commitment in an effort to capitalize on the predicted increased demand.

Existing government and legal forces

Governments cause much change in the business environment by altering interest rates, braking or boosting economies through fiscal and monetary measures. The increased indirect taxation by the Major government 1994–95 has led to fragile consumer confidence and reduced discretionary income. In such situations, it is the luxury items, such as eating out and weekend breaks, that are the first to be abstained from.

Local councils, environmental health departments, public works departments, licensing boards, fire departments, regional and national tourist boards, conservation bodies – the list of bureaucracies keeps on growing – are a formidable obstacle for planning in anticipation of stable conditions for growth. Apart from lobbying various levels of government, individual establishments have little control over their economic and political environments, and most establishments have to ride the changing circumstances.

Ecological influences

The impact of human interference on the planet's physical resources is now a major issue in most people's minds. There is growing concern that we might be destroying the Earth's atmosphere, its oceans and much of the natural environment through a whole range of artificial pollutants. Governments are taking heed, and before developments can occur in most Western countries an 'environmental impact statement' is required.

Ecological concern is restricting mining and building projects. It is seldom possible to embark on large tourist developments, for example, without encountering a series of controls and the protests of 'environmentally conscious' groups. Even small businesses have to be concerned with matters like waste disposal and environmental despoliation.

Technological developments

The way we do business has changed rapidly in the past thirty years as a result of new technology, mostly in the area of electronics. Far more is yet to come, and foremost among these will be computer technology, information transfer and video conferencing. Alvin Toffler's forecasts in his book, *The Third Wave*, concerning the 'electronic cottage', are proving to be imminent. Leading hotels are already catering for the 'new wave' business person with in-house facilities. Toffler predicted that new computer technology, the modem, videophone, facsimile machine and video conferencing facilities would enable increasing numbers of people to work at home in their 'electronic cottages', significantly reducing the 'dead time' of travel and minimizing the need for large office buildings simply to provide space for people to work.

How, when or if these and future developments will affect the hospitality industry, and the way people travel and seek their entertainment, is not clear. However, this is an example of the need to consider change and how it can be turned to advantage before it impacts on the business of the establishment.

Government regulation

Ours is already a highly-regulated society, but the spread of new government rules and regulations in all areas continues unabated as people try to create the perfect society through legislation. Health concerns, especially with alcohol, smoking and food, are the ones which directly affect the hospitality industry as governments again endeavour to provide protection through new Acts of Parliament, such as the Food Safety (General Food Hygiene) Regulations 1994.

However, government deregulation can provide market opportunities; for example, 1995 saw the advent of Children's Certificates, which allow children into the bar area of a pub if they are accompanied by an adult. The industry responds to the changes by turning them into customer benefits or by providing facilities which meet their requirements.

The physical location of the establishment

People's perceptions of a place are dictated by its location. Even being on the wrong side of a road can change people's perceptions. Is the place going to appeal mainly to business people, tourists, locals, the farming community, domestic and overseas visitors, sports enthusiasts, non-drinkers or families? Whomever the hotel targets, the location must match the market's expectation in physical location, size, presentation and facilities.

The competition

No-one has a market to themselves, or not for too long. The competitive environment will materially affect the marketing decisions on a continuing basis. The intensity of the competition, and where it is intruding into the hotel's market base, will determine the reaction which may be required to counter it.

Competition can also come from a different quarter when the market environment changes. For instance, in a recession, a large hotel's competition for accommodation can emerge from guest houses, budget lodges and pubs with rooms, when previously its main competition came from hotels similar to itself.

The organization's resources

Capital and cash flow are vital for survival. The ability to meet the long-term goals of marketing is often under-estimated. For example, there is nothing worse than trying to earn a reputation for a service, a product or a facility when staff, money and supply sources are unreliable. The presentation of the hotel's facilities has to be uniformly impressive, clean, fresh and well maintained. Without cash flow, this can be difficult to maintain.

Each market has expectations which must be met. The ability of the staff to provide the service required by the market being targeted is critical because measurable, consistent service standards are essential in hospitality, which is why careful staff selection and training is vital. Similarly, management and staff must have knowledge and experience of the market in which it intends to operate.

Summary of the marketing environment

All the market environment factors have to be constantly considered. Nothing in marketing remains static. Management's job is to monitor these factors and be prepared to make modifications or changes to the marketing plan. An establishment may have to re-position itself several times during its existence to meet the changing expectations of the market, or to meet the needs of new markets caused by environmental change.

To be successful in business, the following resources are required: a consumer need; a market large enough; an accessible market; a product which can turn a need into a want; a product which is competitive; production means/facilities; continuity of supplies/materials/human resources; a good crystal ball; and money!

Questions for discussion or revision

1   If you won a trip to a tropical tourist resort on an island, which facilities would you expect to find there? What would you think if that was not the case?
2   You are the owner of a three-star hotel. It is recommended that you should change the style of the restaurant to cater for the tastes of an emerging market for Mexican cuisine. How would you react and what would you do about it?
3   Your three-star hotel has had a virtual monopoly of the business traveller's market for years. Suddenly, two highly regarded hotel groups build four-star hotels in your vicinity. What do you do?
4   You have inherited a large house in the country. It is ideal for many hospitality uses. How would you go about making a decision on the best use of the place?
5   New legislation in your city which is aimed at reducing the spread of prostitution and AIDS requires all accommodation places to ask guests for proof of identity and to send a copy of the guest register on a weekly basis to a new government department. This legislation is designed to identify prostitutes and promiscuous people. What are the ramifications of this action and what changes would you make, if any?
6   Your company has been asked to tender for a hotel to be situated on the coast next to a new and very large marina being built by a developer. What are the procedures you would follow before making your bid?

Further reading

Toffler, A. (1981). *The Third Wave*. Toronto: Collins, Bantam.
Drucker, P. (1992). *Managing for the Future*. Oxford: Butterworth-Heinemann.

3 *The marketing mix*

Aims of this chapter

1 To expand the understanding of strategic planning and to show how a business needs various types of goals to cover each stage of the planning process.
2 To explain how the goals are achieved by strategies of the marketing mix.
3 To describe how strategies can be grouped under six main categories called the marketing mix: people, product, price, place, promotion and positioning.
4 To show how the mix of strategies comprises the core of a strategic marketing plan.

The goal of goal-making

A business without goals is like a rudderless ship, likely to go anywhere or nowhere. Goals harness power and set the direction for an organization. They give it purpose, direction and motivation.

However, a goal is virtually useless unless it has a measurable, quantifiable objective. To have a goal which says simply 'To achieve profit' is almost useless. How much profit? A pound? OK, then, how about ten million pounds? Not possible? What, then, is a reasonable expectation for profit that can be quantified and written down as a goal? When that question is answered a goal is created which will generate the activity to attain it. A goal must be feasible and sensible. If it is too high, it may plunge those who have to achieve it into dismay or apathy. If it is too low, it encourages under-achievement.

Athletes constantly strive to go one better than their 'personal best', beat a competitor's time or set a new record. This is the stuff that makes champions. The adage 'I'll give it my best shot!' is the statement of someone who is either being very coy or is already defeated by the prospect of winning. It means that he or she thinks the goal is beyond his or her capacity to achieve.

The other essential component of a goal is to give a time schedule. When is this profit to be achieved? Some time in the vague future, or by the end of the calendar or financial year? Without a quantifiable objective within a time frame, a goal is merely a wish or a hope, and a business won't survive long on wishes and hopes.

Here is a goal which has meaning: 'To achieve a profit of £100 000 by June next year.' Is it feasible? A feasibility study is the only way of saying yes or no to this question. It is an accountable forecast of the likely outcome of marketing activity. Such a study cannot be done without considerable investigation into the market, and this is called market analysis. If this analysis reveals opportunities which make it possible for the goal to be achieved, the next step is to propose some strategies and plan the marketing in sufficient detail to satisfy those who have to decide whether or not to proceed.

Setting marketing objectives is the decision-making time in marketing, the moment when the marketer's credibility is on the line. Fuzzy forecasts and unjustified expenses required to achieve them will be quickly torn apart by the hard-nosed approach of financial people who have to be accountable for the business's prosperity. 'What makes you think you can get this profit and make this number of sales?' is the sort of question bank managers ask before they grant a loan or an overdraft facility. Marketing objectives are a commitment and they have to be accurate and defensible.

Strategies are the means by which marketing objectives are achieved. They are meant to answer the all-important question, 'How are you going to achieve this objective?' Tactics are the working mechanisms of strategies. Strategies are theories. Tactics make the strategies happen, and it is tactics which cost the money in the marketing plan.

When goals and objectives are set, they become the measurement of performance and that is why they must have quantifiable criteria. As a result of the feasibility study, the goals may have to be modified, and possibly even abandoned, until a better set of strategies are proposed. There is always a reason for a goal and that is why goals are required at each step of the business's planning. Let's go through them.

Organization goals, also called corporate goals

These cover the overriding goals of a business which shape its future intentions, and they will change from time to time depending on circumstances. Here are some examples.

'To achieve profit' is the first and most obvious goal of a business; however, in difficult times a goal may have to be written which restricts loss to a certain figure.

'To increase market share' is a corporate goal for an organization in a highly competitive market. When quantified, it will state the amount of business that has to be taken from the opposition. It would have even more meaning if the opposition were named.

'To increase sales' may have an implied profit objective, but it is mainly aimed at building the number of customers to form a customer base.

'To achieve corporate growth' may come about when a company reaches the limit of its existing market and the owners consider moving into other markets, taking over other organizations or diversifying into other products.

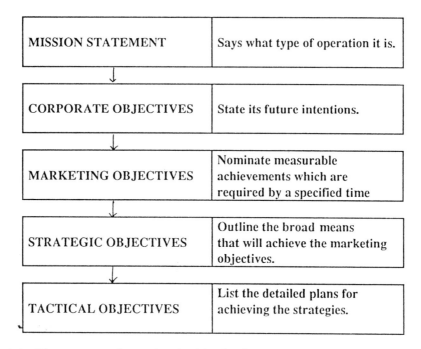

MISSION STATEMENT	Says what type of operation it is.
CORPORATE OBJECTIVES	State its future intentions.
MARKETING OBJECTIVES	Nominate measurable achievements which are required by a specified time
STRATEGIC OBJECTIVES	Outline the broad means that will achieve the marketing objectives.
TACTICAL OBJECTIVES	List the detailed plans for achieving the strategies.

Figure 3.1   *The sequence of steps involved in developing a marketing plan defined by objectives*

'To increase capacity' means that the establishment has reached the limit of growth with its existing facilities and sees merit in adding more rooms or increasing the size of various products such as the restaurants.

Other corporate goals may be: reduction of stock inventories; capitalization of assets; offset competitive activity; achieve takeovers; provide finance or cash flow; increase share prices or values; enter new markets; introduce new products; achieve product or corporate rationalization.

Marketing goals or marketing objectives

Corporate goals are broad in scope. Marketing objectives are more specific and spell out how the corporate goals will be achieved by the marketing mix. Thus a corporate goal concerning profit may have one or several marketing objectives which relate to achieving profit by changing a particular product, promoting it, pricing it differently, offering it to new markets or positioning it in a new way. A marketing objective relating to a corporate goal for profit may read as follows:

'To achieve the corporate profit goal of 25 per cent by 30 June next year we will:

1   Increase food and beverage sales for the Ritz Restaurant by 30 per cent before 30 June next year.
2   Increase sales return from the Club Bar by 21 per cent immediately.
3   Increase the return from room hire by 25 per cent immediately.

Strategic objectives

The strategic objectives state how the increases will be achieved, and they may read as follows:

1 To achieve an increase of food and beverage sales of 30 per cent for the Ritz Restaurant before 30 June next year, we will:
   a) make more tables available (a 'place' strategy);
   b) offer special deals (a 'price' strategy);
   c) double the advertising expenditure (a 'promotion' strategy).
2 To achieve a sales return increase of 21 per cent from the Club Bar immediately, we will:
   a) increase the prices selectively while offering specials to offset negative customer reaction (a 'price' strategy).
3 To achieve the increase of 25 per cent in the room hire rate immediately, we will:
   a) adopt a price-ranging policy by re-grading the rooms so that there is a greater price differential between them (a 'product' and 'price' strategy);
   b) have a range of premium class rooms to attract more people from the senior executive levels (a 'people' strategy).

Tactical objectives

Tactics are the short-term detailed courses of action which follow through from the strategic objectives. Strategies are broad, long-term means of achieving objectives whereas tactics usually involve specific activities and communication. Tactics therefore are concerned with the short-term, immediate needs of implementing product changes, selling, advertising, sales promotions, publicity, direct mail, public relations, signs, brochures, etc.

Hence for the strategic objectives to be achieved, all the component departments of the establishment will have their own objectives in order to carry out the intentions of the strategies, such as:

- sales objectives
- advertising communication objectives
- direct mail objectives
- publicity objectives
- display objectives, etc.

Tactical objectives are written in the same way as strategic objectives and must also have a time frame and measurable, manageable criteria.

Linking the objectives together

The important thing to remember when setting marketing, strategic and tactical goals is that each succeeding set of objectives must relate to the one

Strategies achieve marketing objectives

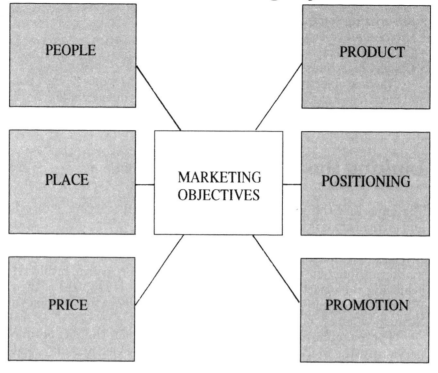

Tactics achieve strategic objectives

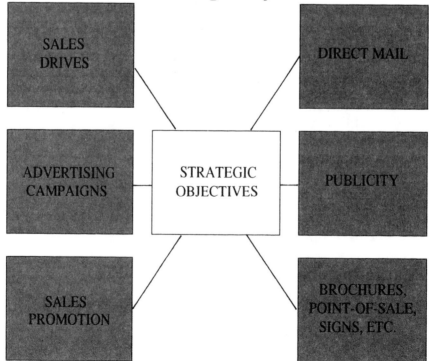

Figure 3.2 *Strategies achieve marketing objectives; tactics achieve strategic objectives*

preceding it so that they link together to form a chain of activity. In a large organization which has separate departments to handle each marketing function, once the objectives are set, every person involved in achieving the objectives has a clear idea of what is required of him or her. When all the objectives are assembled into a document they become the Strategic Plan. For example, to achieve the corporate goals for the Ritz outlined above, the marketing, strategic and tactical objectives may read:

Marketing objective for the Ritz Restaurant:

1 Increase food and beverage sales for the Ritz Restaurant by 30 per cent before 30 June next year.

Strategic objectives for the Ritz Restaurant:

1 Make more tables available (a 'place' strategy).
2 Offer special deals (a 'price' strategy).
3 Double the advertising expenditure (a 'promotion' strategy).

Tactical objectives for the Ritz Restaurant:

1 Increase the table capacity of the Ritz Restaurant by twenty tables by eliminating ten of the private booths.
2 Promote the Ritz by offering a special 'table for four' rate.
3 Offer a low priced carvery buffet alternative for early diners.

Marketing objective for the Club Bar:

1 Increase sales return from the Club Bar by 21 per cent immediately.

Strategic objectives for the Club Bar:

1 Increase the prices selectively while offering specials to offset negative customer reactions.

Tactical objectives for the Club Bar:

1 Increase the prices of spirits and cocktails by 21 per cent.
2 Offer various cocktail and spirit specials to offset the price increases.

Marketing objective for accommodation:

1 Increase the return from room hire by 25 per cent immediately.

Strategic objectives for accommodation:

1 Adopt a price ranging policy by re-grading the rooms so that there is a greater price differential between them (a 'product' and 'price' strategy).

2   Have a range of premium class rooms to attract more people from the senior executive levels (a 'product' and 'people' strategy).

Tactical objectives for accommodation:

1   Upgrade 100 rooms on the fourth and fifth floors to premium rate.
2   Package the present premium rooms and offer added value products.
3   Promote the second and third floor rooms as discount specials and sell up as many clients as possible.

Management by objectives

Management of the strategic plan involves several phases, and the decision-making process for setting marketing objectives follows the steps shown in Figure 3.3.

The story of Joe's place

'I don't have a marketing plan,' explained Joe. 'What do I need with such a thing? I've been running restaurants all my life. People are happy. They like my food. I make the money.'

Joe runs a top London, Italian-style restaurant seating around 250 people, and he is successful. However, whereas he doesn't have a plan in writing he does work to a plan and he carries it in his head. His plan is the result of many years' experience, watching, experimenting and learning. He also has the advantage of coming from a country with a rich culture in hospitality and being from a family with several generations of experience in the restaurant business.

Even so, what Joe didn't say was that he has been broke twice, and he only got his plan right the third time. One wonders about his plan too, because it wasn't just the food that made his place a success.

Joe is like many operators in the hospitality industry; he operates by the 'seat of his pants'. When his business faces a change in circumstances, Joe may not have past experience to help him. Without the discipline of marketing planning, Joe could easily make some wrong decisions.

The marketing mix strategies

There are basically six main strategic elements or groups of strategies used in the marketing mix. Some marketing authorities stipulate four: product, price, place and promotion. But, as all marketing activity involves people and the selection of a target market, there must be strategies aimed at people. In

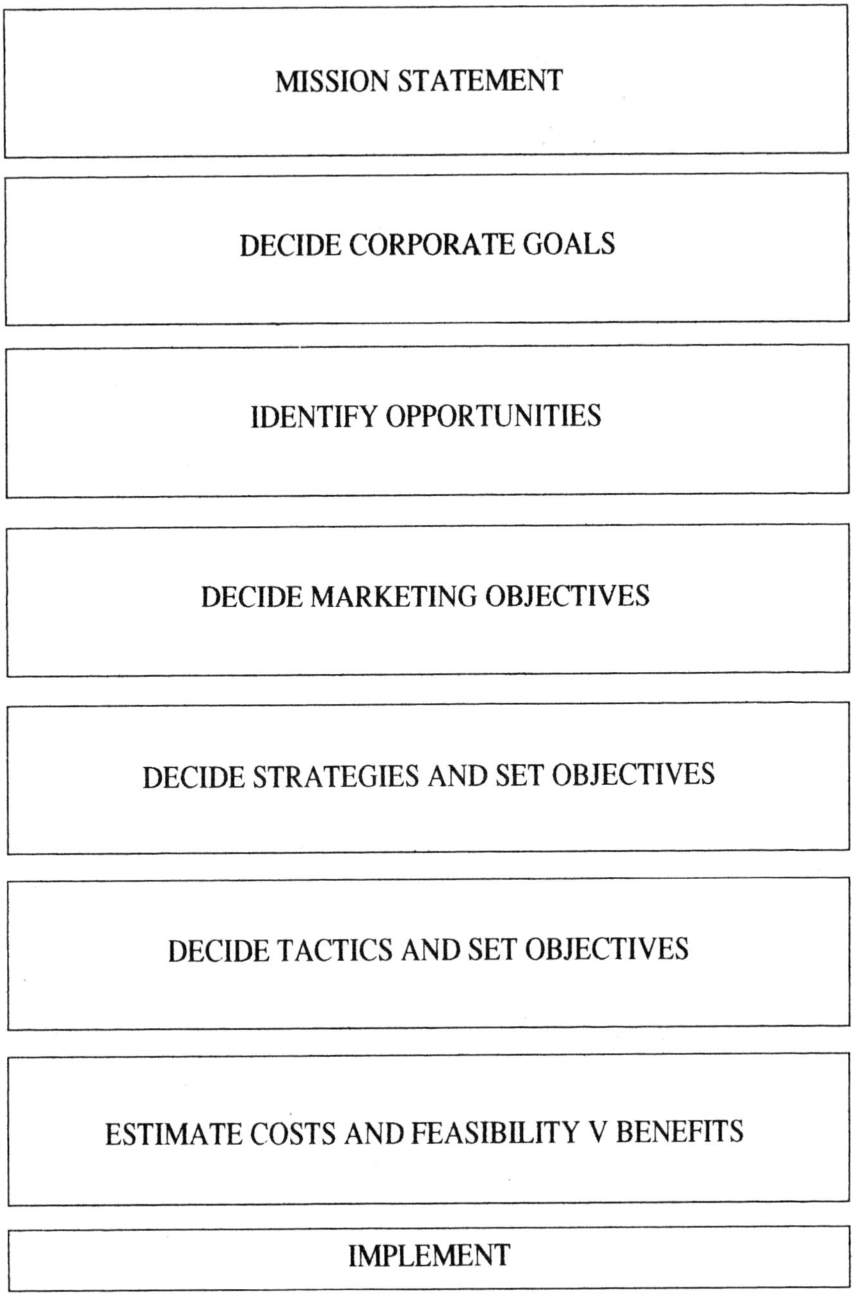

MISSION STATEMENT

DECIDE CORPORATE GOALS

IDENTIFY OPPORTUNITIES

DECIDE MARKETING OBJECTIVES

DECIDE STRATEGIES AND SET OBJECTIVES

DECIDE TACTICS AND SET OBJECTIVES

ESTIMATE COSTS AND FEASIBILITY V BENEFITS

IMPLEMENT

Figure 3.3 *Setting marketing objectives*

addition, as people tend to buy images and not things, and because it is people's minds which are the principal concerns of marketing, there have to be positioning strategies as well. Hence there are six types of strategies involved in marketing planning.

The six strategic elements comprising the marketing mix are described as the 'Marketing Ps' because each one begins with the letter P. It is called the marketing mix because it is a mixture of strategies used by management to produce a marketing plan. In the planning process, management has to make decisions about each element of the mix and determine how people will respond to the strategies separately and in combination.

When devising the most appropriate strategies for a marketing plan, the sequence in which each element is generally considered is as follows.

People

When you begin any marketing assignment, always consider first the People who will be your major customers. It is easier to develop strategies for the remaining Ps of the marketing mix when you focus on a clearly identified target market. A People strategy requires you to choose the groups of People (markets) that you decide to target. People strategies can be broadly classified as being:

- undifferentiated (a mass-marketing approach)
- differentiated (when selective markets are chosen)
- concentrated (when specialized markets are chosen).

Undifferentiated marketing or mass marketing is now a strategy seldom chosen by the large companies around the world. It means one product for everyone, but it is easy to understand why it has fallen out of favour. These days it is hard to imagine a motor vehicle manufacturer, for example, seriously believing that it can produce one model in one colour, like the Ford Model T which was so popular in the 1920s. Even so, there are many operators in the hospitality industry who retain the fond illusion that their market is 'everyone'.

Differentiated marketing occurs when a company produces a product with model and style differences to satisfy selected markets. A five-star hotel, for example, aims at providing a service and experience mainly for a more affluent class of customer.

Concentrated marketing is targeting specific people groups with a product. Examples in the hospitality industry are vegetarian menus, facilities for the disabled and family restaurants.

A thorough knowledge of the people who comprise the segments to be targeted is probably the most essential aspect of successful marketing. It is easier to develop appropriate product, price, place, promotion and positioning strategies when you focus on the needs of specific groups of people, the needs they have and the way in which they want those needs to be satisfied.

Product

Products are the things and the services that happen to and for the customers. It is what they get for their money. Strategies determine the benefits the customers will gain from their purchase. Product strategies can be classified under two broad headings:

1 *Product growth strategies,* which are generally aimed at producing a better or different product to expand the establishment's opportunities for increased market potential by attracting new or different customers. The corporate objective of a growth strategy is to improve its sales figures or to achieve greater profit contributions.
2 *Competitive product strategies,* which are generally aimed at retaining customers by offsetting activity with an improved or different product.

Place

Where and how you sell the products is the purpose of Place strategies. The site chosen for the establishment is a Place strategy because it is from the Place that you will mainly sell your products. However, you may have to sell your products from other places, such as travel agents, central reservations offices or through national tourist boards, so that your products are more accessible for purchase by travellers coming from other regions or countries.

Manufacturers usually sell their products via intermediaries such as wholesalers, retailers and sales agents. In that instance, Place strategies are the means of using 'channels of distribution'. The channels of distribution in the case of hotels are travel agents, tour wholesalers, coach, airline and train companies, etc., each of whom 'sells' rooms on behalf of hotels.

Another important channel of distribution is referral from other hotels in the same chain. Hilton, for example, uses its wide spread of hotels around the world to sell its sister establishments in other cities.

Price

The prices you decide to charge for your products and the reasons for selecting those prices are determined by the expectations of the People you choose to target. However, they are also influenced by the corporate objectives, the activities of the competition, the cost of the product and external factors such as the economic climate prevailing.

Positioning

It is the combination of the other P strategies in the marketing mix which Positions an establishment in people's minds. As it is the market's perceptions and expectations which have a towering influence over its choice of products, great care is required to Position the establishment and its products competitively.

Image and reputation are the result of positioning strategies; hence the information feeds of good Promotion make a major contribution to an establishment's Positioning. Information feeds are the means of getting messages to people, such as talking, writing, broadcasting, putting up signs, displays and many other forms of advertising.

There may be very little difference between two properties in fact, but if in the customers' minds there is a perceived difference, and they believe that one property is better than the other, that perception will be stronger than the reality and it will be the favoured place to go.

Promotion

How you decide to communicate the existence of an establishment and its products are called Promotion strategies. A variety of communication channels, or 'message delivery systems', are available to fulfil Promotion strategies. The main ones are:

- personal contact (sales representation)
- advertising
- sales promotion
- publicity
- point-of-sale displays and signs
- direct mail
- the 'look' of the establishment and its staff.

Promotional strategies usually involve a combination of all the message delivery systems. This is also referred to as 'the tactical mix'.

The effects of goals on marketing mix strategies

It should be clear from the foregoing that one element of the marketing mix cannot be treated in isolation. All the elements of the marketing mix are irrevocably tied together in the pursuit of a corporate goal and every element in the marketing mix has an impact on another. For example, a product change may affect the price of the product. It may also change the positioning of it in people's minds, or even bring different people into the market. It will certainly require promotion, and may even need a separate distribution or place of sale. Similarly, a new target market will necessitate a new strategy for each of the elements involved in the marketing mix, and consequently require different tactics.

Therefore when writing a marketing objective it is essential to consider all the marketing elements involved and the strategies required to achieve the objective. Go back and change the objective if the marketing mix strategies appear to be incapable of achieving it.

Joe's marketing approach explained

Joe said it was his food that was the reason for the success of his restaurant, but actually he had put together all the strategic elements of the marketing mix to form a competent and highly successful operation.

Joe's People strategy was to target middle-class managers, supervisors and secretaries, not a difficult decision to make considering his location in the heart of London's business district. He also attracted young professionals and junior executives.

His Product strategy was good quality Italian food, superbly prepared and presented. He had a team of carefully selected, fast and efficient waiters under the direction of his sons and daughters. Another very important strategy he used was to make absolutely certain that the customers were served and fed within thirty minutes. Everyone knew they could be in and out within their lunch break. All waiters wore white shirts, black ties and trousers. Each one could recite the menu from memory and they used the specials to make it easier for the customers to choose their food.

His Place strategy, apart from the location, was the layout of the restaurant, which enabled rapid access between the tables, the kitchen and the bar facilities.

His Price strategy was to maintain the prices just below or around the same as nearby competitors. Each dish was available as a starter or main course.

His Positioning strategy was to be perceived as a place for high quality food at a reasonable price and with fast, efficient and friendly service. Few were ever disappointed.

His Promotion strategy consisted entirely of an illuminated sign under a striped awning and a very large copy of the menu in the window. He never advertised in main media. Word of mouth advertising was enough. A nice tactical touch was to give everyone a miniature menu with next week's specials when they left the restaurant.

After going broke twice, Joe had learned his lessons. Maybe he didn't know marketing theory, but if he had it would have avoided a lot of pain and he might have got it right first time.

Questions for discussion or revision

1   In order to compete with a price-cutting hotel nearby, a large hotel decides also to cut prices even lower. What impact will this have on other elements of the hotel's marketing mix?

2   If a medium-priced restaurant in the main part of the city decides to upgrade its image and endeavour to capture the top end of the market, why would it do that and what therefore would be its marketing objectives?

3   The marketing objective for an expensive but popular tourist resort in the mountains which appeals mainly to wealthy chief executives reads like this: 'To enlarge our market base by 20 per cent within the next twelve months and target newly-weds from Europe.' Develop some strategies which you consider would help the hotel achieve that objective.

4   The market for a guest house close to the city has been identified as young couples on holiday. The problem is, alcohol cannot be sold or served, and drinkers represent a high percentage of the potential market. In addition, the previous clients of the hotel have been older, conservative people who seek a quiet, restful place to holiday while being close to shops, theatres and restaurants. Prepare a strategic plan which you believe will overcome the dilemma for the owners.

5   Using the example of Joe's restaurant in the text, how would you advise Joe in the event of his rent being raised to the point where he could no longer maintain his price strategy?

Further reading

Buttle, F. (1993). *Hotel and Food Service Marketing: A Managerial Approach.* London: Holt, Rinehart & Winston.

4 *Market analysis*

Aims of this chapter

1 To explain that the purpose of market analysis is to uncover problem areas in a business that need fixing, and to identify opportunities that can be exploited for the future.
2 To describe how to analyse a market by dividing it into small, understandable and measurable segments.
3 To show that marketing has to be based on a continuing flow of reliable information, and that management can never have enough relevant information if their business decisions are to be effective and profitable.
4 To describe the types of information required for market analysis and how this information can be used to identify the segments the property is attracting and which segments it could be chasing.
5 To explain that a diagnosis of product performance is also part of market analysis so that products can be changed, improved or even eliminated so that the property can build a bigger customer base.

This chapter provides an overview of market analysis. There are other chapters which cover the subject in more detail, especially Chapter 5, 'Segmentation by purchase motivations', Chapter 7, 'Target marketing' and Chapter 13, 'The marketing audit'.

The theory of market analysis

Before one can make a decision one must have information. Market analysis is the information base upon which marketing planning decisions are made. Its purpose is to understand the dynamics of a market by segmenting it into convenient components so that it is possible to identify the opportunities that exist. In this way, improvements can be made to a property or its products. It is a detailed examination of the business environment in which a property operates, and has to be comprehensive, otherwise important developments can be overlooked to the detriment of the property's sales and competitive position in the market.

In the continuing search for improved sales performance, a property which is an aggressive marketer will use market analysis to give it direction on how its products can be marketed better and thereby attract new customers. As part of the process, it needs to constantly use market analysis to review and assess the market. This is because the internal and external factors affecting the patrons of an establishment are constantly changing as a result of competitive activities.

Therefore market analysis should be an on-going process of assessment and re-evaluation of a property's performance. This requires an information system so that there is a constant supply of vital information (see Chapter 14, 'The marketing information system').

In marketing analysis, the people forming the market are segmented into various categories. The market's total size in financial terms and sales numbers is measured and market share figures are compared. The external and internal influences on the market are identified in search of any factors likely to affect the marketing mix strategies in the future. When armed with this vital knowledge, management can proceed with its marketing planning and make vital decisions which will ensure its future growth by building a bigger customer base.

The main types of information required

The answers to each of the following questions need to be quantified, compared with previous years or periods, compared with industry averages and, if possible, compared with the competition. Most of this information will come from sales analysis, reservations records and customer surveys.

1 *Market segments.* Who is buying? What types of people are they? From where do the majority of guests and food and beverage patrons come? What products are they buying? How often and when are they buying?
2 *Sales and profit analysis.* What is the size of the customer base? What are the sales figures by numbers of unit sales? What are the sales figures in financial volume terms? Which products are being sold? Which products are returning a profit and which are not?
3 *Market share and product comparisons with competing establishments.* Which establishments are doing well? Which opposition products are selling well? Why? Which segments of the market are they getting? Which market segments do they attract that would suit your property?
4 *Market environment.* What are the tourist attractions, business reasons or other reasons which are attracting hospitality business to the city or region? Who are these people and how are they categorized? In terms of districts, regions or countries, from where are they coming? Which mode of transport do they use to get there? Which motorways do they use, for instance? Are the facilities currently on offer by all the properties in the city or region meeting the customers' needs?

5 *External factors affecting the market.* What government rules and regulations which are in existence or pending are affecting people's purchase decisions for hospitality? What social values or behaviour trends are occurring which may influence events in the future?

6 *Product appraisal.* How does the property compare with the competition?
  - How large is it? How many rooms? What is the composition of the rooms? How many seats in each food and beverage outlet? What are the other facilities, such as meeting rooms, function facilities, bars, business centre, car parking, etc.?
  - What are the entertainment and leisure facilities provided by the property? How do they compare with other properties?
  - Where is the property located and how convenient is it?
  - What is the physical condition of the property, its equipment and facilities?
  - What is the ambience of the property like and how is it positioned in people's minds?

The exciting part about market analysis is that it invariably reveals opportunities and therefore gives direction for marketing decisions. Naturally, it will also unveil unpalatable truths which must be faced and corrective action taken. Frequently, analysis will point to the need for more information. It is a lot of work to gather all the data, but let us repeat: in marketing you can never have enough appropriate information.

Segmentation

People are the core of the hospitality business. Therefore an essential part of market analysis is a thorough examination of the existing and potential customer base. There are many ways of segmenting a market to form a complete picture. All markets consist of buyers who differ from each other by their needs, what they want, how much they are prepared to pay and where they come from. For planning purposes they can be divided into demographic, geographic, psychographic and behavioural segments.

Unsophisticated managers of establishments simply segment their customers into tourists and locals, or even 'foreigners and regulars'. Common industry practice is to segment customers simply as holidaymakers, corporate business clients, groups, packages (people on special packaged deals) or FITS – Frequent Independent Travellers – which means they don't fall into any of the former categories, and that often seems to be the limit of the managers' concern. Their attitude is: 'Why does it matter where they come from as long as they keep coming?'

Of course, that attitude is irresponsible and unprofessional. It does matter where customers come from, where they are travelling to and why they are visiting the area. No-one does anything without a reason. Marketing is about understanding those reasons and using the information to make better use of the opportunities those reasons represent so as to provide greater customer satisfaction and ultimately increased sales.

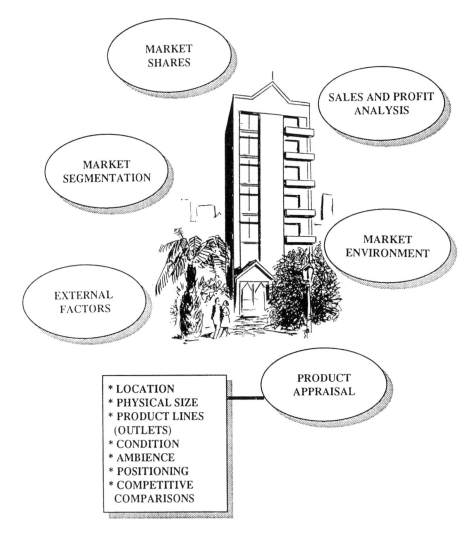

Figure 4.1   *Market analysis*

Some common market segments

Business segments

A clarification of business travel reveals the individual reasons for choice of hospitality. Each category will want different standards and levels of food and accommodation, depending on their occupation, income, lifestyle or position. The main segments are:

- a sales representative calling on company customers;
- an executive, professional person or civil servant attending a meeting or conference;
- a person or group attending a convention or training seminar;

- an itinerant professional or trade person on an assignment for a limited period – a classification which could also include entertainers or sports persons.

Pleasure segments

There is a large combination of factors which can cluster to form the pleasure segments of the market, including age, income, lifestyle, class, nationality, living mode and the customer's means of transport. Some typical segments are:

- people visiting a friend or relative (called the VFR market – Visiting Friends and Relatives);
- honeymoon couples and lovers;
- individual pleasure seekers who want to meet someone, play sport, take part in special events or enjoy the night life;
- couples on holiday with a planned itinerary;
- couples, or single people, with children of varying ages and stages;
- package holidaymakers;
- tour, coach, sporting or social groups.

Demographic market segments

Every age group has its own needs. Young people aged between 18 and 24 have quite different requirements of hospitality from, say, older people aged between 55 and 65. Both groups need to eat and sleep, but they prefer to do both things in environments which have strongly contrasting styles.

Gender changes people's preferences. What a male thinks is an OK place to stay may not be a female's idea of a suitable establishment. Family size changes people's needs. A couple with three children will want a different style and size of accommodation from a young, single man. Income influences choice. What some people want can become severely modified by what they can afford. Occupation will also affect choice. For instance, the corporate business or professional person with an expense account will generally aim for a higher standard of facilities than a self-employed electrician.

People from other countries often have distinct ideas on where they will feel most comfortable. The Hilton group, for example, has endeavoured to appeal to the large number of Japanese tourists and business persons by having bedrooms designed to Japanese specifications, offering a Japanese menu at breakfast and having an interpreter on staff. An odd effect of this seemingly good marketing strategy is that many Japanese report that they are disappointed by this concession. They say it takes away from the glamour of being in a 'foreign country'!

Social class segments

There are several ways of segmenting a market by social distinctions. The two most common forms are (1) demographic, which is subdividing the market by people's ages, gender, occupation, ability to pay and place of origin; and (2) psychographic, which is subdividing people by their personality types, lifestyle aspirations and reasons for wanting a particular kind of hospitality experience.

Figure 4.2   *Market segmentation*

Classifications such as upper class, upper middle, lower middle, upper lower and lower are somewhat dated, but still remain useful. All socio-economic segments are of interest in marketing, depending as they do on people's income, occupation, schooling, place of residence and standing in the community.

Lifestyle segments

Psychographic or motivational segmentation is arguably a more exact form of segmentation because lifestyles are often the reason for choosing a particular hospitality experience. Lifestyle segments offer a marketer the opportunity to target plan more accurately to people's needs and prepare a product mix which will be geared to their wants. This is explained in the next chapter.

Buying stage segments

Holidays and extended business trips are usually 'considered purchases', and there are various stages of readiness to purchase, ranging from being 'aware' of the property, to being 'interested' and then to being 'ready to buy' before people ultimately become customers. Each stage is a market segment and requires careful attention in hospitality marketing so that the transitions are smoothly handled by an establishment without loss of too many potential customers.

'Benefits sought' segments

There are many segments in this category arising from people who seek specific benefits from hospitality, such as their requirements for:

- certain styles of accommodation (quiet, busy, popular, big, small, luxurious, budget, etc.);
- types of meals (gourmet, regional fare, carvery, fast food, vegetarian, etc.);
- locations (near to sea, views, shops, theatres, business, transport, etc.);
- facilities (golf, pool, sauna, tennis, equestrian, etc.).

Purchase cycle and frequency segments

Most products have markets which are cyclical, and this is especially the case with hospitality. There are those who have annual holidays and those for whom it is possible to have more than one holiday in a year. These are 'seasonal' or 'habitual' holidaymaker segments. There are even some lucky ones who manage to holiday all year round. Business travel drops off significantly in July and August.

What constitutes a holiday for people varies considerably, ranging from a camping trip to a world sightseeing tour staying at the largest and most expensive establishments. Types of travellers are grouped into segments depending upon their financial worth to a marketer.

Business travellers are categorized according to their frequency of travel and labelled as either heavy, medium or light users. Airlines promote products to the 'frequent flyer' segment and offer incentives, such as the award of air miles, to attract their membership or custom. Similarly, large hotels target heavy user segments and offer discounts, room up-grading or special privileges to attract their patronage. Restaurants always pay special attention to 'regulars' and endeavour to cherish and nurture this customer base through loyalty award schemes and being responsive to their requests for special products or services.

User segments

There are many with a 'club' mentality who regularly attend a bar, restaurant or hotel, etc, which they particularly like. They can also be dubbed a 'loyal' segment. Others have a routine of drinking or eating, but shift their loyalty from time to time. These are called 'shifting loyals'. Switchers are the ones who have no sense of belonging to one establishment and constantly explore places for new experiences. Another large segment for the hospitality industry is the 'celebratory' or 'special occasion' segments – those people who use outside facilities for weddings, anniversaries, birthdays, reunions and a miscellany of other special occasion reasons.

Price segments

Everyone considers price. Most people seek value. Many are forced to pay less, some pay less because they are careful with their money and there are those who think that if it is expensive it must be good. Hospitality establishments will vary in the way they cater for all the different price segments in the market.

Competing products and their strategic segments

An easy form of segmentation is to label the people which each competitor mainly seems to attract and refer to that market by the competitor's name. Thus we can have the 'Sheraton' market, the 'Inter-Continental' market and so on. Not all products compete in exactly the same way. For example, two budget lodges may be on opposite sides of a motorway with almost identical facilities. However, each will attract a different segment of the available passing traffic. Of course, one will get the north-bound traffic and the other will get the south-bound traffic.

A simple way to segment customers

Where several establishments are similar, say, a group of four- and five-star hotels in a city, a simple way of market analysis is to divide the available customers in the market into 'fors, againsts, indifferents and unawares'.

Those who are *for* an establishment are customers now, or likely to be soon. Many will pass on the good word and attract others.

Those who are *against* the establishment have been there and didn't like it, and they are bad news because the chances are they will tell people they didn't like their experience.

Those who are *indifferent* know about it but see no reason for trying it. They are not convinced and they are going elsewhere.

Those who are *unaware* simply haven't got the message. They don't have enough information.

It is the percentages in each category which are important in this exercise. An establishment with a high 'against' percentage is in deep trouble. The place with a high 'indifferent' percentage is not competitive enough. It is not offering enough benefits. A high 'unaware' percentage means that it is not communicating enough and has to work harder to get the message across.

In summary, one of the main reasons for segmenting a market is because we are concerned with people's minds, understanding what they need and want. It is what existing and potential customers know, think, feel and believe that has formed the market, so if we want to improve our products' chances in the market place we must understand the mind-set of each market segment.

SALES ANALYSIS   DATE:..............   FACILITIES USED

NAME	NO OF PEOPLE	ROOM TYPE	DATE ARRIV	DATE LEAVE	TRAVEL REAS.	FROM WHERE	NEXT DEST.	ACCOM	REST.	BISTRO	BAR	ROOM SERV.	GYM	POOL	COURT	PHONE

£ TOTALS

RATE/PACKAGE:
METHOD OF PAYMENT:
PERSON TYPE:
NEXT BOOKING DATE:
OUTCOME FOR CLIENT:
COMMENTS:

Daily sales analysis sheets like this one provide the basis for accumulating data about guests – the types of people, where they come from, the reason for their stay, what they used and how much they spent. Over time, this data is also used to determine trends, and product strengths and weaknesses.

Figure 4.3 *Daily sales analysis sheet*

Market measurement

The size of geographic market segments

All market segments have to be measured for their viability. Regional market segments are only significant if they have sufficient numbers to warrant special marketing considerations. Japanese, American and German tourists, for instance, are large segments of the total tourism market in the UK. People from the Falkland Islands are not. In a large city, some suburbs will deliver a greater number of customers than others. In order to conserve the marketing effort, it is obviously wise to concentrate on the larger segments unless there is a specific reason for targeting specialized segments.

Sales analysis

The collection and analysis of sales data are the main ways of determining the trends of a business's progression or regression (Figure 4.3). Sales figures are helpful in identifying weaknesses and strengths of products, geographic sales areas, sales representatives' performance, agents' activities, selling methods and advertising. To do this thoroughly, internal sales records and a bookings analysis from each profit-earning centre are required, together with profit and loss results.

Market share comparison

Market share figures are necessary because these demonstrate how the business is doing by comparison with others in the same area of activity. Often in the hospitality industry these figures are shared, to the advantage of all concerned. If not, market share estimates have to be obtained by either market research, observation of supply deliveries or by doing regular customer counts.

Performance comparisons

What is happening to and for the customer is the major concern of hospitality marketing. The reason for market analysis is to identify how well the various services of the property are being delivered. In the hospitality industry, service is everything. How is the customer being treated by the establishment, from initial contact through to paying the bill? Are the products performing to the standards required? More importantly, are the products meeting the expectations of the customers?

Service is a measurable function. Not only does the establishment's performance have to be measured, it also has to be compared with what the competition is doing. For example, Pizza Hut promoted that if the customer's order did not arrive in ten minutes it was free! How would the average restaurant perform with that as an offer? Nine times out of ten, the sum total of the customers' experiences over time will determine an establishment's sales results and its market share.

In a large hotel or holiday complex with many products or profit centres involved in producing a total result, each product in the mix has to be analysed to ascertain strengths and weaknesses. Invariably, some areas will perform better than others, when all should be of a uniform standard if an establishment's market position is to be maintained.

The external influences affecting the market

Government rules and regulations, taxation demands, trade and supplier considerations, etc., all impact on the industry. As part of the analysis, the measures taken by an establishment to meet such requirements must be assessed. Reactions to change are important. For example, if a certain type of food becomes difficult to obtain locally, does the establishment endeavour to obtain supplies from further afield? If the excise on alcoholic beverages suddenly increases, does it pass the additional cost on to the customer immediately, or hold back and allow other establishments to give the customer the bad news?

Competitors' activities

Compiling files of the opposition's advertising, observing and reporting on their sales promotions, seeing their products in action and noticing customer reactions, builds a picture of comparative performances. A market analysis is not complete without this information.

Information sources

A business never works in isolation, and a hospitality establishment is always very visible in the market place. It is necessary to discover how tourist boards, suppliers, bankers, insurers, politicians, government departments and influential people in the industry perceive the market and obtain from them their opinions of how the property is performing. Trade publications, trade and industry reports, government statistics, newspapers and published marketing research are invaluable sources of information. Often they will give advance notice of some industry trends.

The performance of intermediaries (distribution and agency sales outlets) must also be part of the market analysis. A report from and about each agent which makes a significant contribution to an establishment's sales often reveals a goldmine of usable information. Further analysis is needed to examine the leading indicators of the industry in a search for impending building developments, government and legal interference, economic trends, social and cultural trends and even climatic change.

Assessing the data

The value of market analysis is knowledge, and knowledge is power. Market analysis is a fact-gathering process. The sum total of the information gained should provide a picture for management to take action on future marketing changes and improvements. Each market segment therefore has to be measured against the performance of each of the property's products. It should reveal what the property is good at and what the customer thinks it lacks.

No segmentation system is perfect. There will always be some people who don't quite fit into the allowable categories. However, for measurement purposes and ultimate diagnosis of a market condition, provided that the segmentation basis used is logical and covers most contingencies it will be sufficient.

What do you do with the information? How market analysis is used in planning is covered in the chapters dealing with the strategic planning stages of marketing.

Questions for discussion or revision

1 If there is a gradual downturn in sales by a hotel, which areas would you examine and how would you discover the reason for this?
2 Two five-star hotels in the city area are competing for the lucrative business market. Prices have been maintained at a high level. Suddenly, a new contender builds a superior complex. Before it is completed, one of the existing hotels does a full-scale survey and market analysis locally, nationally and internationally. What is this hotel looking for?

3 If your hotel's market analysis reveals that a substantial number of people are unaware of many of your facilities, what does this tell you and what remedial action would you take?

4 A large guest house on the outskirts of the city, with accommodation for 60 people in rooms with bathrooms ensuite, is considering applying for a hotel licence. First, it does a market analysis. How would it go about this, and about which aspects of the market in particular would it want information?

5 Many people complain about a particular hotel being too up-market for them. This is a bit vague. How would you go about ascertaining the real problem?

6 How many segments of the market for champagne can you think of?

5 Segmentation by purchase motivations

Aims of this chapter

1 To explain how to identify the market segments which are motivated by personality, lifestyle and class distinctions.
2 To identify the behaviour characteristics of purchasers and the influences on their decisions to buy a particular style of hospitality experience.

Lifestyle factors

There are huge numbers of people all around the world with the desire and the money to spend on travel, accommodation, entertainment and leisure. They represent a diversity of nations, occupations, incomes and personalities and they have a wide range of reasons for wanting a particular hospitality experience. Obviously, the whole market is too vast and diverse for one establishment to attempt to satisfy.

For practical purposes, therefore, the total market has to be subdivided into many smaller markets, and by the use of market analysis an establishment can determine which segments best suit one's location, property size and type, expertise and resources. The selection of the most appropriate segments is target marketing, and its purpose is to provide a focus for the whole marketing effort.

It is people's preferred lifestyle which determines their behaviour and guides the pattern of their purchases. Not everyone wants to live the same way, and therefore there are lifestyle preferences which can be clustered to form market segments. Once management knows the thinking of each of these market segments, it is in a position to decide which segments to target, and the strategies that are developed for those segments will be more incisive if management is armed with the reasons for their various behavioural attributes and attitudes.

Trying to understand behaviour patterns of a whole market for hospitality has become increasingly difficult in the last five years, and the signs are that it will become more so. For the hospitality industry only one thing is certain: people will continue to want places to eat, drink and sleep. But how, where and when they will want to do these things is a matter of continuing complexity.

It is no longer possible to erect formula hotels on any site in the world and expect them to return dividends on the investment. Too many investors have burnt their fingers. Kleinwort Benson, in their 1995 annual review of Quoted UK Hotel Companies, estimated that in total there are around 35 000 hotel rooms in the UK, accounting for almost 10 per cent of total hotel room stock, which are obsolete and on the market for sale. The large chains are substituting many of them with budget lodges, which are being developed predominantly in secondary and tertiary locations. They are among the best performing hotels in the market and are replacing the full feature and limited feature hotels in these locations.

New-built hotels in major and primary locations in the mid and upper levels of the market are a rarity, and likely to remain so, in the short to medium term at least. In London, in particular, there are no material additions to supply planned in the foreseeable future.

The truth of the markets in the 1990s is that the industry needs to provide travellers with the services and the facilities they really need rather than the five-star luxuries they can no longer afford. What has happened? In a nutshell, change is happening at a speed which has made the unthinkable of yesterday the reality of today. The demographics and lifestyles of most countries are changing quite dramatically. In the UK, for example, the population is increasingly greying, women are having fewer children, and later, there are an increasing number of single-parent homes, higher levels of education achievement and the number of women in employment continues to rise. This, combined with rising unemployment, recession, the widening gap between the haves and the have-nots, is changing consumer expenditure patterns. We also have changes in attitudes to the ecology of the country which are altering demand for many types of products. Advances in technology are allowing the introduction of new products which are rapidly being accepted by consumers.

Significantly, there seems to be a return by many of the younger generation to adopt core cultural values of fifty or more years ago. There is a growing disillusionment with current politics and ideologies, less interest by large numbers of the population in extravagant materialism and a cynicism about advertising claims. There is a large gap between the aspirations of people over 40 and the generation under 30.

The world is becoming multi-cultural, with most societies having similar attitudes towards the things which comprise a civilized existence. There is a growing sameness about cities, with the omnipresent Coca Cola and McDonald's signs, for example, emerging in the most surprising places. The development of satellite communications and the intrusiveness of TV have removed many of the mysteries that once surrounded the political, cultural and geographical features of remote areas.

On the other hand, one would have thought that information and education would bring greater understanding between races and nations, but ancient grievances and ethnic intolerance remain. Rather than the world becoming closer, it seems that these differences between races and nations have been exacerbated in some regions. The removal of the Iron Curtain, and the demise of the political regimes which dominated Eastern Europe and Russia, for example, have created separate states and countries with distinct regional antagonisms which are historical and racial in origin. In the future there may well be a reversion to a tribal border mentality. The warnings uttered by writers such as Nesbitt, in his book *Megatrends*, and Toffler, in his books, *Future Shock* and *The Third Wave*, cannot be taken lightly as, in the main, they continue to be awesomely accurate.

One of the trends these writers identified is the new computerized information transfer technologies which will create a huge employment pool for home-workers. The same technology makes it possible for the home to become the main entertainment source. Shopping can be done from home. Whereas the older generations are not racing towards early adoption of this way of life, the new generations probably will. Already there are ominous signs of them being far less interested in the world around them and possibly a reduced desire to travel. The effects this group will have on travel and tourism have yet to be seen.

These are broad generalizations, of course, but they may explain the slow growth in travel to some countries and the effects it will have for a while on future hospitality demands. Already the styles of eating out being requested are changing and causing the demise of many silver service and fine dining restaurants, as large numbers of people all over the Western world turn to a less formal eating out experience in favour of fast food, brasserie and American diner-style eateries.

Brasseries are big business. As the UK emerges from recession, the trend is to open big, 'buzzy' restaurants, serving high quality, mid-priced food. They aim to be accessible to a far wider audience than would ever walk through the doors of any Michelin-starred establishment. Many of the UK's top chefs have turned their attention to the cooking of simple fare. What they are doing is putting more time, effort and money into new, bigger and bolder restaurants.

The real danger in referring to trends is that they do not apply to everyone. The changes affecting the hospitality business indicate a further fracturing of the overall market into more segments of people with quite different purchase motivations from each other.

Buying influences on behaviour

Before making a purchase, buyers go through a series of decision processes and, in most cases, others are involved in the process. The stages of purchase are the same as those used in selling, and can be remembered by using the acronym A.I.D.A. which stands for:

A. Awareness
I. Interest
D. Desire
A. Action

Before the purchase is finally made there is a nervous period when most would-be buyers require convincing that they are doing the right thing and they look for reassurance from others. Once their doubts are overcome, they usually proceed to buy.

It is interesting to note that there is evidence from work done by several research agencies in the United States which suggests that most advertising is read by purchasers who seek reassurance that they have made the correct decision. The reason for this, the researchers claim, is that after purchase comes another nasty moment: did the purchaser make the right decision? Much luxury car advertising is of this nature.

Post-purchase jitters are the reason why after-sales service is so vital. The key to getting customers to come back, or converting a once-only customer into being a regular client, is to concentrate on making sure of satisfaction after the event. This is why every establishment should know the name and address of every customer and maintain regular contact from immediately after the sale and thereafter.

The lenses of distortion

Despite heated denials when the matter is raised, most people buy to please or impress others. Who they are pleasing or impressing may vary. Spouse, parents, boss, close friends and relatives are the most common influencers. Thus the product is perceived by the purchaser through other people's eyes and this distorts what they are seeing, which is why the attributes of many products are overlooked by the buyer. It explains why some people keep on making the wrong purchases; they are actually being motivated by their desire to impress or please someone else, maybe even a mythical group of peers who exist only in the person's mind. 'Where did you stay?' is a question frequently asked of a returning traveller, followed by 'How was it, any good?' Everyone prefers to give answers that will impress the questioner.

For marketers, just as important as the person actually making the decision are the unseen people who influenced the decision. This is well known to marketers of weekend breaks, for instance. They market to women because they know that the woman is going to either tell the man what to book, go and book it herself or, certainly in the case of most situations, the man is going to ask the woman's opinion before he books.

Who influences the decision where to go for holidays? In the majority of cases it is the wife or girlfriend. When a couple are going out for dinner, who usually gets their way? The family of five is driving along the motorway at lunch-time. Who decides where they will stop to eat? The roles involved in buying motivation are:

- the *initiator*, the one who first suggests or thinks of buying something;
- the *influencer*, the one whose advice or opinion counts most in the decision to buy;
- the *decider*, the one who makes up everybody's mind;
- the *purchaser*, the one who actually makes the purchase;
- the *user or users*, who often have plenty to say about the purchase afterwards.

Figure 5.1 *Who initiated, who influenced and who decided the choice of restaurant? Who paid the bill? Next time, the users may be the deciders*

In hospitality, the person in a group who pays the bill may not be the one you are trying to please, or the one who says whether they are coming back next time. In the corporate scene, the identification of the key people and the roles they play in making a decision is more complicated because there are usually more people involved in both influencing and deliberating over the decision. The secretary phones through the booking, but who was involved in making the choice of establishment?

In the case of a new product, a new service, or a product which is new to the prospective customer, there is always hesitancy. Some people make decisions earlier than others, and they are called early adopters. They are the first to go to a new tourist resort, try out a new bar, or select from the chef's specials. At the opposite end are the laggards, who make sure that everyone else is satisfied before they take the plunge. In between are the early majority and the late majority.

The job of a marketer is to identify these processes and assist the purchaser to make an easy decision, remembering that it is word-of-mouth advertising, or simply the 'good word' being passed on by satisfied customers, which is critical to an establishment's acceptance and eventual success. Therefore every customer has to be seen in the light of his or her ability to affect thousands of future sales.

Purchase behaviour

Most people would like to think that they are masters of their own destiny. The truth is, in most cases people make purchases which are motivated by two major factors:

1 Their aspirations to be a certain type of person who lives a particular way of life.
2 The cultural and social influences which have formed the society in which they live.

The sort of person anyone wants to be is affected by his or her self-perception, personality, desired lifestyle, social class attitudes, intelligence and physical capacity to achieve. These are inner-directed considerations and are usually the result of the genes that made them and the environment into which they were born.

Further modifications of a person's purchase decisions are a result of his or her age-related needs, gender, living mode (where he or she lives and whether he or she is married, single, widowed, or whatever), race or nationality, financial resources and parental, marital or peer group pressures.

People's identities are created by a combination of their possessions and the things they do because they are outward, visible signs of individuality. Their name, family background, nationality, occupation, home and district, car and household possessions, schooling, professional and trade associations, are all possessive factors that give a person a sense of being and belonging. Their 'beingness' is further substantiated by what they 'do', such as their sporting activities, hobbies, interests, work and socializing.

People's identities and self-perceptions are also revealed to us by their personalities. The word personality comes from the Greek *persona*, meaning 'mask'. Oscar Wilde said, 'It's not people themselves who are interesting, it is the masks they wear in society.'

A Greek philosopher, Galen (AD 130–200) recognized that people tended to pursue identity by being either extroverted or introverted, competitive or careful. The combination of these factors, he believed, produces four basic personality types which are generally easy to recognize as customer types.

Performers

These are people who like to be noticed. Often loud and ostentatious, they are talkers, extroverts, gregarious and usually stimulating people to be with. They prefer bright colours, striking fashions, outstanding cars and have lots of friends. They go out a lot and want to be where the action is so that they can be noticed. They are very people-orientated.

Rulers

This group of people are less friendly, cooler and calculating. They like to be in charge of people and situations. They are usually active, hard-working and

PERFORMERS

FOLLOWERS

RULERS

THINKERS

Figure 5.2 *Four basic personality types*

task-dominated. They seek and mostly obtain positions of power. Their dress is formal and their taste in most possessions is restrained, elegant but often lacking in warmth.

Followers

This is a friendly personality group of people who are often shy and like to avoid trouble, facing up to it when they have to and often with considerable determination. They prefer home and a nice comfortable environment without being too noticeable. Essentially cautious and conservative, followers mostly prefer supportive roles in the community. They make good team members, performing tasks willingly and helpfully. They want to be popular and normal, consequently they make safe decisions and purchase reliable, popular brands of everything.

Thinkers

These are independent, usually preoccupied types of people who work at their own pace. They are systematic, task-orientated people who shun the limelight. They work to regulations because they like to know where they stand in most situations, erring on the side of caution. Utility is more important than looks, so sports cars and the bright lights are not for them. They are do-it-yourself types as a rule.

The ancient Greeks referred to the four main types as being melancholic (thinkers), choleric (rulers), phlegmatic (followers) and sanguine (performers).

In addition to the four main personality types, there are six common combinations: Performer/Ruler, Ruler/Follower, Ruler/Thinker, Performer/Thinker, Performer/Follower and Follower/Thinker. These are referred to in Dibb et al (1991) in discussion of the psychological factors influencing the buying decision process.

Social classes

It is probably a combination of personality (mostly set in concrete by the time a person is eight years of age), genes and social/cultural influences which produce the social classes. It is unpopular to talk about social classes, some people preferring to believe that there are only two – the privileged and the disadvantaged. This latter attempt at categorization stems from the belief that class is a consequence of financial opportunity or accident of birth. The evidence of a multifaceted and complex society suggests that people are not forced into a social category, but rather they choose to position themselves in a social category. Only a minority have no choice.

This may be an arguable point of view, but a study by Warner and Lunt, and a subsequent study commissioned by the *Chicago Tribune*, established that:

> there is a social class system and substantial differences exist between classes with respect to their buying habits. The classes do not think the same way and they respond differently to a seller's marketing programmes. Furthermore, money does not necessarily equate with living standards, with some trades people earning more than the professions but having quite different views on how the money should be spent.

The six social classes are termed upper-upper, lower-upper, upper-middle, lower-middle, upper-lower and lower class. The differences are explained in part by the personality types of each group. The upper classes, for example, desire to live an affluent lifestyle which in many cases will disregard their needs or ability to sustain it; whereas many in the lower classes will choose a financially constrained lifestyle even though they could afford to live in a more affluent way.

Social classes have their own set of values and beliefs which serve as criteria for normal behaviour and influence their choice of the brand and the quality of their purchases. This is very apparent in hospitality, with the whole gamut of establishments catering for a class and lifestyle customer mix. Those who would deny the existence of class and lifestyle distinctions fly in the face of the evidence before their eyes in every hospitality establishment in the country.

Some people react to the social box they are in and occasionally may do things which are 'out of character', but most conform to class and personality type.

Bearing in mind the effect of personality, class and lifestyle preferences on purchase behaviour, once the groups are identified it is possible to predict the wants of each group for a hospitality experience. Consequently, when marketing to specific classifications of people, the attributes or benefits of a product should be obvious to each lifestyle classification that is targeted. This enables prospective customers to ascertain quickly from the advertising, the appearance of the establishment, the services and the facilities on offer that it is 'their sort of place'.

It should be noted that corporate motivations are different from private ones. The business executive who uses a suite and entertains lavishly on an expense account considerably modifies the budget when holidaying at the same place with the family.

Summary

When people have a need which can be solved by a purchase, they will usually want that purchase to be reflective of their personality and their class aspirations. Their purchase therefore will be influenced by how they believe others will react to it. People will buy the latest, the most expensive, the best value or the most popular item depending of their personality and class consciousness. There will be some modification of their decisions imposed by financial constraints or their taste. They will want reassurance on their purchase and approval before and after they buy.

As marketing is about satisfying needs and wants, hospitality managers must concentrate their efforts on understanding the segments they intend to target; choosing the ones they can satisfy best and which offer the most opportunity for growth. How to select the right customer mix for an establishment is discussed in the next chapter.

Questions for discussion or revision

1 Apart from thirst, what would be the purchase motivations of a group of office workers who regularly drink at the same pub after work?
2 What would be the most likely product attributes of a cocktail bar in a five-star hotel? Describe what would happen to and for the customer.
3 Name the benefits you think are being sought by a family of four, when they make an unplanned overnight stay en route to their holiday destination. They have not booked any accommodation, have been driving most of the day and don't know the area.

Further reading

Warner, L. and Lunt, P. quoted in *Fundamentals of Marketing*, Stanton, Miller and Layton. Sydney: McGraw-Hill Book Company.
Kleinwort Benson Securities (1995). *Quoted Hotel Companies: The World Markets 1995*, 9th Annual Review, London.

Naisbitt, J. (1982). *Megatrends*. New York: Warner Books.
Toffler, A. (1975). *Future Shock*. London: The Bodley Head.
Toffler, A. (1981). *The Third Wave*. Toronto: Bantam.
Dibb, S., Simkin, L., Pride, W. and Ferrell, O. (1991). *Marketing: Concepts and Strategies*. London: Houghton Mifflin.

6 The customer mix: segmentation by 'reasons for travel or eating out'

Aims of this chapter

1 To explain how to base a customer mix on the people segments which have been revealed by market analysis as the most suitable for the property.
2 To list the various segments which come under the category of 'reasons for travel or eating out' and point out the advantages and disadvantages of each one.
3 To describe how to use the customer matrix to develop a customer mix by identifying how a segment is shared among the competitors in a market region.

Segmentation selection methods

Which available segments of the market revealed by market analysis should management choose to develop, change or eliminate? In other words, of all the many types of people and businesses in the whole of the hospitality market for the region in which the property is located, which ones will suit the resources of the property best?

The type of property, its size, location and facilities will, to a large extent, dictate the customer mix. The intention of management should be to match the resources of the establishment with the most suitable customer mix rather than pursue a market segment which has no links with the existing customer mix or the property's prevailing resource base.

A property which assumes that the total market has a uniform set of needs and wants is adopting a strategy of aggregation. Their belief is that all people are basically the same and that one product mix will suit everyone. The strategy used in segmentation is different. It, more rightly, plans on the fact that people are not all the same and that the hospitality market, even in a small region, comprises many types of people with separate requirements for satisfaction by hospitality services.

The previous chapter on market analysis described how to segment markets by demographic, geographic, behavioural and psychographic criteria, revealing a wide variety of possibilities. Arriving at the best customer mix requires all these possibilities to be sorted and then narrowed to a choice of segments.

All the people in the travel segments do have the same things in common – they want a place to eat and a place to sleep – but, as shown in previous chapters, there are vast differences in each segment's requirements and expectations of a place in which to do these things. Which segments an establishment has now should be checked against those segments which may be more financially attractive and still suit the resources and capabilities of the property.

For hotels and tourist resorts, the best way to select a customer mix is to begin with each segment's 'reasons for travel'. The variables in each segment are then analysed by the targeting process (see Chapter 7) to define and separate the benefits sought by smaller but usually significant sub-markets. Variables affecting the final choice will be the demographics and psychographics of the segments. These can be sorted through until the choice is narrowed to the final customer mix. The customers' reasons for travel create the more obvious market segments such as business, conference, holiday, sport, cultural, compassionate and visiting friends and relatives.

It must be realized that it is not possible to service all segments effectively. They are either too diverse geographically and therefore too difficult to access, or they have particular requirements which are too varied for one establishment to adequately satisfy with the same overall mix of products, facilities or services. The location, resources, experience and competence of an establishment cannot in all cases extend to being able to meet all customers' needs.

Many types of customers do not mix well with each other. For example, the high-profile international business executive is seldom happy to be rubbing shoulders with large families with young children running wild through the hotel and its facilities. There are often ethnic differences, age and lifestyle contrasts, occupation differences and political antagonisms. Bosses don't always want to be with employees and vice versa. A place predominantly occupied by the elderly is not necessarily an attractive environment for young professionals looking for a good night out.

The only situation which makes it possible for a property to be all things to all people is when there is no competition. This can occur in remote villages, for example. Even there, people will often choose not to go at all if the environment and customer mix prevailing at the property is unsuitable for their requirements.

Customer mix percentages

A customer mix for an establishment is determined by the percentages of each market segment it seeks and succeeds in obtaining. An establishment which attempts to satisfy a broad number of segments is said to be indulging in undifferentiated marketing. If it concentrates on several distinctly different segments, it is called differentiated marketing. If it aims at one major segment, it is practising concentrated marketing.

For city establishments, the size of the main market segments it obtains in terms of frequency of usage generally falls in the following order of 'reasons to travel': business; conference/meeting; holiday; visiting friends and relatives; and compassionate (death, illness, accident, etc.). Taken overall, because of their high frequency of usage the business segments are the largest segment of the travel and hospitality market. This is why most centrally located establishments adopt a policy of differentiated marketing and pursue the business segments ahead of other segments.

By contrast, tourist resorts mainly pursue the leisure markets. However, business conferences and seminars still represent a sizeable proportion of their customer mix. Some resorts, such as Blackpool, Brighton and Harrogate, specialize in conferences.

Actually, the total market size in terms of numbers of people is in the following order of 'reasons for travel': holiday; visiting friends and relatives; compassionate; conference/meeting; and business. In other words, the business segment is the smallest in number of people but the largest user of hospitality because business people may make several trips in one year. The leisure segments are larger in numbers of people but most of them make only one trip every several years.

The ranking, or percentages, of each travel type comprising an establishment's customer mix will vary from one region, city or district to another, depending on an establishment's ability to market itself to each segment. In a small city, hotel 'A' might have a customer mix which, when averaged over the year, would have the following percentages favouring the business segments:

Customer mix by reasons for travel

	%
Corporate business	20
Business meetings, conferences	25
Seminars	10
Domestic tourists	5
International tourists	2
Package tours	10
Stopovers	5
Short breaks	5
Miscellaneous and FITS (Frequent Independent Travellers)	18

The customer mix for hotel 'B', which is on the outskirts of a city or in a coastal location, may, by contrast, favour the leisure/pleasure segments and the percentages might be:

Customer mix by reasons for travel

	%
Package tours	20
Miscellaneous and FITS	17
Domestic tourists	15
Corporate business	10
Seminars	10
International tourists	10
Stopovers	8
Short Breaks	7
Business meetings, conferences	3

Customer mix assessment criteria

When choosing the customer mix, each segment has to be assessed on the basis of:

1   *Size*. The corporate market is the first one everyone thinks of because it is composed of a large number of frequent users. For that reason it is also the most competitive. The holiday market is also large. There are many segments and sub-segments worth attention provided that there are sufficient numbers to mount a worthwhile marketing strategy to obtain them.
2   *Location and accessibility*. Most customers heading for the region where the establishment is located come from definable countries and areas. However, it is not always possible to reach them with cost-efficient communication methods.
3   *Homogeneity* of personality types, lifestyle, class, age, occupation and income so that there is an equitable blend. This is mostly sorted out by the customers who will choose the property that has a customer mix with similar lifestyle values to themselves.
4   *Profitability*. The corporate market is the one most often targeted because of its size and frequency of usage. It is also the easiest to access with promotion because it is so prominent. However, it is seldom the most profitable on a pound per unit sale basis. Corporate customers seek discounts and concessions. It is the volume of this segment which makes it attractive and viable.
5   *Durability*. Some segments mushroom into prominence when favourable economic conditions prevail, then disappear at the first sight of hard times. Others are 'trendy' segments. They are hardly good customers around which to build a permanent business.
6   *Expectations of the segment*. Some segments are very demanding and have pre-set ideas of what facilities an establishment should have. For example, people from Islamic cultures have definite requirements for food and beverage and other services. Specialist segments are good business earners if they are of sufficient size, but there is no point in competing for their custom if an establishment's facilities do not match the segment's criteria.

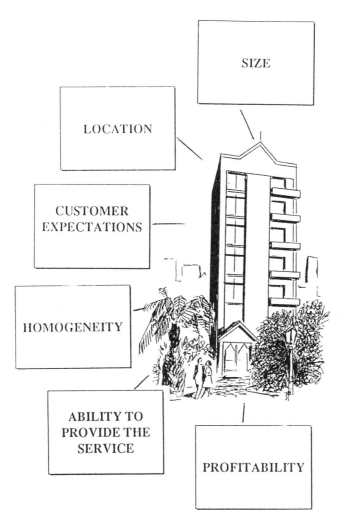

Figure 6.1 *Customer mix assessment criteria*

7 *Ability to service it*. The capacity of the establishment, its resources and competence can be over-stretched; for example, bidding for and winning a conference which fills the place but excludes the regular clientele. Such a move sacrifices long-term customers for short-term profit.

The objective of management should be to get the customer mix right and match it with the right product mix so that the hospitality standards and prices communicate the right message to the chosen market segments. The location of the property, its nearness to entertainment, business centres, special events, holiday infrastructure, etc., its size, facilities and image are factors which will either limit or provide opportunities for the choice of customer mix. How one goes about developing strategies which attract the customer mix is the subject of future chapters.

The reasons for travel

Business travellers

This group provides the largest segment and is therefore the most important. Once dominated by males, the segment has seen more and more women entering it, with different expectations of how establishments should function. Business travellers' needs for accommodation range from a modest room to a suite of rooms with luxurious, self-contained facilities. Many hotels provide special meeting rooms, video conferencing, computers, secretarial assistance and fax facilities. They are virtually offering an office-away-from-the-office to attract the corporate and public service meeting markets.

The traveller's country of origin is an important consideration when targeting the business market. In the UK, the Japanese, US and European markets are being sought by many hotels. Some are offering specific products to suit the expectations of the Japanese in particular.

Conferences and seminars

The conference and seminar business is a huge market requiring a range of small, medium and large conference areas and banqueting facilities. It is a market which is highly competitive and most establishments are keen to bid for it. If an establishment does not have the conference areas to cope, to be adjacent to a conference facility is an advantage in obtaining the accommodation, food and beverage business which is so attractive.

In the case of most large conferences, especially national and international, the bidding is done by a convention and tourist bureau, a promotion or marketing company or a travel consortium. The tender is generally comprehensive and proposes to arrange transport, leisure and shopping opportunities as well as providing a suitable venue. An establishment then has to convince the bidder that it should be included in the package being presented to the conference organizer.

Leisure/pleasure travellers

The reasons for travelling to a holiday destination are varied, and the segments are created by lifestyle, class and demographic considerations. These include single people, couples with children, couples on their own, the young, the elderly, the wealthy, middle income earners and low income earners. The vacation and weekend escape are among the most common reasons for travel. Other reasons for leisure/pleasure travel include sightseeing, health, sport, honeymooning or illicit affairs.

All segments are controlled by their income and the holiday entitlement available to them. In addition, many segments are on a travel schedule which allows for only short stopovers at various places.

The selection of a leisure/pleasure customer mix largely depends on location of the property, its surrounding attractions – the natural and physical tourism infrastructure – and the facilities being offered.

Package holidays

There are many organizations which put together a number of components of a holiday and then sell them as a total package at a special discounted price. These organizations are called 'tour wholesalers'. Airlines, business, rail and travel agent companies are some of the main groups which are involved in wholesaling. The products they create are saleable by anyone with access to a customer base as a rule. The packages can encompass any number of combinations involving travel (sea, air, train, bus or car hire), accommodation, sightseeing, entertainment, sports or special events.

Coach tours

Usually for the young or the elderly, coach tours or bus holidays provide a continuing source of business for hotels, restaurants, coffee shops and tourist attractions of many descriptions.

Motoring holidays

This is the largest of all travel markets because it is cheap and convenient for the majority of people. All that is required is the family car, a map, some money and the will to go. Recent years have seen a resurgence in this market segment as travellers become more independent. Hoteliers have grouped together to provide 'Go-As-You-Please' voucher accommodation schemes where motorists can travel around a number of hotels strategically located on the tourist route. In the UK these have proved particularly popular with the Italian and German markets. Although not a big money spinner for large hotels, its sheer volume feeds numerous small establishments. The quality of the business for a hospitality facility depends on the socio-economic status of the traveller and the benefits sought along the journey.

Caravanning

This is a more serious and planned holiday which is embarked upon by caravanners and campers who are generally dedicated to the freedom and enjoyment of having a 'home on wheels'. Many make the pilgrimage to the same spot year after year. Myriads of caravan parks and adjoining tourist facilities service this segment, but it is a segment undergoing change and being replaced by caravans on a permanent site or self-catering lodges. Restaurants, pubs and coffee shops benefit from this segment, but it does not present much joy for hotels and guest houses.

Group travel

Musicians, entertainers, theatre groups, hobbyists and a variety of special interest types are a large component of this segment. So are sporting associations, social clubs, community service and pensioner groups. They require discounted group rates for everything, but they often fill rooms at off-peak times of the year.

Incentive market

Many organizations reward their employees with travel holidays for good performances, especially sales performances. It is a good market to pursue. In addition, prizes and giveaways for competitions for promotional purposes form part of this segment.

Permanent users

Airlines, construction companies, project developers and many large corporations need a permanent or semi-permanent base for their employees, and request that accommodation always be available either on demand or as a continuing reservation. The level of service required varies, but it is excellent business for most accommodation establishments.

Special events

For festivals, large sporting events, football trips, big concerts, national celebrations and the like, establishments can produce special promotions as a continuing marketing strategy to attract these customers. The usual strategy is to provide tickets, special group rates and packages which include air, bus or train travel. Again, proximity to the venue is a significant advantage. For example, Thistle and Mount Charlotte Hotels was named as the British Legion's official hotel for the 1995 fiftieth anniversary day of Victory in Europe-related events, so its properties offered special packages for those staying at the company's hotels during the weekend commemorations.

Compassionate segment

This is what is called a diffused market, without any identifiable segments of any size. In the main they are individual travellers with a diversity of reasons for travel such as visiting friends and relatives, attending reunions, funerals, private functions and a range of other diverse contacts. The benefits being sought by such travellers are so wide-ranging that it is difficult to single out one group of size worth targeting.

Seasonality

The customer mix of most establishments will vary from weekdays to weekends and change with the months of the year and the seasons. Business and conference segments mainly want accommodation on working days, perhaps booking in on a Sunday night and leaving Friday morning. The weekends usually attract a holiday or short break market. In the UK, January, February, July and August are traditionally slow months for business travel. If you mainly target a business/management/upper-class clientele, and your strategies have been effective in reaching this group, your holiday and weekend markets should be the same types of people because yours is the sort of place they like.

Many establishments offer inducements for the business traveller to 'stay over' or come back another time. Attractive inducements are special rates, up-grading, entertainment such as theatre, concerts, sporting events, or special sightseeing tours. They make it easy for people to accept by offering family plan rates, concert tickets, tour packages and discounted facilities, which are tangible reasons for customers to amend plans or at least make plans for future arrangements.

The local market

For many establishments, the local market is the main or only user of the leisure facilities and food and beverage outlets. If the property is geared towards the domestic business travellers, the local market can be targeted for weekend use of the facilities.

Depending on the country, around half of the adult population never travel away from their region, and a similar percentage seldom venture from home to use the facilities of a hotel restaurant or bar and, believe it or not, do not even visit a McDonalds. Such people are not potential customers. Nevertheless, a substantial number of patrons exist in local areas, and whichever segments an establishment attracts from the travel market, the same segments can be targeted locally.

Some places spurn the locals, forgetting their role as potential influencers. Travellers going to an unfamiliar area want information and reassurance on where to stay or which hospitality places to visit. If they know someone at the destination, it is common for them to phone, fax or write and seek advice.

The places which spurn the locals do so to preserve their guests from unwarranted intrusions or to maintain exclusivity for their guests. Most international hotels, for example, do not have public bars. Some make the restaurant prohibitively expensive as a means of restricting the access of all but the wealthiest of the locals, whom they regard as a captive market. However, the most profitable of properties know that it pays to familiarize and encourage the indigenous markets and offer full access to the establishment's facilities.

Modes of transport

Another way of choosing a customer mix is to assess the modes of transport used by various segments. This makes sense for budget lodges, for example, which are mostly dependent on car and commercial travellers. Hotels adjacent to airports would naturally target plane travellers. Resorts are dependent on their location and this depends on customer travel access to the property.

Points to remember

- Choosing the customer mix begins with the market segments' reasons for travel. The final selection of segments is adjusted by considering the demographic and psychographic market variables of each segment.

- The customer mix is dictated by the establishment's resources, experience and location.
- Assess each segment on the basis of its size, location and accessibility, homogeneity, profitability, durability, the segment's expectations and the ability of the establishment to meet those expectations.
- The usage rate by each segment of the market will vary according to the environmental variables of the market, the most dynamic of which are economic and political.
- Analyse the city, region and country the customers come from. This knowledge assists in the appointment of sales staff, agents, promotion and publicity and the provision of facilities which best suit the customers' requirements.
- Consider the attitudes of the local market and its ability to influence the customer mix.

The customer matrix

Nearly all governments maintain records of tourists and travellers and sometimes, through customers and visa records, their reasons for travel to the country or region. These statistical data can be used to compare an establishment's customer mix with the total market potential. When customer records are kept over a period of time, a complete picture of the existing customer mix emerges, which can be compared with the competition's customer mixes. It will show which types of customers are being lost to the competition and which market segments offer the best potential and the least potential. Modification to products and facilities can be the result, or the provision of new facilities to cater for a missing market.

The purpose of the customer matrix or market grid is to provide a means of analysing each market segment and, on the basis of comparison with the competition, choose the segments which can be expanded or added to the establishment's customer mix.

Restaurant segmentation selection

The method for selecting a customer mix for a restaurant is very similar to that used for selecting an accommodation customer mix. It begins with the reasons why people eat out and the benefits being sought by them. The selection of segments is then narrowed by the variable of each segment's demographic and psychographic attributes. Essentially, the customer mix will be affected by the establishment's location, its physical and human resources and the experience of management.

Each reason for dining out is a market segment. In the course of a year, some people can find cause to eat out for several different reasons. Consequently, over a period it is possible to find the same group of people eating fast food, dining in a luxury, fine dining restaurant or going out for an 'Indian'. The

Reason for travel..

Benefits sought..

(A customer matrix can be completed for each travel reason segment, and each cluster of benefits sought)

TOTAL MARKET PROFILE	TOTAL SALES	SHARE OF SALES (EXPRESS IN NUMBERS OR PERCENTAGE OF TOTAL SALES)					
		A	B	C	D	E	YOURS
MALES							
FEMALES							
AGED 16-18							
19-24							
25-34							
35-44							
45-54							
55-64							
65-74							
75+							
EXECUTIVE							
PROFESSIONAL							
MIDDLE MANAGER							
SELF EMPLOYED TRADE							
SMALL BUSINESS OWNER							
SUPERVISOR							
SKILLED WORKER							
RETIRED							
INDEPENDENT MEANS							
SINGLE							
COUPLE							
FAMILY							
GROUP							
LOCAL ORIGIN							
COUNTRY							
OVERSEAS							
UPPER-UPPER							
LOWER-UPPER							
UPPER-MIDDLE							
LOWER-MIDDLE							
UPPER-LOW							

Figure 6.2   *The customer matrix or market grid*

majority, though, dine out from habit. They find a restaurant which suits them and, for varying lengths of time, will consistently use the facilities of a few establishments, only moving on when they become disappointed or bored with one outlet and want a change.

The reasons people eat out

In each of the following examples a different benefit is being sought. In some cases, several reasons are combined:

Convenience: this means 'somewhere quick', a place close to the hotel, home or office. It also can mean car parking nearby.

Escape: to get away from it all. Whether it is the home, the office, a difficult situation or person, we are all familiar with the need for a haven or retreat. Escape is also offered by unique places, including a ship, a castle or a train that has been turned into a restaurant, a place with a panoramic view, a farmhouse, even a cave. There are many imaginative options for this segment.

'Where there's a crowd': music or entertainment, somewhere different and possibly exciting is the requirement here. As well as a pianist or jazz group, there are some places which offer a play while the customers eat, a murder mystery, or fun characters waiting on the tables.

To be with others: where people might find someone they know. In the words of the theme tune from the well known situation comedy series 'Cheers', 'Everyone likes to go where everybody knows their name.' This is a typical club approach, and some restaurants and pubs fill this requirement because they have secured a band of regulars with like needs and habits. Noise, activity and companionship are the needs of this segment.

A meeting place: seclusion and exclusion are the needs of this occasion, and they are often the requirements of a business group who want to have a serious discussion while eating. There are also personal reasons such as 'somewhere quiet, where we can talk', or 'where we can be alone together'.

A food experience: here the reason is for a food style, such as a steak, fish, vegetarian, or frequently to taste the delights of food themes such as Thai, Indian, Italian, Chinese, Japanese, etc. A few are also entranced by the concept of an expensive gourmet fine dining experience.

A special occasion: a celebration of any sort, such as the finalizing of a business deal, an anniversary, birthday, visiting guests to be impressed, a win at the races, etc.

Somewhere casual: this does not mean that this segment wants cheap food. It could be as simple as not wanting to change out of leisure clothes. Most likely they are seeking a casual, relaxed environment which offers value for money. This is a growing segment all over the world. Their requirements may range from fast food to a moderately expensive establishment as long as it meets the criterion of being 'hassle-free'.

There are sub-segments of each of these 'reasons-for-eating-out' markets caused by demographic and psychographic variables. The key variables would be the income and class distinctions of the segments. Another variable will be

Figure 6.3 *The reasons people eat out*

the type of food service, such as buffet, carvery, brasserie or more formal silver service.

Hotels should consider the overall or 'umbrella' image of their property when deciding on a customer mix for their restaurants or bars. For example, a luxury hotel does not have to have an expensive restaurant with formal service, especially with the trend towards a more relaxed dining experience. Perhaps casual elegance would be more suitable.

Questions for discussion or revision

1 If you were sales manager of a five-star hotel with a large business and professional clientele, how would you handle an enquiry from an amateur football club which wants a group discount for a five-day stay? Explain the reasons for your decision.
2 Assume you are the manager of a five-star hotel which has five floors of accommodation with four suites and 100 rooms on each floor. Would you segment your guests by floors? If so, describe the criteria you would apply to differentiate the customers from each other on the various floors.
3 If you were the manager of a hotel with three bars, how would you organize the attributes of the bars to suit the four main people types identified by Galen? Describe the decor and service experiences you would offer. Which of the four types would you combine in your deliberations?

7 *Target marketing*

Aims of this chapter

1 To explain how to target viable market segments by using the Market Menu and Target Market Grid.
2 To explain that the basic purpose of targeting is to choose market segments which best suit the property's resources and capabilities and then build a customer base around these segments by offering a clearly sustainable competitive advantage.

Opportunities from market analysis

A hospitality establishment, like any business venture, can either create a market, discover one, join one, specialize in one, or target several segments. It can be said that a tourist resort commencing in a new area and offering unique facilities is creating a market. A hotel which thinks it is catering for one type of customer can 'discover' it is gaining most of its business from an unexpected source. A hotel which sets out to capture a well-established market in the same location as several others is joining a market if it does no more than offer the same services. A hotel which caters only for the health-conscious is specializing in one market.

Targeting is selective. It fixes on market segments and makes it possible for products and strategies to be developed which are specific to the needs and wants of the people comprising the segments for a price they are prepared to pay. It is more cost-efficient for the marketer's promotions than a broad or undifferentiated marketing approach. It is about customizing products and services. In targeting, management develops strategies for each market. The rule is – one market, one strategy.

A single market for everyone does not exist. Even a universally used product like Coca-Cola cannot and does not target everyone. Coca-Cola changes its strategies for each market it targets, including its container type and size, promotion, price and distribution. It targets different age groups, genders, lifestyles and people with various diet preferences. It is interesting to observe that commercials aimed at one group are seldom noticed or recalled by another.

The purpose of market analysis therefore is not only to establish the segments that form a market, but also to search for and identify segments capable of being targeted and then exploited. The objective is to either consolidate, expand or increase profitability.

One can have several, even dozens, of target markets for the same product with each segment responding to different persuasions. When choosing the target markets that suit a property or a product best, you can define the people you want by their needs, wants, preferred benefits and features and price. You can also select them according to their demographics (age, income, occupation and gender) or their psychographics (personality, lifestyle and class).

Needs arise from people who seek security, ego gratification, bodily comfort, escape and the basics of food, shelter and clothing.

Wants are individual expressions of needs which are translated into things and experiences that suit people's ideas of colour, size, fashion, shape and performance.

Targeting is crucial to good marketing because it recognizes the differences between people types and generates new products or changes to existing products which satisfy individual preferences. The reason for being so precise when determining target markets is because the attitudes of masses of people are often difficult to understand. Small groups are more understandable and predictable and therefore easier to satisfy with separate marketing solutions. Target marketing is the opposite of mass marketing (undifferentiated or aggregation marketing), which does not recognize separate preferences.

So much in hospitality relies on understanding and appreciating people; it should be easy to see why targeting is the platform of a marketing plan.

Case example

'Our customers come from all over the world,' said the manager of a large Paris hotel, proudly waving his arms to encompass the universe. 'All types, all nationalities you will find here. That is why we do not target anyone in particular. How could we?'

'How many people have you had from Rwanda in the last two years?' asked the interviewer. 'From where?' 'Precisely. How about Iceland? Andorra? Burundi?'

The perplexed look of the manager was replaced with triumph. 'No, not them but Japan, yes! America, yes! Germany, yes! All the important countries!'

'That's the point,' exclaimed the interviewer. 'Targeting is about concentrating on those countries and segments which are important, ignoring the segments which offer insufficient return. It would be senseless to have a sales office or to advertise in Burundi, but I bet you have plenty of dialogue with the travel agents and tour wholesalers in the countries you have mentioned.'

'Well, it is good business to do that. I see what you mean. . .'

The selection process used in targeting

The way to use target marketing at the planning stage is to follow the steps explained in the previous chapters:

- Conduct a market analysis and identify the key segments that make up the total market.
- Sort them according to their demographic, geographic, psychographic and behavioural characteristics.
- Establish the sales volume of each product used by the various market segments.
- Find out the reasons for each segment's product preferences.
- Determine the segments that the property is now servicing.
- Identify segments that the property is not servicing and decide which ones would be attractive to target.

The information gained from the market analysis will usually throw up some segments which represent opportunities for the property to expand its customer base. *Definition*: a customer base is the hard core of customers who make up the bulk of an establishment's clientele.

- Establish which competing properties are successful with the segments which are attractive for targeting. Find out whether the people comprising those segments are happy with the level of service they are receiving.

When a group of people seem not to have their requirements or expectations of hospitality fully satisfied, there is an opportunity for exploitation by providing a better service.

Before embarking on a plan, first be sure that your property is located in the right place and has the resources and capabilities to win the segments over. If it has, perhaps with some reasonable modifications to products, consider some strategies which might move a significant number of people in those segments over to your property.

- Conduct a feasibility study. Make certain that the segments you have targeted are worthwhile. Assess each segment on the basis of its size, location and accessibility, profitability, durability, the segment's expectations and the establishment's ability to service the segment.
- Commission research to fill in information gaps necessary to answer any questions arising from the assessment procedures.
- Armed with the appropriate information, you are now in a position to confirm the segments which are to be targeted because they offer the most potential for the property.
- It is probable that, in order to meet the targeted segment's needs, it will be necessary to develop, change or modify the facilities or product mix. The cost of making these changes has to be weighed against the profits likely to be obtained and the time it will take to recoup the outlay. This too is part of the feasibility study.

- If all criteria are satisfactory, the marketing planning process then continues with the development of marketing mix strategies for each of the targeted segments.

How to use the grid or matrix

The customer mix matrix or Target Market Grid uses a Market Menu as a means of narrowing the selection process to one or several market segments. In the case of hotel establishments, the process begins by selecting the reasons for travel. For restaurants, it begins with the reasons for dining out.

The Market Menu is the list of variable factors which have to be considered when selecting a market segment. From each list one factor is selected to go into the Target Market Grid. When complete, a picture emerges of the people comprising the market segment to be targeted. The purpose of the process is to bring the segment into focus so that it features recognizable and understandable people, not just a broad-sweeping demographic category.

The danger of generalization is ever apparent in marketing. A group defined as men aged 18 and over is not even a market, let alone a target market. Whereas there are a few very basic things that a young man of 18 might have in common with an 80-year-old, the vast majority of needs and wants of the two are a long way apart. Even a group defined as '18-year-old students' will have enormously different wants from each other.

In the selection process, each item on every list has to be thought about carefully. Not every list will be applicable, of course. Religion, for example, does not always become a factor in the various products used in hospitality, but sometimes it is important.

Do not be concerned that, by targeting a narrowly defined segment of people, those outside the target will miss the message. This is not a problem. There is a radiation effect from any public promotion like advertising, and nearly everyone knows whether or not a product or service is meant for them.

When a segment is properly targeted, the people become a reality – tangible, understandable human beings whose particular traits have been recognized and acknowledged.

The hospitality market menu

Market segments

Business	Vacation, leisure, pleasure
Package holidays, tours	Backpackers
Conference, seminar	Honeymooners
Coach tours	Hill walkers, climbers
Meeting	Sport
Motoring holiday	Incentive

Special event

Caravanners

FITs

Sightseeing

Compassionate

Group travel

Mode of travel

Plane

Train

Coach

Car and caravan

Self-drive

Hire car

Sea

Reasons for dining out

Convenience

Escape

Entertainment

Somewhere casual

A meeting

Food experience

Special occasion

Permanent user

Local

To be with others

Age

0–12	25–34	55–64
13–18	35–44	65–74
19–24	45–54	75–85

Gender

Male

Female

Desired price range

Least expensive

Medium/high

Low

Top of the range

Middle of the range

Social class

Upper-upper

Lower-upper

Upper-middle

Lower-middle

Upper-lower

Lower

Occupation

Small business owner

Self-employed trade

Self-employed professional

Employed professional

Senior executive

Senior management

Middle management

Supervisor/foreperson

Clerical

Skilled worker

Unskilled worker

Student

Unemployed

Casual worker

Home manager

Retired

Pensioner

Income

£0–6999	£22,000–31,999	£52,000–70,999	£100,000–149,999
£7,000–13,999	£32,000–41,999	£71,000–85,999	£150,000 +
£14,000–21,999	£42,000–51,999	£86,000–99,999	

Living mode

Dependent child   Young single
Mature single   Young couple without children
Couple with young children   Couple with adult children
Mature-aged empty nesters

Departure place

Local   Region
Domestic   Overseas

Personality type

Ruler   Performer
Follower   Thinker

Religion

Nationality

Name country or ethnic origin

Questions for discussion or revision

1   A large hotel chain is building a new hotel in a big city already serviced by sixteen international standard hotels, all aiming at the business and professional markets. Would you advise the new hotel owners to join, create, specialize or target a market? Describe the differences in the strategies and give the reason for your advice.
2   Imagine that a large international hotel in a city which has a big tourist trade has decided to develop a restaurant featuring Japanese cuisine. Which three target markets would you recommend the hotel to target using the Market Menu and Target Market Grid?
3   Describe the process that would enable a hospitality establishment to determine which markets it should target.

MARKET SEGMENT ....

NEED ....

WANT ....

PRICE RANGE ....

COMPETITION ....

MARKET'S PRESENT PURCHASE BEHAVIOUR AND REASONS

....

SEX ....   NATIONALITY ....

PERSONALITY LIFE STYLE ....   SOCIAL CLASS ....

HOBBY INTEREST ....   OCCUPATION ....

RELIGION ....   MARITAL STATUS ....

(Select one group from each Market Menu category:)

	£0–7	8–14	15–21	22–31	32–41	42–51	52–70	71+
65 +								
55–64								
45–54								
35–44								
25–34								
19–24								
13–18								
0–12								

A G E

INCOME £000

(Select one group from each Market Menu category:)

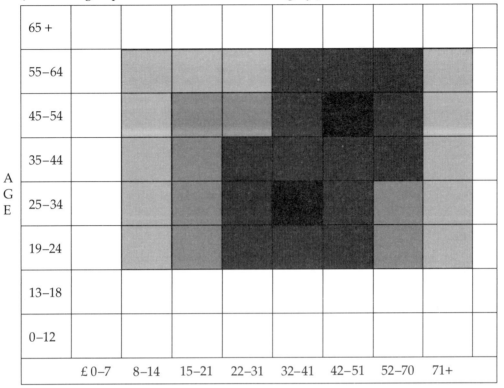

INCOME £000

An example of the radiation effect from the epicentre of
the target maket. A broader cover of the total market is
achieved by two target markets, with some cross-over effect.

Figure 7.1 *The target market grid*

8 The product mix: assessment and decisions

Aims of this chapter

1 To explain how to make assessments about a product mix so that it matches the customer mix.
2 To describe the product life cycle and when to change the product mix.

Achieving the right mix

A product mix is the range of facilities and the quality level of services that an establishment offers to its customers. Each customer is in the position of asking, 'What do I get when I stay at this place and how much will it cost?' At a five-star world-class hotel the customer will probably get the lot, including the tennis court, fitness centre, spa and sauna, as part of the daily room hire. The customer will also be paying a portion towards the cost recovery of the luxuries which will surround him or her during the stay – the marble, plush lounges, chandeliers and fountains. At another hotel, the customer may get a cheaper rate, and the tennis court, fitness centre, spa and sauna can be purchased separately. In this case each product on offer has to be regarded by management as a profit-earning centre for the property to justify its existence.

Because of the expense involved in building and providing these products, a property has to be reasonably assured that the customers want the extras. The management of a five-star hotel may perceive the extras as being a necessary part of their product mix to attract custom. A de-luxe property generally believes that having a wide range of products is an important aspect of its quality image and that the upper-upper or lower-upper class attitudes of its targeted customer mix would be mortified if they were not available. But what about the tired business person who wants nothing more than a bit of attention, a nice meal and a good night's sleep in a quiet, comfortable bed without paying the earth?

Matching the customer mix with a carefully planned product mix is a series of decisions crucial to a hospitality establishment. It has to be sure which products to have as part of the normal room rate, which ones to offer as extras and which ones not to have at all. It all depends on the customer mix that the property decides to target and the expectations of each customer segment.

Essentially, having completed a market analysis and then selected the mix of customer segments for targeting, the facilities provided have to attract the customers wanted. This is customizing the product for the needs and wants of known customers as opposed to creating the products first, then looking for customers later.

Product lines

A product mix has width, depth and consistency. A product line is a group of product items which are similar in their purpose and function. Every major hotel usually has three main product lines: accommodation, restaurant facilities, and bars.

The product width depends on how many additional product lines a hotel offers, such as shops, sports and leisure facilities and hire cars. Some resorts have a wide product line and embrace an extensive range of services. Others keep it simple and inexpensive.

The number of items in each product line determines the establishment's product depth of choice. A hotel with a choice of four restaurants, for instance, has a depth of four items.

Consistency relates to the similarity of the product lines to each other in their appeal to the customer mix.

Each product line requires a marketing strategy, especially if the items are chargeable extras and have to pay for themselves. Some lines are subsidiary to the main promotion of the establishment, such as the availability of a swimming pool; just by 'being there' they meet the needs of the customers and are not expected to make a profit contribution. The costs are covered by the room-hire sales as part of doing business.

The style and size of an establishment generally dictates its product lines, depth and consistency.

The basis of any hospitality business is to provide a place where one can sleep, eat, meet, have sex, drink a beverage, drink alcohol, talk business, exchange gossip, rest, relax, be private, be noticed, play sport, wash oneself, wash clothes, escape, celebrate, entertain, impress, shop, have fun, do nothing, do anything, be waited on, be massaged, have a sauna, dance, listen to music, spend money, feel important, see important people – nearly the whole gamut of human experience can be had in a place of hospitality. No-one wants to do all these things, of course, so does management try to offer everything, or only a selected choice?

As one hotel manager aptly put it, 'Sometimes you have to be prepared to walk away from business.' Some customers are not worth pursuing because to provide for them is an investment which is unlikely to return a profit.

For instance, a large hotel will probably have a swimming pool, an item which most managers consider to be a mandatory item in their leisure product-line.

However, what if the pool is only used by a handful of customers each week? A pool is expensive to build and maintain, and occupies a large area of valuable space which perhaps could be put to better profit-making purposes. Many product lines are merely the result of management making marketing decisions based on industry habits, pandering to a customer demand that may not exist. The establishment without a pool, for instance, may lose some customers, but pick up a lot more by using the space for something else.

Similarly, having a fitness centre seems like a good idea, but a customer count of those who use it often reveals that only a few of the customers want it. Nevertheless, having these extras may be important for the total image of the property.

Styles of operation

The primary accommodation places are termed hotels, guest houses, bed and breakfasts, budget lodges and resorts. Each term is meant to describe a type of place where one can expect a certain product mix and style of service. There are some grey areas in these classifications, though, with some guest houses providing services competitive with highly ranked hotels, and some hotels verging on offering resort-type facilities.

Applying a star rating is a broad classification used by the industry for positioning a lodging place's product mix, price and level of service. Management believe that they have to live up to a rating label which they have either given themselves or which has been assigned to them by an independent organization which publishes a hotel guide, such as the Automobile Association.

Although customers may use a star rating as an initial guide, ultimately they will base their choice on personal experience and the recommendations of others. A hotel's reputation is earned by quality service, and a star rating may have no relevance to its occupancy rate or numbers of satisfied customers.

The size of an establishment has a bearing on the appeal to the customer only if a large place has the width of product lines, and this is not always the case. Some of the largest merely have a lot of rooms. Some of the smallest, such as boutique hotels, offer more personalized service and comfort.

The 'value engineering' concept of hotel construction (a phrase to describe the concept of arranging a standard product mix which will offer value to any customer anywhere) seems to produce a sameness in hotel design. The attempt to provide a multi-purpose operation to suit everyone in the end pleases no-one in particular. This formula approach to marketing is not using targeting to effect and is unlikely to produce a breed of satisfied loyal customers who are going to go away and 'sell' the place to their colleagues and friends. However, a current exception to this viewpoint is the success of the budget lodge formula, where customers are seeking convenience and accessibility in terms of location and price, and the occasion of use does not warrant personalized, 'high-touch' service.

World-class hotels are aimed at the top end of the travel market. After a period of high growth, a large number of these towering structures which have risen almost everywhere in the last twenty years have hit the wall of dwindling customer demand. They remain desperately quiet in many locations due to a global economic down-turn and because the growth segments of the hospitality market are cost-conscious and want less glitz and more value.

The trend of travellers in the 1990s suggests a growing demand from people who want to stay where they feel most comfortable and at a place which best suits their pocket and needs. The simple, cost-saving benefit of building a property around customers instead of expensive facilities seems to have escaped many investors. The return from a million-pound investment in a marble-lined foyer may be zero in comparison to a less expensive, smiling, helpful and interested concierge supported by a willing staff. The customers will probably never come back to look at the marble foyer again, but they will come back to experience the dignity and comfort provided by caring service.

The keys to success

Michael Hurst, one of the best educators in the world on hospitality, stipulates that for an establishment to be successful the customer has to be given an experience beyond his or her expectations and become an unpaid sales person for the place. As he says, 'The majority of custom comes from word-of-mouth recommendation.' He cites the case of a 130-room property that he managed with his partners which opened in a poor location with only two paying customers the first night. He never spent a penny on advertising and yet within the first year it had a 93 per cent occupancy rate.

There is always a new property which seems to be brighter, bigger and glitzier than the ones before it, and it will drag in the early adopters who like change and want to be 'where the latest action is'. Long-term survival, however, will always depend on the lasting quality of the guest experience. While the big places spend their money in a bid to gain the fickle 'switchers', a small guest house close by can be attracting regular custom and making money consistently while watching with curiosity as the bigger places go into an ever increasing debt spiral.

Location and distance

Location and distance will always be the primary determinants of an establishment's success. Not everyone can do a 'Michael Hurst' and recover from being in a back street in the wrong end of town. Proximity to places where customers want to engage in other activities is always best, such as being near an airport, on a major motorway, next to shopping, sporting or conference facilities, close to a business centre, in the heart of a local community or part of an attractive holiday destination. Wherever the property is located, more business will come from the nearest customer sources than the distant ones. And the customers will keep coming back if they get what they want.

Product assessment

An establishment's facilities need to be constantly reviewed. There are two sets of criteria – economic and strategic. The two work together.

Economic

Any establishment requires a huge investment in money and time. The investors are invariably looking for an early return even though they know that planning through to actualization takes years. Management seeks to use the property and its products to achieve growth, sales, profit, market share and to make the best use of its capital and human resources. Each product therefore has to be assessed on its ability to make a contribution to management's objectives, and that is dependent on market size – the availability of customers.

Strategic

In the pursuit of economic objectives, management has to consider the competitive intensity and the customers' expectations. It has to plan for maximum retention of customer loyalty, customer attraction and how that will lead to other purchases. All of these considerations are reliant upon product and market homogeneity. Decisions about products should be made strategically on what the customers want and how the customer mix feels about each one, as well as considering the more pragmatic economic approach.

   If product mix is altered to achieve an economic objective, management faces the consequences of a change in the customer mix. For example, a hotel which abandons room service because it is not making money, or allows it to run down so badly that it is a customer turn-off, may be 'penny wise and pound foolish'. It is sometimes better to recover losses on a product which is essential to the needs of a market segment with profit from other products.

The product mix formula

The simplest method for developing a product mix to match the customer mix is to ask the customers. Why sit around guessing what the customer wants? If management has targeted a segment, it should have a good idea why. The decision has presumably been based on that segment's reasons for travel and its expectations of product/service and price. To fill in the gaps of knowledge, a consumer survey of the targeted segment will provide the missing pieces.

   Armed with knowledge about the groups comprising the targeted customer mix, the product mix becomes a combination of items selected from the following product lines. Remember that each item must satisfy the economic and strategic objectives of the property.

Accommodation product lines

Large, medium or small self-contained, fully serviced apartment or suite, separate self-catering accommodation, two- or three-room self-service suite, large, medium or small room with en-suite bathroom, family bed layout, twin double beds, double or single beds.

Catering product lines

Banquet halls, restaurants of varying nature, coffee shops and brasseries, room service.

Beverage and bar product lines

Room service, room mini-bar, cocktail bar, lounge bar, private bar, club bar, public bar, restaurant bars.

Entertainment product lines

Nightclub, band, dancing, live theatre, cabaret, movie hire, arcade games.

Business services product lines

Meeting rooms, conference facilities, computers, fax, secretarial, photocopying, translators, etc.

Shops (wide variety of items)

Personal services product lines

Valet, hairdressing, nail care, grooming, dry cleaning, laundry, ironing, clothes hire, creche, baby minding, playgrounds, nannies, in-house doctor, chemist, nurse.

Leisure facilities product lines

Swimming pool, sauna, massage, fitness centre, aerobics, etc.

Sport facilities product lines

Tennis, golf, squash, skiing, sailing, equestrian, etc.

Leisure/pleasure product lines

Hire cars, limousines, mini-buses, boats, sightseeing tours, theatre, sport, concert booking service.

Signature product lines

Toiletries, towels, bathrobes, slippers, T-shirts, gifts, souvenirs, etc.

When choosing the product mix, bear in mind that each product line comes with a cost for the customer one way or another, either in the total charge-out rate or by separate charges for each product used during the stay. How many will be willing to pay the price? By using targeting to arrive at an ideal customer mix, the profile of the segment's basic wants and the product mix can be decided with a strong measure of assurance. The customer knows what is the value to him or her. The bottom line is always cost, and the customer value is arrived at by the simple equation:

$$\text{Value} = \frac{\text{Costs}}{\text{Benefits}}$$

Product life cycles

Any establishment seems to have a limited life cycle, and so do its products. Hospitality, even though it is a fundamental aspect of civilized life, is subject to fashions, moods and trends.

The four stages of the life cycle are introduction, growth, maturity and decline. At the introduction stage, the property is new, and having gone through the early assessment stages of market analysis and feasibility it is launched and brought to the attention of the targeted customer mix by promotion. If the property and its products are acceptable, it will achieve growth and, hopefully, some degree of prosperity. At the maturity stage, the property will have reached its maximum growth and stabilize. It should then be returning some profit on the original investment. This may take several years. The decline stage is generally reached when other places enter the market, the facilities become tired and need refurbishing, the market's needs and wants alter, or changes to the establishment's surrounding location occur.

The length of the product's life cycle varies, and some concepts have more durability than others. For example, Claridges in London, Raffles in Singapore, Gleneagles in Scotland, George V in Paris have not changed their basic formats, but there have been subtle adaptations to the needs of the customers over time.

How to handle change

Sometimes it is better for a property to target a new customer mix, or subtly phase one segment out in favour of another. This will probably lead to some changes to the product mix, the dropping of some items in a line or adding new ones. A restaurant which is no longer serving the needs of most segments can be refurbished, restyled and renamed.

A property and its product mix should be constantly under review. When the point is reached for a change to any of its product line items, there are four basic decisions to be made: build; hold; harvest; or divest.

If the market demand for a product is increasing and the product can be expanded to cope with the additional business, it makes sense to build or extend the product. This would depend on assurances from various market, economic and industry indicators that the upward trend will continue. In some cases, when the demand warrants it, management will line extend and add more items to the product line, such as increasing the number of bars, perhaps with differing prices and themes. Another example would be a hotel line extending its leisure facilities, adding to an existing golf course some tennis and squash courts, etc., thereby providing a full mix of sports alternatives.

Holding, or maintaining, a facility would make sense if, for economic and strategic reasons, nothing is to be gained by making any change. Unfortunately, sometimes management holds on to a product too long, despite dwindling customer numbers, for sentimental reasons or fear of change. Often there is a belief that additional promotion will solve the problem, and then management is throwing good money after bad.

Harvesting makes sense if more profit can be gathered by simply maintaining a facility. For instance, this would apply in the case of a restaurant which fills regularly and where patronage would not suffer if the prices were raised marginally over a period.

Where a facility is losing money and has no strategic advantage, it may be time to divest it. This may apply to a hotel function room, for example, which occupies valuable space in the building. If it is under-utilized for its original purpose, catering for concerts, displays, meetings or functions, the space may be better used for another purpose. Another approach is to franchise out a facility to a supplier; for instance, a number of London hotels have done this with their restaurant outlets.

A drastic change for a declining property to make is to refurbish, rename and reposition the property and target an entirely different customer mix. Sometimes it is better to sell the property and start afresh with a new one.

Most properties need redecorating, but not just when the place starts to look tired and worn. Redecorating is required whenever it is necessary to maintain a contemporary sense of style that is compatible with its customer mix.

Drastic change to the property or its product mix can lose customers. Customers develop a feeling of ownership about a property they use a lot, and, like an old friend, they do not like to see it change.

The problem for management is that nothing stands still in the hospitality business. To not meet the challenge of external changes is fatal. However, the important detail is to recognize what the changes mean so that change is made for a reason. That reason should always be to meet the existing customers' expectations and attract new customers. Change is a bad word to use with loyal customers. If you improve or do things better, that is OK. Customers understand and appreciate that.

Toffler's prophecies in his book *The Third Wave* have become today's realities. The splintering of society has created 'customizing'. There is no blanket strategy for all, only a custom-designed product mix that suits groups which can be clustered into a customer mix with like requirements.

Questions for discussion or revision

1 Your hotel has only one public bar and it is always overcrowded at peak times of the day. Someone has suggested a line-extending strategy. What did they mean by that term?

2   You have been asked to make an assessment of a hotel's leisure product mix – its swimming pool, squash and tennis courts and its snooker room. Describe the criteria you would employ for this task.
3   Devise a product mix for a new hotel which is targeting the non-drinking, non-smoking, health-conscious segment of the market.

Further reading

Toffler, A. (1981). *The Third Wave*. Toronto: Bantam.

9 *The service concept*

Aims of this chapter

1 To explain what service really is and how a service culture in an organization works.
2 To describe what is involved in developing strategies and management procedures for a service product.

The theory

There is a lot of talk about service. Everyone says how important it is in the hospitality business. And yet customer complaints and disappointment in the 'service' they have received are still prevalent in an industry which claims to be totally committed to service. What is the problem? Are customers expecting too much? Are they being educated to expect service over and above that which can reasonably be supplied?

It is probable that many of the problems are caused by the fallibility of the human condition, our inability to consistently work to a standard. However, the truth more likely lies in the fact that management does not know what service is. They think it is something 'the staff' does, and that it means being nice and helpful to the customer.

Nine out of ten books on management and marketing fail to give it more than a passing mention, merely acknowledging its importance. Only a few books set out to define service as a product requiring objectives, strategies and measurable management criteria.

Service: both a product and a strategic imperative

The objective of a hospitality business is to provide guests with a place where they feel welcome, appreciated, relaxed and have an enjoyable experience. Service is what an establishment does to and for its guests to achieve this objective. Service is not about smiling and servility. It is a strategy which considers the customer while serving the interests of the establishment.

It is service excellence which gives an organization a competitive edge. Outstanding service makes a lot of money for a hospitality establishment because business is people. The success of such a commitment to excellence is illustrated in Peters and Waterman's renowned book *In Search of Excellence*.

The intention of a service strategy is to manage the customer's experience. The services that an establishment provides are products, and, like a product which is manufactured, a service has to perform to a measurable standard and fulfil its purpose all the time, every time. Who would buy a washing machine that only works on some days, and, when it does work, washes better on some occasions than others?

It is not something which only the staff does, either. It requires commitment from the top. In an organization which is committed to a service strategy there are only two types of staff – those who serve the customer and those who help those who serve the customer. It inverts the hierarchical management pyramid where the managing director is at the top and there are levels of seniority leading down to the customer at the base of the pyramid. Instead, the customer is at the top and full responsibility for the customers and those who serve and help to serve them rests on the managing director on the sharp end. It promotes a 'flatter' management structure, emphasizes team work and makes the chambermaid and the dishwasher as important as the managing director.

Imagine being in a high-class restaurant and just as the meal arrives you notice that the fork has a piece of old meat stuck to it. If that is not enough, the wine glass still has a ring of lipstick. It is hard to feel the same about the food, isn't it? And all because the dishwashers failed to do their job properly, and, worse still, no-one checked the glass and the cutlery when they set the table.

The products which are provided by a hospitality establishment are nearly all service-orientated. The product mix, consisting mostly of accommodation, restaurants, bars and a range of ancillary products which vary with the establishment, have to perform to a level of satisfaction, otherwise the customer will not return. They cannot be good some days and poor on others.

Accommodation, restaurants and bars are obvious service products because they are direct profit earners. Less obvious, but just as important to the customer, are the products which indirectly make money by substantially contributing to the customers' service experiences.

Safety standards

Safety does not make any money, but without adequate safety procedures an establishment can lose a considerable amount of money and a hard-earned reputation. Safety for the employees and the customer is a product that performs without it always being seen to perform.

Stock and inventory control

There is nothing worse than running out of a customer's favourite wine, the kitchen running short of eggs, replacement crockery not being there when it is wanted, etc.

Cleanliness

No-one considers cleaning a profit-maker for a place, and yet it can either earn a reputation for an establishment or ruin one. Most of us expect cleanliness as a norm from the place where we stay and eat. When it is obviously dirty, the establishment has failed to meet our expectations.

Financial planning

Repairs to the premises, the plumbing, renovations to the kitchen and its equipment – there is a long list of things that do not happen or get fixed because there is not enough money – the age-old excuse of management. Do not believe that the customers do not notice, they do. It is not only the fixtures and fittings they see, either, it is the sudden breakdown of a little service that did not happen because a piece of equipment was too old or was not fixed. Customers will be understanding once, but not when it happens again and again.

Credit control

The places that will not take certain credit cards, or ask for deposits, or insult the customer in many ways simply because someone is too lazy or inefficient to check a credit rating in advance, give reasons for customers to go away and never return. Proper credit checks are sound business practice, but when they become unreasonable impositions on the customer's patience and understanding such systems are stupid. Attempting to achieve 100 per cent credit control will cost the establishment money. By being diplomatic and sensitive the customer credit control can be enforced, bad debts minimized and customers retained.

Operational systems

Too many of these are designed for the convenience of the staff or management. These include room cleaning which must be done at prescribed times and to hell with the customer who does not want to be disturbed; the tables which have to be arranged for another function while the customers are still eating; a docket system for meal ordering which is designed to prevent items being missed on the bill and petty fraud but which causes a five-minute delay to the customers' meals. Systems are fine as long as they improve the experience for the customer.

Layout appeal and efficiency

Many places seat the customers near to the kitchen so that the staff do not have to walk so far, or close to the windows to make the place look busier than it is. The reception desk is just outside the general office not because it is closer for the customers but because it is closer to the manager's office. A lot of establishments make their front desk staff responsible for answering incoming phone calls as well as serving the customers face to face. As a consequence, time and time again customers are left standing and waiting while the phones are being answered – the phone call always taking precedence. In reality, these establishments would be better advised to have the manager and the manager's secretary answer the phones. Which is more important, to avoid interrupting the manager or to service the needs of the customer at the desk?

Managing the service products

In the course of their stay, customers are part of a whole cycle of activities from the front door through to their eventual departure. Each activity is handled by a different department and the customer is passed from one to the other. Lots of service products are involved, but in far too many places no-one is responsible for making sure that the transitions happen smoothly. The duty manager waits for a complaint, meanwhile assuming that all is functioning as it should. The whole experience for the customer becomes a sum total of a myriad of little experiences.

For all the service products to happen effectively and concurrently to the guest's complete satisfaction, several control factors are necessary:

- There has to be a strategy which identifies when, where and how the service product shall perform.
- There have to be systems with measurable criteria for each of the working procedures involved in providing the service. If a service is to be managed, it must be capable of being measured.
- The people providing the service have to be 'people people', those who are interested in others, caring for their welfare and making the comfort and satisfaction of the customer top priority. Procedures are only as effective as the people performing them.
- The people providing the service directly to the customer must have the support of everyone else. Albrecht and Zemke emphasize that the organization exists to serve the needs of the people who are serving the customer.
- Management's primary function is to monitor and maintain the service standards. Management must make sure that nothing and no-one prevents the service product from happening. In a service organization, management's role is not merely giving instructions, it is to help those providing the service. If there are delays or upsets, what or who is causing them? Is it a procedural problem? Is there a weak link in the staff chain? Is more training needed? Perhaps the person is wrong for that job? Would a new or different item of equipment solve the problem?

Services that satisfy wants

Some consider the service culture to be reactive to customers rather than proactive. This is wrong. Customers recognize that the establishment has to make profit. They look for leadership from the establishment and want it to provide the magic that gives them a quality experience. With a service strategy, you are involving the customers and the staff so that the strategic service mix works to everyone's satisfaction. It is a process of drawing together the expectations, needs and wants of the customer and the provider so that the customer gets value and the provider gets money. It sounds so simple, doesn't it? Then why does it not always happen?

Part of the answer lies in the arrogance of a large percentage of human beings who are not really interested in other people's thinking. It is a 'We-know-what-is-best-for-you' attitude. Such types are rarely successful in the hospitality business. It results in a general preoccupation by management with putting products in place which they think are for the benefit of the customers, when often they are not what the customer wants or expects at all.

For example, a restaurant put on a special three-course meal for a very low price in anticipation of creating an influx of business, only to be disappointed because the customers did not come and those that did never came back. The restaurateur added more choices, but still failed to increase business. After two or three weeks of this he finally snapped at a table of uninterested customers, 'Well, what the hell do you want then?' They proceeded to tell him, and he finally realized that he had not been taking notice of what the customers wanted. He had not taken the trouble to review what the customers were consistently choosing from his normal menu. Nor had he ever bothered to talk to his customers about their preferences.

The wants of the customer mix should always drive the service strategies. Equally important, though, is to anticipate the customers' wants and occasionally provide something delightful that they did not expect. Michael Hurst experiments with various dishes and consults his customers before including the dishes on the menu.

It costs money to do something new or differently. Why do it unless there is some certainty that the change will be appreciated and bring in more money?

Secondary services – the competitive edge

Effective service products achieve increased business by 'laddering'. This is drawing from the total market a number of people who are transformed from potential customers into advocates for the establishments. The objective of laddering is to identify suspects and target the best prospects (potential customers). With the help of promotion a percentage of them will become customers. From this point the objective of service products is to provide customers with a quality experience that turns them into regular patrons of the establishment. Consequently, they will soon become firm advocates and go out and 'sell' the place to their friends and acquaintances.

Most restaurants provide good food, reasonable service and charge average prices or prices which suit their customer mix. This is called a 'primary service'. Michael Hurst states that it is the small extras, the 'secondary services', which take an average customer experience and elevate it into something beyond his or her expectations. It may be the special brand of coffee, the bread and shortbread that have been made on the premises, the appetiser at the beginning of the meal which is not charged for.

Hurst claims quite rightly that there are many ways of doing things that are better and different which become the main factors in the customers' minds. The primary service product usually does its job of satisfying the customers without much comment. It is the extras that give the customers something to go away and talk about, giving the establishment the competitive edge.

Planning by working to an objective: measurement by outcome

Service has to have measurable criteria. It has to have objectives and perform to a prescribed set of rules and standards. Its purpose is to define precisely what will happen to, or for, a customer by when and by whom. Measurement is achieved by deciding the required outcome of the service. The standard criteria are as follows.

Set the service standard objective

What is it you want the product to do to and for the customers? It is the answer to this question which determines the objective. Forget the money objective. That is an overall corporate objective. This is a product objective, and it is its outcome, what actually happens and how that happening is accepted in the minds of the customers which counts. It may take several statements to sum up the outcome that the objective is set to achieve. Remember, for an objective to have meaning it must contain measurable criteria of achievement within a stipulated time frame.

Set the tasks to be done in the time allocated

For example, a restaurant allocates staff numbers by customer numbers depending on the style of service of the establishment. So one waiter may be allocated to fifteen customers. Three chefs may be required to cook for 150 customers. The service standard which is set requires each customer to be served with drinks within two minutes of sitting down, to have the first course on the table within five minutes of ordering, to have the second course on the table no later than twelve minutes, and so on. If it is not being achieved, management must find out why, isolate the difficulty and remedy it. 'Whatever it takes' is the rule that governs the provision of a service standard.

The measuring criterion in this instance is keeping account of individual performances and comparing them with the average. Those who lag are trained, encouraged or helped until they come up to the standard required.

Describe the team work required

Hospitality is team work, people working together to jointly achieve the objectives of an excellent guest experience. A team leader is essential; a catalyst for the smooth functioning of the procedures required in delivering the product. Each person must know exactly what is expected of him or her and be constantly acknowledged as he or she performs. Achievement is a reward on its own, but nothing beats the rewards of money and extra privilege for a job that goes beyond the standard required.

Set quality standards

Not every action or function can be directly translated into money terms or measured by customer reaction. Much of what happens in a service product goes unseen by the customer. As it is the culmination of little things that ultimately counts in the final assessment by the customer, the contributing functions need a points rating system ranging from poor up to excellent. It is surprising how standards are lifted and enthusiasm develops when staff are performing to known criteria. Everyone likes to know where they stand in a situation.

Measure the level of satisfaction

The desired outcome of a range of service strategies is the extent of the customers' consistent satisfaction. This can be measured in terms of increased sales made, and repeat business, which is the real measure of a product's success. There is another way, and that is to constantly research customer attitudes to find out if the number of complaints are reduced and whether the customers appreciate the various experiences being provided. Guests, in the main, do not mind filling in brief questionnaires, particularly if a prize incentive is offered.

Set a goal for money earned

Whereas the objective is to meet the satisfaction of the customer, money has to be made. At the end of a service period the money required from a product has to be added to make sure that it meets the corporate objectives. A non-profit product such as cleaning can be measured by a points rating system and judged by what it does not cost in terms of lost or disappointed customers.

Analyse costs involved

There is always an accountant adding up the costs of a product. That person has a job to do, which is to make sure that more money does not go out than is coming in. An accountant performs the function of being management's conscience. A product service has to be cost-efficient, with the customer satisfaction level being measured against the costs incurred and the profits made.

Figure 9.1   *Developing a service strategy*

The answer to the accountant's concern for profit is invariably turnover, looking at the end result rather than cost-consciousness of individual items.

Develop a service strategy

Albrecht and Zemte conclude that a high-quality service orientation is such a powerful competitive weapon that it will soon come to be regarded as an essential part of business strategy, not a frill or a 'nice-to-have' feature. Organizations which cannot demonstrate a significant commitment to the needs of their customers will be left further and further behind. Quality of service is now a top management issue.

The steps to be taken that provide a sustainable competitive advantage over the competition by using a product-service-orientated approach to marketing are as follows:

- *Establish customer needs and wants.* This is done by market analysis and segmentation. It will lead to a target market whose particular needs and wants the establishment intends to satisfy.
- *Ask the customers.* Nothing beats the simple research technique of talking to a representative sample of customers, existing and potential, and asking for their opinions and advice.
- *Set down objectives for improvements or changes.* Decide the outcome you want from a product or series of products.
- *Identify key strategies.* Decide how you are going to achieve the objectives and realize the outcomes required.

- *Establish measurable criteria for strategy*. If it cannot be measured it cannot be managed.
- *Allocate tasks and responsibilities*. Decide who is going to perform the functions involved in producing the outcome. Choose 'people people', those who can share the 'gift of friendship'. Look for catalysts which lead and encourage a team effort.
- *Train staff*. Anything new requires comprehensive explanation and careful supervision to begin with. Monitor what happens thereafter. Even high-quality service can deteriorate into mediocrity if left unmanaged.
- *Remove demotivating systems and staff*. Every organization has a number of systems which are designed for the convenience of operators. Seldom do they help the customer. In fact, most of them will be 'customer-hostile' in the sense that they will create adverse reactions from the customer in many instances. These must go! So must the people who insist on tasks before people.
- *Gain commitment to the objectives and strategies*. Without the active support of all the staff, service becomes a bore and a nuisance. Only by involving the staff totally can this problem be overcome. Communication at all times is critical. Never hold back information. Praise those who are doing it right, help those who do not come up to standard. Always make it a team effort. Lead by example.
- *Make physical changes where necessary*. Any physical object, part of a building, piece of equipment or whatever which prevents a service product from performing properly should be changed, moved or replaced. Never allow a physical problem to be an excuse for lack of service.
- *Experiment with the changes*. Do not go charging in with a whole host of new concepts. Test each one first. Involve both the staff and the customers to see if it will work and perform as expected. When it works to expectations and performs according to the desired outcome and to the customers' satisfaction, then make it happen as a permanent operation.
- *Measure and manage*. Management's role is to monitor and step in to help and train whenever it is necessary. Continue with the measuring criteria laid down. The moment you stop it will start to come unstuck.
- *Ask the customers*. The ultimate test of a service product is its satisfactory performance for the customers. Maintain a regular research programme with the customers so that you are informed of progress at all times.
- *Modify where necessary, measure again*. Not every product will service the customers' wants indefinitely. Conditions change, expectations change, moods and fashions change. A viable establishment committed to the service culture for its customers will change with the customers and not sit on past achievements. If the organization does not move with its customers, the customers will move elsewhere.

The training strategy

One of the principal laments of managers about implementing a service strategy is about the lack of cooperation and consistency of their staff. 'We tell them how to do it. We spend money on training. We try to motivate and enthuse, but in the end we find the staff going back to their old habits and we give up in despair. What's the use? It's a nice idea, but it isn't realistic. People are people.'

One has to feel sympathetic with this lament, which is about as consistent as the inconsistency of hospitality staff's ability to perform consistently. The problem lies with management, and we will come to that in a moment.

There is another management attitude which says: 'Our staff know what is expected of them. They don't always do what they should, but they know.' Experience shows that this is a false premise. The truth from research and a series of random interviews of staff reveals that in most cases they do not know what is expected of them. They may know the rules and they may know the procedures they have been taught, but in the majority of cases they think that what is expected is only to perform to those rules and procedures.

This is an open invitation to rebel. It is human to buck the system, so as human beings occasionally they deliberately flout the rules and procedures just to prove that they are individuals in their own right and not a bunch of robots caught up in a system. After a while, flouting the rules becomes a habit and then they feel a bit guilty. As the guilt rises, so do the defence mechanisms, and then it is someone else's fault, not theirs.

What does one do? Most service people think that they are doing their job for a remote, cold and uncaring manager, or a bunch of shareholders they will never meet and who have no interest in whether they live or die. Anyone who works in that sort of environment knows that as long as they do enough to not get fired they will get paid, and that is all that matters. That sort of knowledge takes precedence over any other knowledge because it is the truth.

The answer therefore is to give them responsibility for their customers. When they realize that the people they serve could be theirs for a long time and that their real job is to keep them as their own customers it helps to change their attitude to the procedures. If, in addition, they are given a financial incentive for every customer they retain, and each time that customer spends money they get a little part of it for themselves and they get praised for their efforts, you have a person who is working for him or herself as well as for you. If the right people are hired, they will know that the procedures are there to help them build their own customer base.

Notice what happens when customers request to be served by a particular waiter that they like. It is a funny type of waiter who is not flattered, and naturally he or she responds with additional, personalized touches of service. Often a handsome tip is the reward. However, it is better if management supplies the reward so that there is a standard recognition for retaining a customer and providing outstanding service.

This approach does two things. One, it personalizes the service. The staff get to know the customers by name. Two, the customers get service because every person who walks in, phones in or writes in is worth money. All of a sudden, the staff are scrambling to get to the customers first and claim them for their own! The ones who do not scramble are the ones you do not want. So, instead of management saying that staff are all the same, it becomes apparent that they are not all the same. If you want staff who give service you need to retain the scramblers and keep them motivated.

Some managers may balk at this concept because they think that service people are mercenaries, merely hired for a job. In the case of waiters and commis chefs, they are often hired on a casual basis so that they can be laid on and off at will. And here is the real problem – management's attitude to staff. Until that changes, and the staff are given individuality and respect by managers as being vital contributors to the joint prosperity of themselves and the property, the customers will be at the mercy of a high percentage of mostly unmotivated and uncaring staff. The staff are an integral part of the product being sold.

Most motivational training is wasted. The staff see this type of training as an insult to their intelligence, and often it is. They think, 'Here we go again.' Most staff want to be nice to customers if they can, and they think that they already provide 'service'. Many of them want to do better, and often they know how it can be improved, but frequently they are restrained or demotivated by systems and uncooperative attitudes born from management which does not respect them as individuals. No-one asks them for their opinion. All too often there is little management supervision, only authoritarian direction. Systems and procedures are put into place without staff consultation or understanding of the problems that they often pose. Profit and expediency come first and the staff come second. Usually there is no means of measuring service or what the staff do except by casual observations.

As a consequence, most service training begins with the premise that it is the front line 'sales and customer service people' who need to have the right attitude. Wrong. Service is a marketing product which requires strategies that begin at the top, and it is management which has to respect, support and service the front-line people.

Training should be conducted around the strategies and involve the people who will implement them, and that requires staff acceptance and commitment to the concept. To achieve this commitment it cannot be an 'us and them' approach. It has to be a joint deal for mutual benefit, with the guest's satisfaction from the total experience of the property being the primary objective.

Questions for discussion or revision

1 List some of the most common examples of service failure in a hotel restaurant.
2 Is the customer always right? Give some examples of occasions when the customer's demands can go beyond the provision of normal service and when additional attention is necessary.
3 Explain how service strategies can overcome the shortcomings of room size, tired decor and worn furnishings.

Further reading

Albrecht, K. and Zemke, R. (1990). *Service America*. New York: Warner Books.
Peters, T. and Waterman, R. (1982). *In Search of Excellence*. London: Harper Row.

10 Service strategies: achieving a competitive advantage

Aim of this chapter

To explain the processes involved in developing service product strategies for hospitality establishments which achieve a sustainable competitive advantage.

Service first, property second

A good business should be constructed from the service strategies up with a specific series of target markets in mind, not from the property and its facilities down. Many investors like to believe that if the property looks good, has the right style and is cleverly located, lots of people are going to want to stay there, eat there and do everything else one does in a hotel. They are not altogether wrong. Their belief is well founded, it is just that they are not altogether right.

Where are they wrong? Well, there are many places which have a great-looking, really impressive facade. They have lots of style. There is style everywhere you look. Some places drip with opulence and style. Usually they are well located too, either next to the business centres, the shopping and entertainment streets or, in the case of resorts, adjacent to rivers, lakes, seas, mountains or on islands. The trouble is that not all of them are full or even remotely close to being full. Some are, but a whole lot are not. So there has to be something else in the equation that makes a place a success which investors do not always know about or take into consideration.

The answer lies in the fact that the property itself is really only the shell in which the total service experience for the guest happens. It may be hard for some people in the hospitality industry to appreciate that marketing is part of product development. The view held by many in management is that marketing people should only be concerned with selling. They think that their 'grand design', the location and the style of the property will dictate the customer mix, and that marketing people are merely the communication tools which bring their property and the customers together. Their belief is that such matters as the environmental theatre of the place (impressive design features) and all its products and facilities are solely management decisions. This attitude overlooks entirely the fact that the choice of markets and the development of products for those markets are essentially marketing processes. It also explains why some properties are destined to fail before the first surveyor's peg is put into the ground.

As a consequence, management's solution to a down period is fairly predictable. They say to the sales people, 'Go out there and sell your hearts out! Do deals, cut prices, do what you can to bring in the customers!' So the sales people go into top gear. They ring up their main customers, they contact the travel agents, they brief the advertising agency and the PR firm, they do all the things that have to be done to promote the place.

The drive and impetus of the sales team, backed up by some sharp deals, can and often does bring in a stream of customers. But where is the service and the special series of experiences for the customers that will retain their patronage? All too often, all the customers get in terms of service is more of the same which they have been getting nearly everywhere else. And, as they drift away to other places, the downturn resumes and the expensive selling drives have to start all over again.

Sales people need something more than just a story about size, style and location because all the competitors have these. The competitors have most of the other same things too, the loyalty club discounts, the special rates, the upgrades, the special room hire rates. The lot. So, what does retain the customers?

The points of difference in service

The things that make a property really successful are the points of difference. The unique selling proposition, if you like. The well known guru of hospitality marketing, Melvyn Greene, describes it as the 'Wow factor' – the point of difference which makes the customers walk away from the establishment saying, 'Wow! That was something else. Did you see...' Or the phrase which most aptly describes it, the sustainable competitive advantage. For example, price cutting is not sustainable; continuous quality service is.

Points of difference are in the products that you sell. There are other means by which you can establish points of difference. Two important means are: (1) the way you do things; and (2) the people who do these things. These are service strategies. Some of them are small by comparison with the huge investment in building, style, glitz, glamour and location, but they usually work a lot better for a lot longer.

The people who do these things

Here is an example of a point of difference that made the almost impossible possible. A hotel group in 1992 ran a chain of 67 hotels of varying descriptions.

One of the hotels in the group did not fit the slick image of the majority of the groups' hotels. It was an old, small property (about 100 rooms) called the Parkroyal located in London. The group purchased another hotel in London with a similar name, the Kensington Parkroyal. It was newer, bigger, closer to the business centre and the shopping and entertainment areas of the city.

There was not much they could do to refurbish the Parkroyal property to make it fit the group's style, so they decided to sell it and convince as many customers as possible to use the Kensington Parkroyal next time. This was a tricky situation because the old Parkroyal had a strong and loyal following of customers who had been using it for many years. If it was true that the building itself is what attracts and retains customers, then the hotel group was going to have a lot of trouble converting people to the new property. In any case, when there is a major change to any business there is a loss rate because it is always an opportunity for many customers to seek fresh fields and experiences.

Within twelve months, 90 per cent of the old Parkroyal customers had made the transition to the Kensington Parkroyal, a phenomenal result! How was it possible? A lot of the credit went to one person, James Millar, the concierge. When James went to the Kensington Parkroyal a large percentage of the customers moved too. What was so special about James Millar? Yes, he had a unique personality. He bubbled with enthusiasm, but, what was more important, he liked and knew his customers, every one of them by name. He treated them with respect and interest, asking after their families or their hobbies at every opportunity. He was the perfect concierge.

There are other 'perfect concierges' around the world, and their secret is always the same – a deep interest in other people and a marvellous faculty for remembering names. Imagine walking into the leading hotel in a city which you haven't visited for over a year and the concierge calls you by name and welcomes you back. You are flattered and you feel important and welcome. Regrettably, in too many places this sense of welcome stops after the concierge hands you over to other staff. It is back to 'ordinary' from then on as indifferent employees go through the motions of service.

Personalizing the service

A service strategy is required for each product in an establishment's 'product line'. Yes, of course there should be an umbrella strategy for the whole establishment, but as each product is aimed at a segment of the customer mix, each one needs its own strategic plan. With a product like accommodation, the service strategy begins with the initial hotel contact because being welcomed by name is the first service a customer notices. This is before he or she has had a chance to see a room, drink in a bar, anything. This is where a James Millar becomes so important. The point of difference in some places may simply be the concierge.

You can build a whole strategy very simply around a smiling, happy concierge by extending the rapport he or she establishes and spreading it throughout the organization. It is so easy. It starts with calling the customer by name and remembering that name and the important details about that person's preferences. Let us say the customer's name is Mr Smith. The porter carries up 'Mr Smith's bags' and puts them into Mr Smith's room. When the chambermaid comes the next day it is to clean Mr Smith's room, not THE room, but Mr Smith's room. Mr Smith is not just a guest, but has hired his room which can only be invaded with his permission. A different staff attitude emerges. The chambermaid therefore ASKS when it would be convenient to clean the room; it is no longer an automatic function.

Similarly, with a dinner reservation, the table does not have a 'reserved' sign on it, it has 'Mr Smith's table' written on it. The waiters, everyone, calls him by his name. In turn, everyone in the place wears a name tag so that Mr Smith can return the compliment and call the staff by name. A side benefit of this strategy is that in a large organization with many people carrying out different functions, it is far easier to build a sense of belonging and being appreciated. In so many places, most people working there do not even know each other by name.

Years ago, James Lavenson gave a speech to the Executives' Club of Chicago and recited many amusing stories about his experiences when he first took charge of the Plaza Hotel in New York. Lavenson made a very strong case for the simple stratagem of calling a guest by his or her name and for the staff to wear name tags. When he moved to his new position things were far from right at the hotel. There were 1400 staff members, and as he said, 'How would they ever know all the people working there, who were the guests, who was just a burglar smiling his way through the hotel while he ripped us off? I can assure you that in the beginning if he smiled and said "hello" he was a crook. He certainly wasn't one of us.'

Lavenson went on to explain that after the Plaza name tag was born and affixed to everyone's chests:

> Believe it or not, Plaza people began saying hello to each other by name when they passed in the hall or in the offices. At first, of course, our regular guests at the Plaza thought we had lost our cool and that we were having some gigantic convention there. But now the guests are also able to call the bell person, the maids, room clerks and the manager by name. And we began to build an atmosphere of welcome with the most precious commodity in the world, our names and our guests' names. When someone calls you by name, and you don't know his or hers, another funny thing happens. A feeling of discomfort comes over you: if he calls you by your name twice, and you know you're not world famous, you have to find out his name. And this is the phenomenon we saw happening with the Plaza staff name tags. When a guest calls a waiter by name, because it is there to be read, the waiter wants to call the guest by name.

The staff's product knowledge

There is another very simple strategy that anyone in the hospitality business can employ which does not cost very much money, and that is teaching the staff about the products the place has to offer. If you want the staff to sell they have to know what they are supposed to sell. The additional business created by staff information and recommendations is huge. Familiarizing the staff with the products not only helps the selling process, it also builds a sense of pride in the whole organization.

'Selling' is a bad word. It implies pressuring clients into buying something they may not want. Michael Hurst does not believe that staff should 'sell', but they do have to inform and advise, and to do this they must have an intimate knowledge of the products they are offering. Informing customers about what is available and asking them if they would like it is not selling, it is first, simple courtesy; and secondly, supplying knowledge which can be gratefully used by the customer to make a decision.

James Lavenson reported in his speech that when he took over the Plaza Hotel he made a few calls to the various departments and made casual enquiries as if he were a potential customer. He did this before the staff could recognize his voice over the phone. Here are some of the examples.

'What's the difference between your $85 suite and your $125 suite?'

The answer was, you guessed it, 'Forty dollars'.

'What's the entertainment in your Persian room tonight?'

'Some singer', was the answer.

'A man or a woman?' Lavenson asked.

'I'm not sure,' was the reply. It made Lavenson wonder whether he would be safe going there. Why was it, he asked, that a hotel staff does not act like a family of hosts to the guests who have been invited, after all, to stay at their house?

Lavenson introduced a week of orientation for the staff which included a visit to the nightclub, a night in one of the rooms, just like a guest, and a meal in each of the restaurants. Today, everyone knows who is singing in the nightclub and everyone knows the difference between the $85 and $125 rooms.

In the restaurant, another 'moment of truth' for an establishment is often reached when the customer asks the waiter about the wine. A frequent answer is along the lines of 'Wouldn't know, sir. Don't drink wine myself.' How bad is that? What is the point of a drinks waiter who cannot advise the customer on the choice of wine? Another favourite customer question is, 'What is this menu item? Can you tell me something about it?' How many times have you watched as the waiter frowns, desperately trying to remember something about it and finally admitting with a sense of despair (or indifference) that he or she has never tried it, then adding with a smile, 'But it looks nice!' Waiters are not order-takers. They are there to advise and assist the customer with his or her product selection. How can they do that if they do not know the menu or the wine list?

Like Lavenson and the leading operators around the world, Michael Hurst makes sure that every waiter tries every dish before he or she serves a customer. You cannot sell or tell somebody about products that you know little or nothing about. Before the waiters go on the floor the kitchen must tell them about the whole meal and how it has been designed and prepared. If there is something new they must try it so that they can tell the customers.

When everyone in an establishment is an expert on its products, sales soar, because if the staff are enthusiastic the advice they give is infectious and the customer gets the message that it could be a fun thing to try. Teaching the staff about products and encouraging them to tell the customers is a very simple strategy for management to use to build a business.

The little extras that make a big impression: the way you do things

Michael Hurst tells the story about a man who sat next to him on a flight to Denver. Without knowing where Michael was staying, his companion proceeded to sell him on staying at the hotel where he was staying, which happened to be the same hotel. One of the main reasons for his companion's enthusiasm for the place was the special things they did, and the one that stood out most of all for him was the hotel's lemon soap!

That is silly, you might think, but it is lots of seemingly 'silly' little things like a special lemon soap that make the all-important points of difference between places to stay. It is not the large issues that concern the average human being so much as a sequence of seemingly inconsequential small issues. Think of the silly little aggravations that have broken many a relationship or even a marriage, like men who do not put the cap back on the toothpaste tube, or women who shave their legs with the man's razor.

It is the little things that can beat the competition. At the Knockomie Lodge Hotel in Scotland a red squirrel features as the hotel's logo. Not only that, but ceramic figures of the little creature appear in all the nooks and crannies around the hotel, peeking out at the fascinated guests. On departure, each guest is presented with a small ceramic version of the friendly mascot – a little detail which translates into a 'Wow factor', powerful in the ability to promote positive word-of-mouth publicity and encourage repeat business.

Whisky which is specially blended to the specifications of the hotel and labelled with the hotel's uniquely designed label, that is a point of difference. Flowers which are always fresh and imaginatively arranged, that is another good talking point. The flamboyantly dressed, slightly eccentric, but nevertheless efficient and friendly chef/patron sticks in the customers' memories.

John and Mary McMenemie own and operate the charming Knockendarroch House Hotel in the Scottish Highland town of Pitlochry. The Victorian manor has the atmosphere of a large country house and home. There is no bar, guests are not permitted to smoke, lunches are not offered to the passing public nor to residents, and only residents are offered dinner from a limited menu.

You may think that the Knockendarroch has not got much going for it and that it is even a little impertinent to call it a 'hotel'. Well, you would be wrong. John and Mary have a very special way of offering genuine, warm, authentic hospitality. The hotel is very much an extension of their own home. Mary creates superb quality food, drawing on her Irish roots for inspiring recipes. John welcomes the guests in a real, timeless 'mine host' fashion, drawing them into the spacious hall with its roaring log fire. 'We treat our customers as guests in our own home, which the hotel is,' says John. When evening comes and a fine meal has been enjoyed, guests, host and hostess gather in the drawing room to chat, play chess or enjoy a song at the piano from John. Nothing is too much trouble. What the customers need to make themselves comfortable they get.

All the stationery, point of sale materials, menus and children's activity materials play a part in the overall image of the Littlejohn group of family restaurants. The children's menu is available also to senior citizens. As well as featuring the adventures of Little John the cat, the questions included on the menu's kids' club quiz are intended to encourage youngsters to ask their parents and grandparents for answers. The restaurants themselves feature raised model railways, station signs and other rail memorabilia. Other wall-mounted conversation pieces include adverts for branded goods also taken from the time which many would regard as the golden years of rail.

Michael Hurst makes the point that when we are children we are told to come to the table the moment the food is ready. We sit down to eat. That does not happen in most restaurants. We sit down to wait. We wait to order our food, we wait to order a drink and then we wait for someone to bring it to us. That gives the word 'waiter' a totally different meaning. In too many places it is bad luck if you are hungry, dying for a drink or have children who need occupying to pass the time. Meanwhile the waiter performs the meaningless task of putting a napkin on our laps. What for? It may be twenty minutes before it is needed, and as you sit and perhaps talk or just watch everyone else if there is nothing to say, the useless napkin keeps falling on the floor. A nice thing about Littlejohn's is that the children are kept occupied, there is a source of conversation and plenty of eye-catching furnishings to make whatever time you need to wait fly by.

Whitbread's conspicuously successful restaurant division TGI Friday has made a feature out of training bartenders to read the guest's needs to establish what type of experience they want. For example, a group of girls on a night out may be treated to some ice-juggling, whereas less riotous patrons may be offered a matchstick brain-teaser. Here the point of difference is concern with responding, in all sorts of unexpectedly personal and fun ways, to the customer who buys your wares.

There is no doubt that these little extras make a big impression in their own very unique ways.

The secret strategy that can make a place great

When customers go to stay somewhere or when they go out to a restaurant, they hope they will be given a bit of fun; maybe entertained, perhaps excited, but certainly they expect to be given some special treatment and be made to feel good. Mostly it is a distraction they want, a temporary refuge from business, work, home or some situation that they would prefer to put to one side for a while. If you are paying a large amount of money to stay or eat in an expensive place you should be treated as though you really matter. In the best hotels around the world you can get that kind of treatment; however, it is not really dependent upon how much you pay but how much you get in return.

For most people, the places that really stand out are not always the most expensive, biggest or in the most glamorous locations. Julie's Sunset Bar in Clearwater, Florida, is a two-storey shack of a building situated on the coast in a run-down end of the town. Food is simple 'surf and turf', steaks and seafood, and the only drink served is bottled beer, drunk 'by the neck'. So what makes it special? The atmosphere is electric, full of people of all ages, enjoying the simple, honest good value of the product. The operation is controlled by Julie herself, a colourful character, and service is by young, lively staff glowing with the Floridan sun. All of a sudden the hustle and bustle stop, there is silence as patrons and staff alike stop all activity to gaze in awe at the sensational sunset which has enveloped the sea and the skyline. Julie's Sunset Bar is not expensive, certainly not glamorous, but definitely fun, exciting and the thread from which the fabric of special moments is woven.

Fun and excitement, the joys of staying somewhere are provided mostly by people, not things. Sure, the marble, the fountains, the imposing atrium rising to the heights above you are impressive and they provide a sense of occasion. But you cannot sleep on marble and you cannot eat the fountain. If you want an imposing and impressive ambience you can visit a cathedral and stand in the nave with its soaring arches, stained glass windows and vaulted ceilings.

The value-added package you buy which offers a free bottle of champagne, discounted restaurant rates and free use of the leisure club is all great. What happens, though, when warm champagne is brought by a depressing-looking waiter? 'Here's your champagne,' he says, placing the tray on a side table. 'Sign here to say you got it!' The champagne is now flat and so is the sense of occasion. Services performed in a perfunctory fashion with feigned smiles take the sparkle from the enjoyment of an experience in even the most fantastic of places and situations.

It is people who make an occasion special. Which is why the secret of a successful establishment is nearly always its people. Yes, the foyer, the procedures, the efficient service, the value you get, the location, the extras of pool, spa, sauna and massage are all important, but to make the occasion really happen people have to make it happen. It is the staff with the 'gift of friendship', the charm, wit and engaging personalities who make an experience memorable. There are plenty of staff who can whiz through the orders and get the work done faster than most, but if they leave a trail of disaster of ruffled guests and irritated cooks behind them, what is the point? When someone turns up for work and he or she has the flu, a friend or relative has died, or there has been an argument of some sort at home, do not let him or her near a customer! That cloud around the head may ruin the experience for some guest. It is better to pay the staff member to stay at home than to lose a customer.

Michael Hurst hired an Irish lady for a specialized task – to sell Irish coffees. He hired her because of her beautiful accent and her fascinating personality and the ability to spin the most charming tales about the effects the various Irish whiskies would have on the customers. She talked about ancient spells and the drop of magic from old Ireland that was in every nip. It was all nonsense, of course, but the customers loved her and wanted a little bit of the magic to rub off on them. Michael Hurst said she had to sell a quota of Irish coffees to justify her place on the staff, but she had no trouble at all in meeting that quota.

Some in the hospitality industry say that good service should go unnoticed. Although there is a lot of truth in that, it suggests that service is an expectation and that it is only noticed when it is not there. The trouble with a lot of places is that it is more likely to be noticed if it is there. It takes a lot of hard work for a place to achieve that smooth-running excellence which realizes the customers' expectations. Exceptional service, that extra something in the way in which a place does things and gives it that competitive point of difference, is usually provided by the personalities of the people who provide it.

Making the whole service experience work for the customer

Service for the customer begins from the very first contact with the establishment. This initial contact may be with a travel agent. A property cannot directly control what a travel agent says or does, but it can indirectly control it by making sure that the travel agent is armed with information to pass on to the customer. That information has to be more than a description of the property, the number of rooms and the going rates. It must include the points of difference and the benefits, the reasons why the travel agent can recommend it to the enquiring customer. Proper briefing of the travel agent is not just a selling strategy, it is also a service to potential customers via an intermediary.

The handling of an enquiry by an establishment should also be perceived as a service to the customer. Let us take out the mercenary considerations of 'getting-what-you-can' for the room for a moment. Sure, that is part of the business of being in business, and most experienced travellers know that. What most of them want is helpful information so that they make a decision, whether to stay at your place or another place.

However, it seems that for a number of establishments this does not always work the way it should. A ring-around of hotels in London and Manchester once produced some interesting results. Despite the fact that the world was in a recession at the time, in most instances the answer to the simple enquiry about rates resulted in a single reply, 'so much a room'. Nothing more. No additional helpful information, and this from some of the best in the country. In one case the phone just rang without being answered.

Those who responded properly to the enquiry handled the situation by first quoting the rack rate and then going on to mention some of the packages they had. Not one respondent added any reasons why the enquiring customer should consider their establishment ahead of the rest. No benefits or points of difference were mentioned. Apart from being a bad example of selling, it also showed a lack of interest.

First impressions

When this situation was related to some hotel managers the response was mostly a rejection that it had happened. They used an excuse such as: 'must have been busy', 'it was an off night, we all have them', 'probably struck the wrong person', 'I'm really surprised, our people are excellent as a rule.' No-one seriously considered what could be done to improve the situation, nor did they admit that something should be done.

The moment of truth for customers occurs when they arrive at a property. How much preparation has there been for the guest's arrival? Were they told in advance what to do about parking, for example?

Most establishments are very good at making first impressions when guests arrive. Building appearance, decor, cleanliness, the door person, the reception by the concierge or receptionist and the booking-in procedures are normally fine. This is where the place's well-oiled machinery goes into operation. There is usually evidence of good training at this point, and seldom does it go off the rails unless a reservation is lost. The porterage and room-delivery systems also work OK in most cases. Why is this? Perhaps it is because the front desk is like the cockpit of an plane where everything is controlled. The more likely reason is probably because it is right outside the manager's door.

For a new customer there is the initial impact of the room – its decor, lighting, size, layout, cleanliness and tidiness, the bed, the smell, the music, TV, mini-bar, tea and coffee-making facilities, bathroom and toilet, linen fresh and crisp, etc. All of these items make their impression. The customer either feels at home at this stage or wants to run screaming from the building and catch the first taxi out of there. It is a very sensitive moment for the customer and the quality of the hotel is often judged on how that moment is handled. In a good place the service strategy is to explain how the room works: an induction course on where things are and how they work, such as switches and appliances, then information is given about the facilities and additional services which are available.

This is the opportunity for reassurance on the customer's decision. More than that, though, it is the time to establish rapport with the customer and prepare the way for 'selling' other services. Ideally, the person doing the induction should be the continuing contact for the guest during his or her stay so that advice, information and 'fix-it' situations can be readily handled by one person or another designated person when the original contact is off duty. This contrasts with most establishments which divide the hotel into a number of departments working as separate profit-earning outlets without anyone assisting the customer in his or her use or choice.

The list of service items that form part of the overall strategy can be extended according to the size and nature of the establishment. Every detail is significant. A service strategy is not someone else's job, it is a total commitment by everyone. The objective of a commitment to sustainable competitive service strategies is obvious – management and staff want the guests to return and to recommend the place to others.

The restaurant

The proximity of a hotel's restaurants to its accommodation should ensure that a very high percentage of guests use the facilities such as fine dining room, bistro, carvery or coffee shop. The problem is, such places are also competing with others in the streets nearby. So it is not enough just to be there. Each hotel eatery has to offer a really exciting benefit to win a share of its own guests and add a number of customers from outside the hotel.

Food is interesting and can be fun. Dining should be an important part of the total guest experience of an establishment. A strategy for this product requires close attention to first impressions, the guest's comfort, familiarity, welcoming staff, easy on the eye decor and style. It should build on the ambience and quality experience provided by the rest of the hotel.

Again, it is all the extra touches – hiring personality people especially – that make the competitive difference for the customers. Details matter, such as having a baby high chair, cushions for the elderly, music which is used to create an ambience for the place (not merely to fill a sound vacuum), perhaps the smell of freshly ground coffee, newly baked bread and rolls and, most of all, the food quality – all add up to a place being a really great experience.

Getting the fundamentals of food and wine right and served well is basic to the business of a restaurant. It is not enough, however. There are many establishments which do the same. Doing the ordinary things in a better and different way is about style, and style combined with attention to every small need of the guest causes guest satisfaction.

The bar facilities, for example. The bar does not have to be just a place where the guest can have a drink. A service strategy can be developed around it so that it is the beginning of a dining experience, not just a place to wait for guests. For example, while the customers drink, the food order can be decided so that they go to the table as soon as the meal is ready. Meanwhile, a skilled and personable bartender could be offering cocktails which enhance the anticipation and enjoyment of the food to come. The wine list can be a feature, offering distinctive wines of a specific country or region, wines of selected vintages, or special house wines of the month.

Meals and presentation which exemplify the regional tastes can be a talking point for guests, with gourmet experiences that no-one else offers. Special theme nights and promotions lend interest and excitement to the eating occasions and provide reasons for guest participation. Celebrity speakers and performances by entertainers are further suggestions for making the dining experience special.

It is the sum total of these experiences which is the strategy for attracting and retaining customers. Michael Hurst and Melvyn Greene emphasize that you must have points of difference. You must look at the operation and figure out what is unique about it, what is special, what is exciting, what is distinctive, what is there worth talking about in your business. And, if you have nothing to talk about, you have a problem! You are not going to get word-of-mouth advertising in that case. You get people because it is convenient. You have some business which may be financially successful, but in terms of building an establishment that is truly a vibrant, living thing, you have to have the 'Wow factor' for people to talk about.

Questions for discussion or revision

1   Describe the strategies you would employ for a real ale pub that mainly caters for American tourists.
2   The hotel you manage has a small kitchen that can only cope with 100 guests at a time. Renovations are twelve months away. Without losing customers, explain the service strategies you believe could satisfy the needs of 300 guests requiring to dine at the restaurant on a busy night.

3 Some people are better at giving service than others. When training people for front desk reception work, describe the service strategies you would regard as being essential for them to do their job effectively.

Further reading

Greene, M. (1987). *Marketing Hotels – Restaurants in the '90s*. London: Heinemann.
Hurst, M. *Pizzaz*, a training videotape sponsored by South Pacific Hotel Corporation.

11 *Marketing management*

Aims of this chapter

1 To explain how to implement the necessary control procedures to keep a marketing plan running.
2 To explain various corporate approaches to marketing management.
3 To outline the different job functions in the marketing department of an organization.

Part One: Service control procedures

A marketing plan can only be effective if:

- management has the ability to manage;
- the organization has the right staff to service the customers;
- the staff have the capability to implement the marketing programme.

In the hospitality business, because it is so directly dependent upon service, organizational control and the maintenance of standards is critical. Any establishment is totally in the hands of its people and their skills. Hiring the right staff is therefore vital.

Michael Hurst insists that if you treat labour as a commodity that is what you get as staff – commodities. The hospitality business is about people. The customers and the people who serve the customers have to like each other. This means employing staff who can share the gift of friendship with their customers.

As Hurst says, 'A lot of places accidentally have good people.' The secret of a successful operation is having nothing else but good people. 'You can always teach procedures to a friendly person, but you can't teach friendliness to an unfriendly person.' A person without the right personality for the work can go through the motions of smiling and saying, 'Enjoy your meal' or 'Have a nice day', but that is what they are doing, going through the motions. The customers know the difference.

Michael Hurst's restaurant, The 15th Street Fisheries, has a slogan which epitomizes the operation's attitude to its staff and customers. It says, 'We're glad you're here'. It is a message which everyone on the staff wears in the form of a lapel badge. The staff believe it and so do the customers, because for them friendly service is a planned reality.

Management by measurement

A good manager does not 'control' people in the sense of using fear as a control mechanism, nor does a good manager use heavy authoritarian direction. Effective management is about giving direction by setting goals, allocating tasks and then facilitating, making it possible for the staff to do their work effectively and efficiently. This is management by measurement. It also uses negotiation with individuals when there is conflict.

In a restaurant each person's work is particularly dependent upon someone else doing theirs. It is team work that makes an operation 'click'. If one person is causing a hitch in the procedures, not only will others in the chain be affected but ultimately so will the customer.

According to Blanchard, author of *The One Minute Manager*, the following management systems are effective:

- *Acceptability*: everyone has to be clear on what they are being asked to do.
- *Data system*: performance information must be gathered to determine how well people are doing.
- *Feedback*: feedback must be provided to people so that they can continue to do well or re-direct their efforts.
- *Recognition*: good performance must make a difference, so good performance must be recognized.
- *Training*: people must have the skills to perform well. High expectations without skills (or ability) will only lead to frustration and poor performance.

Management's job is to make sure that each of the five systems is in place and happening the way it should. Management has to constantly observe and monitor each person's work and step in to help a person who is in trouble. To achieve this there has to be a description of each person's function which can be measured against a norm, an average expectation of how and by when the activity should happen. The degree of competence required to perform a task has to be measurable. The adage to be observed is, 'If it can't be measured it can't be managed.'

The Employee Performance Appraisal illustrated at the end of this chapter is one of several types of forms that can be completed by a supervisor for the purpose of assessing an employee in a general way. Far more precise is the form that can be used to assess a job function, which outlines a customer outcome and the performance criteria necessary to achieve it. The gradings are 'U' (unsatisfactory), 'S' (satisfactory) and 'E' (exceptional). Those who are 'unsatisfactory' need counselling or training.

However, on some occasions, a person performing to an unsatisfactory level is unable to perform because of factors beyond his or her control. For example, sometimes other people in the service team are obstructing the procedures, or it may be a piece of unreliable equipment. Another problem may be the procedure itself which is incapable of fulfilment in the time allocated.

Measuring performance reveals problems. If a person proves to be unable to perform the task according to the performance criteria, other tasks will have to be allocated or the person dismissed. The customer outcome must be achieved.

The purpose of 'control' in the sense of 'managing' is the development of a working culture, easing the interaction between people, smoothing the handling of procedures and maintaining the service momentum. In the capacity of 'facilitator', whoever is responsible for supervising the service functions has to provide information and advice, training skills and staff development, and make changes when necessary to bring the marketing process into line with the marketing plan.

In most service teams there are people who are natural catalysts around whom the service tasks flow more easily. They should be constantly acknowledged and rewarded. Unfortunately, there are also the odd 'rotten apples' who may be efficient enough at what they do but who are critical of management, find fault with others and are generally disagreeable. Regrettably, people like that have to be removed because their presence has the opposite effect of the catalysts, causing friction and unfriendly feelings.

Objectives of marketing control

These objectives can be listed, as follows:

- To make it possible for each person involved in the marketing mix to perform efficiently and effectively to achieve the marketing goals.
- To measure the performance of each element in the marketing mix and take the appropriate action to correct divergences from the marketing plan.
- To have an efficient marketing information system with regular and accurate reporting and a strict timetable. To be effective, the reporting system must be regular and transmitted without delay to avoid damage to the plan.
- To have a friendly environment for both customers and employees. Friendliness, pride and willingness to do what is required are the attributes that an employer must instil in the staff. Employing the right people in the first instance is how to start the process.
- To offer praise and reward good performances.

Management by motivation

Management or the directors, having approved the marketing plan, then have to keep up the required resources to fuel the plan's ultimate realization. A shrug of the shoulders and an acceptance of unavoidable difficulties is seldom appreciated by disgruntled clients, quickly leading to a rapid down-turn in sales and profit. The decision-making process of control involves the setting of realistic sales and profit objectives and the ability to measure those objectives with:

- internal information
- external information
- performance comparisons
- advice and opinions from those concerned with the marketing function and its implementation
- the decision maker's knowledge and judgement
- timing of the action.

Here, financial management and marketing management have to be resolved together. Systems are in place in any well-run establishment for a reason other than keeping the customers; they are also essential to avoid unnecessary losses. Lax management can lead to staff dispensing free drinks or pilfering. However, staff who are motivated by friendly, caring management are less likely to be subject to petty pilfering.

Staff motivation

Motivation and control go together. What motivates people? Apart from the primary motivations of thirst, hunger, fear and anger, etc., the secondary motivations are the ones which most organizations have to deal with, and these are:

- a need for approval
- a need to belong
- a need for achievement
- a purpose
- an interest in the tasks to be performed
- pride in what one does and for whom one works.

Is there a person in this world who does not like being 'stroked', to be appreciated, either by being told that he or she is doing a good job or simply a friendly acknowledgement of his or her existence? Who does not want that proud feeling of belonging or being part of something worthwhile? It is the reason for family loyalty, the existence of clubs, the reason for people adopting causes, national fervour, joining groups and, of course, company loyalty. It is to achieve, to have a purpose or to have an interest in what one is doing which makes life and work worthwhile.

So how come so many organizations ignore these fundamental human needs? The answer probably lies in the common management trap of regarding employees as functionaries, human robots who are 'paid to do what they are told'. Ignorance of the basic human motivations leads to staff discontent, which in turn leads to indifference, dissatisfaction and poor service, often with disastrous financial consequences.

Figure 11.1   *Staff motivation*

Organizational control therefore requires management to put into place the following:

- Staff-orientated policies and administration
- Appropriate salaries and incentives
- Helpful supervision
- Friendly working conditions
- Understanding of the individual's personal life
- People-handling skills of supervisors
- Proper recognition of status
- Job security.

Whereas these factors are generally considered to be the province of general management, the unions, human resource management and not marketing, the absolute reliance in the hospitality industry on these factors working well indicates that the marketing plan cannot function without them.

Fear and coercion are the last resort motivators. A working culture and environment which provides people with esteem, pride and satisfaction will always prevail. However, wages, fringe benefits and good, safe, working conditions do not by themselves bring satisfaction which lasts. Motivation comes from the implementation of recognition and rewards commensurate with contribution, high organizational standards, good internal communications and the opportunity for self-control. People will correct their own mistakes more quickly and effectively if they spot them first.

Pride and competition

Many car manufacturers around the world are throwing out the production-line approach to building cars and are using the team method. Self-managing work units are formed to make up a team which builds a car from beginning to end. The units compete against other teams for productivity and quality control, to build a better car and build it more quickly than the others. There are incentives for the teams to do better.

The results have been outstanding in most cases. The team members are happier, there is less sickness, they earn more and they have pride in what they do because they are involved and are rewarded for their efforts.

Michael Hurst, at his 15th Street Fisheries restaurant, builds the same pride among his staff. At the beginning of each busy Saturday night, the chefs want to know how many meals they have to do, and at the end of the night they want to know how many they did. The waiting staff are the same. Everyone is imbued with the desire to do better and reach a standard of excellence, to keep improving on their personal best.

Pride, ego gratification if you like, is a basic human emotion. An organization which does not allow pride to take hold and grow among its employees is missing out on the rewards of increased productivity and achievement. The much vaunted and probably over-used term, productivity, is not achieved by systems alone. It is nurtured and encouraged by competition, job satisfaction, acknowledgement (praise, if you like) and rewards.

Part Two: Organization control

Business consultants and hospitality industry specialists Horwath and Horwath are well aware of the large number of businesses which have failed over the recessionary years. In the past, investors were attracted to the hospitality industry by the notion that running a pub or a small hotel was romantic. In many cases, investors believed that little more than a convivial spirit was needed to ensure success. In the 1990s Horwath and Horwath observe that survival depends upon well-balanced management expertise, traditional values of hospitality, value for money, high quality, investment in staff training and strategic marketing.

A successful organization requires management of the marketing plan as well as good marketing strategies. A number of establishments begin with the right ideas and lose their way because they become opportunistic instead of sticking to the original game plan and controlling the strategies that made them successful.

Here is an example which is as old as the hospitality business. It is about a restaurant which originally targets a low-income, aspiring group of young executives and professional people aged between 25 and 35, a market that eats out frequently. Let us assume that the owners get their service strategies right and the target market appreciates the casual style and the modest prices they implement. Before long, the business succeeds and makes a profit.

After a year or so of steady gains in customer numbers, greed then steps in and the management inches up the prices a few pounds, limits the meal portions and reduces staff hours. What invariably happens? Before long, the customers realize that they are not getting the same value for their money and begin to drift away. 'It isn't the same any more,' the customers say. 'The place is going downhill.'

Management does not really know what is happening or why, so it blames the customers for being fickle and resorts to advertising to 'get the customers back'. This does not work, so the restaurant goes into a slide and becomes just another restaurant struggling for survival.

The point of the example is that management does not really know what is happening because it does not have the necessary checking and control procedures in place.

A marketing plan has to be constantly monitored, otherwise it goes off track. The only difference between the marketing management of a large establishment and a small one is that the larger organization has more people to attend to the various marketing functions. Someone running the small place has to wear several hats or, in many cases, all the hats. This makes it harder on the small business operation because many skills are required. But that is not an excuse. On the other hand, with the larger operation, even though the load is shared the efforts have to be coordinated, placing a special responsibility on additional people to 'manage' the people who manage.

Elements of successful performance strategy

In the nucleus of a business, three specialized skills are needed – financial management, marketing and product and production knowledge. Each is equally important, but all must contribute towards a 'performance strategy'.

According to McKinsey & Co, seven elements are required for a successful performance strategy – objectives, structure, systems, skills, staff, style and values:

- *Objectives* determine what the organization wants to achieve.
- *Structure* determines the human and physical resources which are required to achieve the objectives.
- *Systems* determine the methods it will use to achieve the objectives and how it will deploy its human and physical resources.
- *Skills* determine the knowledge and information required of its human resources and the training needed to fill the gaps.
- *Staff* determines the numbers, experience and skills levels required of the human resources.
- *Style* determines the type of operation and how it wants to be perceived by its customers and its many publics.

- *Values* appropriate a degree of importance to customer satisfaction, staff loyalty, occupational health and safety, maintenance, progress and profit.

A sympathetic managerial climate and sound, open communications are essential. This can be called 'the corporate culture'. Staff have to work with a management style that will determine both consciously and unconsciously how they regard themselves, their employer, their customers and their work colleagues.

The marketing organization structure

A performance strategy requires an organization structure, and the structure in the case of marketing can take several forms. The structure chosen is directly related to who has the authority or power and therefore who allocates the responsibilities. In marketing, there are several primary functions to be performed:

- Marketing planning (development and overview)
- New product development (future planning)
- Direct sales representation (to corporate customers and travel agents, locally, nationally and internationally)
- Advertising (direct with media or using an advertising agency)
- Sales promotions ⎫ Usually assisted
- Direct mail ⎪ by outside
- Market research ⎬ consultants
- Public relations and publicity ⎭ or agencies
- Product management (overview or separate product managers for each profit-earning outlet)
- Customer services.

Who performs them depends on the size of the operation, the structure and the systems decided by the owners. Sometimes the structure and the systems evolve as the needs arise or growth occurs. In the case of a marketing organization structure for a large property there are five main alternatives for a marketing management system.

A sales only department

The managing director handles most of the marketing functions and requires only a sales force to make direct contact with existing and potential customers.

A sales department with ancillary advertising and promotions

In this instance, the managing director appoints a sales manager to handle a sales staff and the advertising and sales promotions. The main planning functions are controlled by the managing director.

A marketing department separate from sales

This structure usually occurs when an operation grows in size and the managing director (or the board) realizes that specialized assistance is required for most of the marketing functions. A marketing manager is appointed to work with the sales manager. The managing director retains control of planning. In this case, marketing and sales are seen as separate and equal functions.

A marketing department with sales as a subsidiary

Marketing in this variation of structure is perceived to be a holistic function, with sales being one of several functions. This is close to the modern concept of a marketing structure.

A modern marketing structure

A marketing director is appointed with full responsibility for all marketing activities and may have several specialists for each of the various functions reporting to him or her.

Organizing the marketing function

There are four ways of organizing the marketing functions and, again, it depends on the size of the operation and from where it draws the majority of its business.

1 *Functional departments* – various marketing specialists reporting to a marketing manager. This simply means dividing the ten marketing functions into people or departments. If it is a large international hotel group, for example, the advertising manager plans for all markets and regions. This is centralized control.
2 *Regional management* – each region is self-sufficient and responsible for itself. In this case, for example, London would have a complete marketing structure and control all functions for the south-east of England. Edinburgh would have its own separate marketing structure. Sheffield and Leeds, being smaller markets, may share the functions, and so on. This is decentralized control.
3 *Product line management* – a product manager is responsible for the marketing functions affecting each product. This approach would probably appeal to most middle line managers. It means, for example, that the food and beverage manager does his or her own marketing without direct interference. The person is given a target and a budget. The conference and banqueting managers, restaurant managers, etc., all work on the same basis. The overall marketing of the hotel as a corporate umbrella campaign may be vested in either the managing director, marketing director or sales manager.

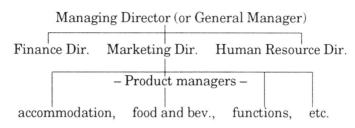

Figure 11.2 *A typical hotel organization structure*

4 *Market management* – separate marketing for customer groups. This approach divides the hotel's customers into groups, with a separate person responsible for the marketing functions affecting those groups. Thus the corporate market would be handled by one department, the holiday package market another, the meetings, seminars, groups and function markets by another, and so on.

Management control approaches

The owners and senior executives of operations often have differing views on marketing and how it should be controlled, even what part it plays in the total running of the operation. Some owners believe that marketing is just another function, and that it ranks equally in importance with financial, operational and human resource control. Others see marketing as being a 'selling' function, and give precedence to operations and finance. The attitudes of senior management, and therefore the management systems that they put into place in large hospitality establishments, affect both the structure of the marketing division and the roles of the managers of each function.

These are the main control approaches:

- *Market control* – sales, markets, market share and profitability are viewed together by senior management as being interrelated, which they are.
- *Profitability control* – senior management's emphasis is on sales and profits, the belief being that high sales mean high profits. This is a simplistic approach with in-built problems.
- *Strategic control* – markets, product mix, market mix, market shares, sales and profitability are constantly monitored and analysed using a marketing audit. This is usually the best method.
- *Product control* – senior management places most emphasis on the productivity, cost-efficiency and profitability of each line in the product mix. Even with a corporate overview, this approach does not always allow for customer satisfaction.

Whichever structure and system are employed to achieve the corporate goals they will change the order of the line management and the responsibilities or power vested in each job description. The classic organization structure to be found in a majority of the leading hotels around the world is as shown in Figure 11.2.

Marketing department:
Marketing director or manager

Adver- tising manager	Sales promo- tion manager	Sales manager	Public relations manager	Data base or systems manager	Cus- tomer services manager	Region manager etc.

Figure 11.3   *A typical marketing department structure*

A typical marketing department structure is organized like the one shown in Figure 11.3 (bear in mind that in some establishments the position does not exist and is covered by another job description).

The job description in brief

Marketing director/manager or director of marketing and sales

The title 'director' is sometimes loosely applied. It does not always mean that the person is on the board of the company. However, it is deemed to have more seniority as a title than manager even though the job descriptions are the same. The person has the responsibility of fulfilling all the marketing functions and endeavours to achieve the sales objectives set by senior management. Usually reporting to the managing director, the marketing director/manager has to coordinate his or her activities with those of the finance controller (finance director, chief accountant) and an administration manager.

In many hotels, the product managers, such as the food and beverage manager, conference and banqueting manager and rooms manager, have equal status, and the marketing manager has to liaise with them. In a modern marketing structure, the marketing director/manager has control over the product managers and, in addition, has department heads who handle sales, advertising, market research, customer services, sales promotions and public relations.

Sales director or sales manager

A sales director or sales manager would report to the managing director and may also be responsible for the whole marketing function in a sales-orientated organization. In a modern marketing structure, the sales manager would report to the marketing director. The person would be responsible for all the direct contact functions and would have a staff of sales representatives (also called account executives) and sales assistants. The department would be required to develop corporate customers, groups, seminars, functions and meetings, organize packages and contact travel agents and tour wholesalers.

Operations manager

This is an optional position. It refers to someone who is in charge of all the products or outlets in a large property.

Customer services manager

This person has the task of looking after the customer from the moment he or she makes a booking. Often also called accommodation manager (mainly because in a hotel accommodation is the premium product), and may also be the administration manager.

Public relations manager

The responsibility for the image of the hotel rests on this person's shoulders. Contact with the organizers of conferences, visiting celebrities, large parties, big accounts, politicians and government departments, all senior-level contact is part of this function. In addition, liaison with the media and a variety of publics is required to ensure favourable publicity whenever possible.

Advertising manager

Arranging for the development and placement of all forms of advertising in the media is this person's responsibility. In addition, he or she must organize the creation of brochures and literature for the establishment. An advertising agency is generally employed for creating campaigns, preparing the material and placing it in the media.

Sales promotions manager

With promotions being a large stimulant for business, this person has to create the promotional concepts and follow them through. The position is often included in the duties of the public relations manager and sometimes the advertising manager, as these two functions normally work together.

Direct mail manager

This is a specialist area, and one which is growing as establishments use direct mail techniques more and more to maintain contact with existing customers and endeavour to achieve further market penetration. Maintaining a database of customers and potential customers is part of this function. Great skill is needed to gain the maximum results. Direct mail agencies are often employed. Frequently, this job is included in the duties of the advertising or sales promotion manager.

Telemarketing manager

Another area of specialization for some places, used to back up the direct mail functions, sales promotions and advertised package offers, or to make direct contact with customers to sell particular products. The person in charge usually has a team of telesales people to control, advise and encourage.

Product line (or outlet) managers

Managers of accommodation, food and beverages, conferences and banquets, restaurants, entertainment and leisure divisions of a large property are also members of the marketing team, even though in most cases they will report to the general manager or an operations manager.

The importance of interaction

Every function in a large property is mostly directly involved or affected by each marketing activity. A close working relationship is therefore required because the customer is part of a transference of skills (doorperson to concierge to porter and so on) and there is often scope for communication problems, ambiguity or demarcation disputes unless the communication lines are carefully planned. This is another reason why the modern marketing department structure, with a key person responsible for directing and coordinating the various functions, is best.

Using competency-based strategies

Service is a product. It is a property's means of providing the customers with an experience which is special and unique. A service strategy has to state precisely what will happen to and for the establishment's customers. It has to be consistent and measurable. The best way of achieving these objectives is to translate the strategies into competency-based criteria which detail every action involved in providing the service.

The establishment of a competency-based service strategy requires a series of decisions which answer the following questions:

- What is the desired outcome for the customer?
- What are the details of the service that can be itemized as performance criteria?

Evidence of satisfactory performance of the service strategy is obtained from:

- observation by management;
- customer reactions from surveys or discussion;
- improved sales or customer numbers;
- staff feedback from discussions with management.

The success of the strategy relies on the abilities of the staff performing the service and the feasibility of the demands of the performance criteria. Some amendments may have to be made at the beginning to achieve consistency.

The concept of competency focuses on what is expected of the service and the people who provide it. To be competent, the staff must:

- have the skills to perform the service functions;
- provide the service to the satisfaction of the customers in the time allowed;
- handle irregularities and respond to special guest requirements;

- work as a team member and interact with others so that the customer benefits from the smooth transfer of information from everyone in the service chain – reception, waiter, kitchen, bar, and so on.

Three grades of evaluation of the outcomes and the performance criteria are recommended:

U – unsatisfactory, meaning that the service is not being effectively provided as stipulated by the performance criteria.
S – satisfactory, meaning that the service is meeting the performance criteria.
E – exceeding, meaning that the service is exceeding the expectations of the performance criteria, indicating that praise is required.

Each person involved in providing the service has to have a written chart which outlines the desired customer outcome and the performance criteria. The 'Restaurant Reception Service assessment' form in Figure 11.4 shows how it should be written.

A service strategy is not a 'holy writ' directive. It is a guide to be followed as closely as possible, but should never be an inflexible system. The customer is not processed like a piece of food.

The real skill of management is the creation of a service procedure which is a happy, interesting and even exciting outcome for the customers. That should always be the objective of a service strategy. Innovation is necessary so that in the end the establishment is offering an experience which is not only different but far better than that provided by other establishments.

Fast food places and chains like McDonalds, Pizza Hut, KFC and Taco Bell work to a formula which is highly successful. However, it is not that the customers are 'processed' which is the clue to their success, it is the fact that there is a satisfactory and consistent outcome for the customers. In the case of such places customers get a fast, convenient and cheap eating gratification. A fine dining establishment is different because it is offering an eating environment and service experience. The outcome for both sets of customers, however, has to be just as carefully planned.

Questions for discussion or revision

1 For a commercial organization, three skills are essential to its success. What are they, and, expressed as a percentage, how important is each one?
2 What are the respective advantages and disadvantages of each of the four ways of organizing the marketing function?
3 There are three management control approaches. Each one places an emphasis on one aspect of management. Which approach would work best for a hotel that is targeting the business traveller?
4 List the objectives of marketing control.
5 What are the assessment procedures required for an effective management control system?

Customer outcome	Performance criteria	Grading		
		U	S	E
1 To be greeted on arrival	Reception person • Customers to be greeted within 30 seconds of arrival. • Open the door for customers • Greet cordially. If customers not known by name, say: 'Hello, my name is....... May I have your name?' • When name supplied, check against reservations book. Acknowledge if there is a reservation: 'Of course! Mr & Mrs . . .' • If no reservation, enter name in book.			
2 To be given a table	• Make out a table place name. • Indicate a table and ask: 'I have a table (describe location) will that be all right?' • Escort customers to the table while making conversation. • Beckon to waiter who is in charge of the table.			
3 To be introduced to a waiter who will arrange food and drinks	• Introduce customers to waiter by name: 'This is Mr and Mrs. . . . Please meet Jane who is your waiter. She will assist you during the meal with food and drinks.' • If there are no other customers waiting, at the reception point, remain while the waiter seats the customers to make sure they are comfortable. • Before departing, wish the customers an 'enjoyable meal'. • Return to the reception point.			

Figure 11.4   *Restaurant reception service*

6   What are the procedures that need to be put into place to ensure that the staff are reasonably well motivated?
7   List the three types of management control factors and explain the purpose of each one.

Further reading

Blanchard, K. and Johnson, S. (1990). *The One Minute Manager*. London: Fontana.
Horwath and Horwath Consulting (1994). *Business Review*, No. 13, Spring.

12　*The planning discipline*

Aims of this chapter

1　To explain the components of a marketing plan and how to use a step-by-step process to bring them together to market a property or a product.
2　To describe how to write a marketing plan.

Why have a plan?

What is it meant to achieve?

The planning discipline is the way that management handles change. Change may not always represent growth, but often be simply an adjustment to new or altered circumstances. Anyone involved in business should always be thinking of ways and means (strategies) for improving or maintaining it. This is marketing planning, and it has to cover the short, medium and long term. Good marketing planning should allow for contingencies, to cover 'what if?' situations. It is the marketing of the property overall which usually involves the long-term view, as well as considering immediate short-term progress – especially true of a large property which can take up to ten years before it returns a worthwhile profit for its investors. Product lines are considered to be medium-term and product items tend to be more short-term because they can be changed without affecting the customers' overall perceptions of the property.

It is worth remembering that in business, as in war, failures have a common cause – growing too fast and entering additional territories with inadequate resources. In a word, greed. It is advisable to secure the base of the business and then, with careful planning, expand or extend the operation.

The outcome of planning is a master plan which guides and directs the operation through change. The purpose of a marketing plan is to apply discipline to the strategic process and avoid costly errors, but mostly to make sure that nothing is overlooked. The benefits of a master plan are:

* It demands up-to-date facts upon which marketing strategies can be based.
* It pulls together all the available information and the thinking behind the marketing efforts to create a documented plan of action.

- It offers a challenge to all involved to question existing practices and seek improvement.
- It integrates all elements of the marketing mix which must be considered in relationship to each other. All must contribute to the overall corporate goals.

In plain English, planning is a business process which encompasses an appraisal of what has been achieved in the recent past, a debate about how improvements can be made for the future and how they can be achieved (Teare et al 1994). There is a tendency in the hospitality industry to think that marketing planning is only for larger hotels and that writing a plan for a hotel with a very limited staff is a waste of time. However, because jobs are not as well defined in smaller properties it may be even more vital for the small property to commit its marketing plan to writing (Hart and Troy 1986). The high failure rate among small businesses can be attributed directly to either inadequate finance or the inability of the operators to prepare a business plan. In only a small percentage of cases can failure be attributed to bad luck or external forces (Storey 1994).

The critical path

A marketing plan must be produced as a written document, and address these issues:

- Consider the company's mission and its corporate goals.
- Recognize the financial, physical and human resources available.
- Examine and review all the available market and marketing information.
- Analyse comparative strengths and weaknesses of each product in the mix.
- Identify problems and opportunities.
- Target the most appropriate customer mix.
- Select the best match of products with the customer mix.
- Decide on realizable marketing objectives.
- Set marketing budgets.
- Develop strategies for each of the elements in the marketing mix to achieve the marketing objectives.
- Outline detailed operational tactics and costing for each element.
- Establish management controls and review procedures of the marketing plan.
- Propose long-term future developments.

(The discipline of 'ORGANISATION' described in Chapter 1 is an easy way of remembering the main steps.)

The planning procedures are flexible

A marketing plan should be completed at least annually. However, when an opportunity is presented by an altered circumstance in the operation's micro-environment (internal factors), such as a failing product, or the macro-environment (external factors), such as new legislation, the demise of a competitor, a market or product opportunity, the plan may have to be revised or a new plan drawn up to cope with the change. In each case, the planning discipline should be followed for the reasons outlined earlier – to avoid costly mistakes. However, the planning discipline does not always follow the critical path in the same sequence. Nevertheless, it is essential that ALL steps are considered before approval by management.

Similarly, the process of generating the plan – the planning discipline – need not follow the procedures used to write a report. The planning process may start with a market opportunity and lead to an examination of target markets and the development of strategies. In that case, the planner must work backwards and test the feasibility of the market opportunity and all the other factors along the critical path requiring analysis before finalization and the preparation of a documented report.

Nykiel (1983) outlines the following questions which clearly spell out specific steps to include in the marketing programme to be viewed both internally and externally.

Customers and markets

- Which market segments relate best to your product or service?
- In which areas of need are your products perceived by your current customer mix segments to be strong? In which areas are they weak?
- Are there operational weaknesses that have contributed to the perceived weaknesses, or are they simply an awareness or image problem?
- In the areas where you have strong competition, what are their major strengths and weaknesses as perceived by your customer segments?
- With which products can you exploit a competitive weakness or capitalize on your own strengths?
- Which existing product lines offer an opportunity for expansion?
- Which new product lines or items show growth trends and could be introduced to your existing customer mix? Or used to attract new customers?
- Are there any growing markets that can be exploited?
- Are there declining markets for some products requiring replacement or scaling down?
- What new developments are coming which represent either a threat or an opportunity?

Internal operations

- Are there selling difficulties with some products?
- Are there service and quality problems?
- Are the pricing levels and deals being offered attractive and competitive?
- Are some sections of the property in need of refurbishing?
- Is a change of image needed to re-position the property or a product line or item?

- Are costs exceeding expectations in some areas? Therefore, which areas of the marketing can be turned to more cost-effective use?

The master plan

A marketing plan makes a set of recommendations. Upon approval, it becomes the final marketing plan or 'master plan'. When completed, a written master marketing plan must incorporate all marketing activities, and all marketing activities must subscribe to a common corporate objective. It should be a living, working document which is referred to daily.

In a way, having a working document is as basic as the old joke about the highly successful accountant who eventually became a multi-millionaire. His staff observed over the years that he had the habit of beginning every day furtively unlocking the top drawer of his desk and carefully scrutinizing a piece of paper. Everyone considered it to be the secret of his success. When the old accountant died, his ambitious assistant forced open the drawer to obtain the secret and make a fortune for himself. The document in the drawer which the greedy assistant read with shaking hands and disbelief simply said, 'Debts left, credits right'.

Truly, surviving in business is mostly a matter of sticking to the basics of business, 'making sure more comes in than goes out'.

The need for separate product plans

Each product in the mix should be dealt with separately and have its own plan which can be either contained in the master document or be individually documented. This is because each product which is a profit-earning entity requires its own situation analysis, a marketing objective, target markets, a budget, strategies for the elements of the marketing mix and a detailed set of operational tactics.

In the case of a large hotel, there should be a master plan for the whole hotel and then separate plans for marketing the restaurants, bars, meetings and conferences, groups, tour wholesalers, and so on, for every line in the product mix. New products launched or introduced during the planning period get their own plan too. Advertising, sales promotions or selling plans are subsidiary plans which may follow the same format and fulfil the master plan.

Thus a marketing plan for a large property with a complexity of product lines can be an extensive document because a different set of strategies is required for:

- the property as a complete entity;
- each product line and item;
- each target market.

If there is a change of company policy or philosophy, the document has to be re-drawn to incorporate the change in strategic direction.

The fundamentals of planning

When an opportunity arises, or when change becomes necessary, the initial step is to review the company's mission statement, to orientate it with existing circumstances. Too often, management forgets what business it is really in.

As marketing is the process of developing products and services to satisfy people's needs and wants and arranging for them to be sold at a profit, the question must be asked, Is the business doing this according to its original mission? For example, hospitality is concerned with people experiences, therefore hospitality marketing is mostly about understanding people. Before proceeding, does management know enough about the current state of mind of its customers, potential customers, staff and the myriads of intermediaries and others who influence the purchase decision?

The next significant question to be asked is, Would the change contemplated fit with the corporate objectives? If it does not, then a consultative process is necessary to abandon the project or re-align the corporate objectives. Business history is littered with examples of failures and near failures resulting from marketing moves which diverged from or exceeded the corporate brief, remembering that it is objectives which are the engine of achievement.

In most product failures, or new ventures which 'don't quite work out' (which means they cost the company a pile of money), more often than not it is the senior executive who has a bright idea and then arrogantly implements it. In such cases it is done without the proper planning procedures and probably against the advice of less timorous employees, the majority being hesitant to go against the wishes of their superior.

In the planning process, package all the information and have a good, hard look at it. Market analysis is the beginning of the planning process. Its job is to gather all the information together and arrange it in a clear manner so that planning decisions can be made. The information to be assembled is covered in the chapters on market analysis and segmentation and also in Chapter 13, The marketing audit. There can never be enough appropriate information.

Once all the information is assembled, it has to be analysed for problems and opportunities. Almost invariably, the analysis highlights the need for limited or extensive change to products or markets, such as:

- a market opportunity;
- a product line or item opportunity;
- a product line or item which has to be changed, modified or improved;
- a re-positioning of the establishment's image.

(See Chapter 21, 'Growth strategies', for further explanation.)

The checkpoints of planning

Let us assume that a hotel has a problem with one of its restaurants, which means that a product item has to be changed. Furthermore, let us say that research suggests that a new Thai food theme restaurant may be popular. Using this example, let us now follow it through all the checkpoints.

- Is there a need for the product which the establishment intends to market? (Thai food has become very popular and it is a growth area of the market.)
- Is there an idea for the product which will give it a sustainable competitive advantage? (There are an increasing number of Thai restaurants, what is going to be special about this one?)
- Is there a market large enough to justify the investment? (Is there really a market for another Thai place? A primary cause of failure or frustration in business is the discovery that the market that someone thought worthwhile was either non-existent or too small to make the enterprise viable.)
- Is the market accessible, that is, is it physically close and can it be communicated to with relative ease? (Apart from the hotel guests, a resort, for instance, may not have a large enough local population to support the required number of sales. If the hotel is in the main city area, advertising and promotion would be simpler.)
- Is there the production means or the facilities for making or preparing the product or service? (Who has the skills to cook and prepare Thai food? What additional equipment is required? What is necessary in the way of decor and presentation?)
- Does the establishment have the ability to maintain the service and the production standards? (The place could be vulnerable if it achieves rapid success. Continuity of supplies and staff with the right credentials need to be considered.)
- Is there the money to develop the project properly and follow it through? (The place would have to look and play the part to be successful. In a competitive environment, a half-hearted investment in furbishing, staff and equipment could spoil the whole concept.)
- Is there enough knowledge about the people who comprise the market? (The devotees of Thai food are a certain type. Their expectations have to be understood.)
- Has a feasibility study been completed? (The costs of setting up have to be weighed against the forecasted income and profit.)
- Does management have the experience to control the project successfully? (Who has run or worked in a Thai restaurant before? It is not something one 'picks up'. The skill and expertise have to be evident to the customers from the beginning.)
- Does management have the marketing budget to promote it? (Selling, promotion and public relations are expensive exercises. Will the costs justify the results?)
- Does it make sense to do it? (Would a Thai restaurant 'fit' with the overall positioning of the hotel establishment and the customer mix?)
- How much business in terms of sales, market share or profit is possible from the new development or change? What are the marketing objectives which will drive the endeavour? (When writing down the marketing objectives, measurable results have to be decided and a time frame allocated.)
- Which segments of people should be targeted to form the customer mix? (The answer to this question should come from the market analysis.)
- What will be the product strategies? What will happen to and for the customers? (The service style, the menu, meal portions, plate presentation and so on all have to be decided.)

- How will the place look? (The decor theme, the music and general ambience have to be appealing to the target market.)
- What are the price strategies? (The price levels that will be charged will determine its perception of service and meal standards for the customer.)
- How will the product be positioned in the minds of the customers? (Promotion is necessary to communicate the place to the potential customers using a mix of advertising, direct contact, sales promotions and publicity. What will be the message?)

Writing the marketing plan

Once a project passes all the checks, the planner can proceed to prepare the plan in the form of a written document – a marketing report. A marketing document must take the reader from a state of ignorance through to awareness and understanding. Even if the majority of readers are conversant with the subject and have a reasonable knowledge of its purpose and content, there will be others who will read it who will not have that advantage. But, more importantly, the document's purpose is also to present the rationale behind the conclusions and provide meaning to the recommendations.

The writer must provide the background to the recommendations and the reasons for each step. Do not leave the reader wondering, 'How did the writer reach that conclusion?' Remember, there is a difference between observations and facts. In the main the writer should present facts, make observations about the facts and then draw conclusions in a logical sequence.

The order of presentation

1 Begin with an introduction that explains the purpose of the document, what it is about and what it intends to explain.
2 Provide a list of contents so that readers can refer forward or back to points of interest.
3 Include an executive summary, which usually occurs early in the document. This is for readers who are impatient and want the conclusions immediately, leaving the contents to be more closely scrutinized by others.
4 Recite the history or background behind the organization or product.
5 Present the market analysis information and quote its sources as you proceed. The topics which are covered by market analysis may be as follows:
   - How the product fits into the operation as a line or item
   - The product's positioning (the public's perceptions of the property)
   - Sales history
   - Market share information
   - Product trends
   - Profile of the market segments of the product's customer mix
   - Competitive activity
   - Product assessment, comparisons of performance strengths and weaknesses with the market as a whole and individual competitors

- Marketing activities and the results of previous strategies affecting the product's selling, pricing and promotion
- Internal factors affecting the product
- External factors affecting the product
- Market and marketing research data
- Internal observations by staff
- External observations, informed opinions from the industry and trade sources, etc.

6 The assessment provides an analysis of the situation and the main findings from the analysis. Here you can draw some conclusions and, based on the information gathered, put forward the reasons for your marketing recommendations to follow.

7 The marketing recommendations. This is where you outline the plan for introducing a product, or making product changes. The order of topics is usually as follows:
- The marketing objectives
- The markets to be targeted (People)
- The Positioning of the product
- The Product strategies
- The Pricing strategies
- The Place strategies
- The Promotion strategies.

8 The operational tactics. This is where you outline the details of the plan and stipulate the financial and physical requirements to implement it.

9 Your management proposals to measure the effects of the plan.

10 Your proposals for the future of the property or its products, if any, when the project proceeds according to plan.

11 Summary, where conclusions are drawn.

The creative part of marketing

A large number of decisions are required in marketing planning. The planning procedures outlined in this chapter are designed to assist the planning and therefore the thinking process.

There is a very definite place for creative thinking in marketing. The person who is capable of 'lateral thinking', of grabbing a 'great idea' from the cosmos, can often run away with a wild success. More often than not, though, it is the tried and proven formulas in business which are most likely to bring success.

Some people claim that they go by 'gut' feeling. The gut feeling is, in reality, the individual mentally scanning a reference area of experience gained from the marketplace. In effect, they do their marketing planning in their head and do not write down or reveal the process. The person who 'shoots from the hip' without any proper planning is the one who places the organization at risk.

Then there are those in management who manage by inactivity, failing to recognize the imperatives for change and ultimately being forced to react rather than plan to act when the opportunities arise.

The best operator is the one who has a competent mixture of pragmatism

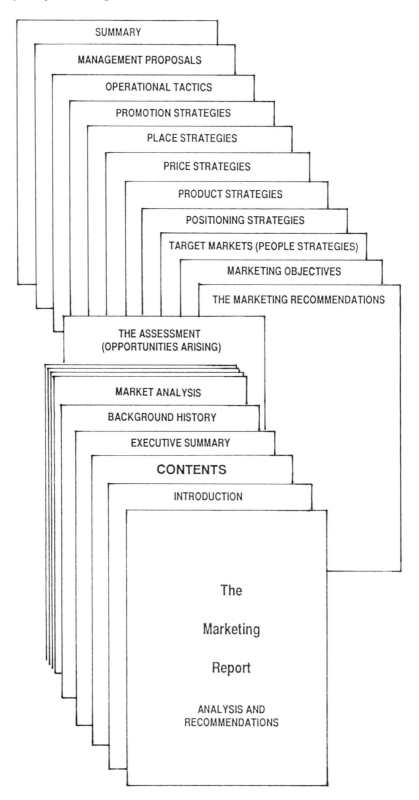

Figure 12.1   *The marketing report*

and creativity and who plans carefully, justifying each step of the process. They always please the customers, shareholders and bank managers.

Questions for discussion or revision

1 What are the main reasons for having a marketing plan?
2 List the various aspects of an organization that need to be considered in the planning process.
3 Who should have access to the marketing plan in a hospitality establishment and why would they need to refer to it?

Further reading

Hart, G. and Troy, J. (1986). *Strategic Hotel/Motel Marketing*. Educational Institute, American Hotel and Motel Association, Michigan.
Nykiel, R. (1983). *Marketing in the Hospitality Industry*. New York: Van Nostrand Reinhold.
Storey, D. (1994). *Understanding the Small Business Sector*. London: Routledge.
Teare, R., Calver, S. and Costa, J. (1994). *Marketing Management: A Resource-Based Approach for the Hospitality and Tourism Industries*. London: Cassell.

13 *The marketing audit*

Aim of this chapter

To explain how to dissect and analyse a company's marketing situation.

'Too many managers manage with hope instead of managing with facts'

The approach to a marketing audit is similar to doing a market analysis, but the intention is different. A marketing audit is a critical, outside-in investigation which is aimed at establishing an organization's exact market position and examining the effectiveness of its strategies and operational procedures.

To conduct an efficient marketing audit, the person has to think like a company auditor, or a detective. The auditor's task is to look for facts, reasons or motives regarding the company's market position and the performance of its products in the marketplace. A good auditor should consider possible solutions, or alternatives, as the audit proceeds.

A marketing audit process is used to understand an organization. It is an ideal process to use in the following circumstances:

* If you are thinking of purchasing a business
* If you are entering an industry you know little about
* If you are a newly appointed outside consultant
* If you want to introduce a new product
* As part of an annual review before planning begins.

Aspects which are examined by the auditor

The Murray brothers are very experienced hotel and restaurant operators. Over the years they have excelled in taking over properties which are failing and have then built them into thriving businesses. Their success story is not dissimilar to that of several hotel chains which have done the same thing.

The Murray brothers have developed and refined a format for assessing properties to test their suitability for improvement. They leave nothing to chance because they know that there are sometimes millions of pounds at stake. They do not like making mistakes, although they admit to the odd blunder with a property which did not prosper as well as they would have liked.

> A marketing audit is a systematic examination of the organisation's objectives, strategies, organisation and performance. Its primary purpose is to identify weaknesses in on-going marketing operations and plan the necessary improvements to correct these weaknesses. (Dibb et al 1991)

The Murray brothers do an audit for their own purposes, but as Philip Murray, the older brother, states: 'If the company under examination by us had done their own independent audit and reacted to what they had found, they may not have been in the position of being forced to sell. There is nothing very smart about what we do. A lot of managers could do the same. The trouble begins with too many operators managing with hope instead of managing with facts.'

Marketing audit procedures

The following procedures are recognized marketing audit methods used by many companies and documented by various marketing authorities.

Macro-environment

The Murray brothers begin by carefully examining the marketing environment in which the business operates. In each case they look for market factors likely to have affected the operation of the property in the immediate past and which may affect it in the not so distant future. The aspects they check are as follows.

Markets

Are the markets for hospitality growing, contracting or altering in some way? Are there new market segments emerging and others dispersing?

Demographic

Where is the property situated and what major changes have occurred in the way of building development or population shifts?

Economic

How is the economy of the country and the region doing? What effect is the economy having on the standard of living and people's discretionary income, their attitudes to hospitality, especially holiday travel, business travel and entertaining?

Environmental

What is happening in the physical environment? Are there conservation plans likely to affect the property?

Technological

Have there been or are there going to be any advances in technology which will affect the way the property is operating? For instance, development of the Internet in the UK has interesting implications for on-line commerce, and thus the way in which customers will reserve the hospitality product.

Political

What is the government doing or planning which could affect the property? Governments are always doing something with regulations which cause change to a business and the way it operates.

Cultural

What changes are occurring to people's lifestyles? How have their attitudes to hospitality changed?

Micro-environment

The state of the property

Where is it located and how does the property's position affect the perceptions of potential customers? What initial physical impression does the property make? What does its appearance convey to the customers? What expectations does the property arouse for the casual observer? What is the condition of the property externally and internally? What are the physical attributes of the place in terms of size, customer capacity and the standard and quality of its equipment?

Customer mix

Which market segments has the property targeted to comprise its customer mix? Which segments dominate? What types of people are not currently attracted to the property?

Product mix

What product lines and product items does the property have? Which ones are showing high usage and good returns and which ones are languishing?

Competition

Who are the main competitors? How are they performing by comparison with the property? Who has gained which proportions of the various segments?

Agents and tour wholesaler activities

How do travel agents and tour wholesalers regard the property? How much business is generated through them? What type of business is it?

Outside suppliers

What is the attitude of suppliers to the property? How efficient are they and how costly are their supplies? What deals are being done? What is the situation regarding future supplies? How much credit is being offered and what are the trading terms? How much money is owed by the property?

Corporate publics

What does the business community think of the property? Does the place have a high or low profile? How are relations with banks, insurers, media and the public in general?

Strategic planning

Business mission

Is there a written mission statement? What does it say? How closely has it been followed? Is it still viable?

Corporate goals and strategies

What have been the short- and long-term corporate strategies and how has management set about achieving them?

Marketing objectives

What have been the marketing objectives over the period of the property's existence? Have they been achieved? What is the management's explanation for any shortfalls?

Market position

What is the property's actual position with regard to market shares, sales and profits?

People strategies

Which markets has the property chased for each of its product lines or outlets, and what share of those markets has it secured?

Product strategies

What have been the strategies of the property for achieving market penetration and growth for each product line and item over the period and, when graphed, how do the results reflect the success of those strategies?

Service strategies

Which strategies are in place that are designed to provide a consistent, measurable and effective series of experiences that happen to and for every customer? How are these strategies measured and managed?

Product positioning

How has management endeavoured to position the property and its products? Are the perceptions of customers in line with the objectives of the positioning strategies?

Promotion strategies

What advertising and promotional strategies has the property pursued, and with what degree of success? What is the annual budget for promotion and how is it spent? Are the effects of promotional spending being measured against the budgets?

Pricing strategies

How has the property priced its various products? Has it adjusted to market realities, practised a uniform pricing policy, adopted a flexible pricing strategy or has it discounted extensively to gain business and remain competitive? Are the property's various products perceived by the customers to represent value?

The organization

The organizational structure

How has management structured itself? How have authority and responsibility been distributed? Who does what? How good is the management standard overall and which members are performing to an optimum level? How are they monitored?

Lines of communication

How do the managers communicate with each other vertically and horizontally? What communication systems and meeting procedures are in place? How good is the functional efficiency of management? In other words, is management effective in achieving the marketing goals?

Company rules and policies

What are the company policies regarding customers and staff? What is the basis for them, and how are the rules and policies implemented? Who governs them? How do customers and staff react to them?

Human resources management

What is management's attitude to staff? How do staff regard management? How does management interact with the staff? What training is provided and how is it provided? How are relationships with the unions? How good are the occupational health and safety measures? What are the staff amenities and privileges?

The market systems

Marketing information system (MKIS)

Does management have a way of gathering and assessing market and marketing information? Which sources are used and what is done with the information gathered? (This subject is covered in Chapter 14.)

Market and marketing research

How much research is conducted by management and how often? To what extent is management guided by the researched attitudes of its customers? What are the sources used by management to access data? To what extent does it refer to the staff for input?

Marketing planning system

How is marketing planning organized and how often is it updated? How are sales forecasted for budgeting purposes? Does everyone work with a coordinated marketing plan, or are growth and market penetration opportunistic and haphazard?

Marketing control system

Are marketing activities checked progressively by management? Is a sales analysis conducted regularly? Are quotas set and, if so, on what basis? Are there strategic, profit and tactical operations controls in place, and how are they monitored? For example, is there a customer attitude tracking system?

New product development, future planning

How does management decide on improvements and changes to products, or plan new products? Does management plan for change, or is it simply being reactive to circumstances and opportunity?

Marketing profitability

How does management analyse the property's cost-effectiveness and profitability? Are the following regular checking procedures in place:

- Return on investment?
- Cash flows?
- Profit and loss account by each product line and item?
- Market share comparisons?
- Profit margin contributions by products?
- Cost-effectiveness analysis of products and staff?
- Probability analysis?

Marketing functions

How well does the property perform? The day-to-day functioning of the property is the final check carried out by the Murray brothers. This is a two-way check of:

- the staff and their operational procedures, their attitudes to customers and their ability to provide service, the service strategies they follow, the service systems in place, the standards of the equipment they use and overall efficiency levels achieved;
- the reactions from customers resulting from their experiences of the staff's services and their level of satisfaction with each of the products.

The Murray brothers gather this information by talking to staff and a random selection of customers. From these interviews they also seek to determine:

- staff and customer awareness of the property's products, attributes and benefits;
- the effectiveness of service strategies and their ability to achieve the sum total of experiences which will satisfy and retain a high percentage of customers;
- attitudes to prices and whether there is a perception of value.

Further information about the property's ability to function effectively is gained by outside interviews to ascertain:

- tour wholesalers' and travel agency representation knowledge of the property;
- advertising effectiveness, the standard and presentation quality of what the Americans call 'collateral material' (brochures, factsheets, folders and merchandising aids);
- sales promotions and their effectiveness in increasing new business;
- publicity. How often does the property gain a mention?
- sales force effectiveness. How good are they in securing corporate customers, organizing tours groups and achieving repeat business?
- the standard of property maintenance.

Summary

'The sad fact is', claims Philip Murray, 'each marketing audit we conduct reveals not one but usually several shortcomings. Which I guess is the reason why we always have many properties on the market to choose from. Hospitality is a tough business to be in. It is a service business and all the factors we audit have to be going right for a property to perform well and succeed. It would be good to say some factors are important and the rest don't really matter. The truth is, every damn one of these factors has to be spot-on. A failing property is one that has failed too many times in too many areas.'

Financial factors are an essential part of the marketing audit. Marketing is the cause of the property's condition as measured by customer numbers, cash flow, corporate profit and debt. The best way to analyse the condition of a property is to examine it in a cause and effect way. It is not possible to separate the financial concerns from the marketing concerns when doing an audit. Both are irrevocably locked together when assessing a property's performance because the ultimate aim of marketing is to achieve a profitable result for investors.

A prospering property almost invariably has strong forecasting and control measures in place so that it cannot stray too far from its corporate objectives and its marketing planning. The outside-in view provided by a marketing audit is a valuable tool to be used in addition to management control procedures as it tends to focus on matters which can be overlooked from within the organization.

Questions for discussion or revision

1 In which circumstances would one use a marketing audit as opposed to a marketing analysis? Explain the difference between them.
2 List the main categories in a marketing audit which require attention.
3 Of all the marketing audit categories, which group of factors are the most crucial when determining a property's future prospect for survival?

Further reading

Dibb, S., Simkin, L., Pride, W. and Ferrell, O. (1991). *Marketing Concepts and Strategies*. London: Houghton Mifflin.

14 The marketing information system

Aim of this chapter

To explain the need for management to have information systems for effective control and how to set up a marketing information system (MKIS) which meets the requirements of a property.

A worst case scenario example

Scott had been appointed as the new chief executive of a failing company. In an attempt to discover its actual position from its records he ran into the dilemma faced by many chief executives – there is either too much information of an unusable kind or not enough information upon which to make decisions.

Tuesday promised to be an exciting day for Scott. He arrived at the office eager to go over all the reports Johnson and Locke were going to bring him.

At 8.00 sharp, Johnson knocked at Scott's door and brought in twenty binders of reports, each about two inches thick. He said, 'These are financial reports for each division for the last month. If you want the breakdowns at the plant level, there are a hundred reports like this in my office. I'll have them brought in. I'll also bring you the operation reports in a few minutes.'

Johnson left Scott's room and returned with a trolley carrying stacks of thick computer reports. He carefully placed them in a neat row on Scott's conference table, then turned and walked out.

Scott was in shock when he saw the masses of reports. He had expected to see several reports but not quite so many. He couldn't make much sense out of this information even if he could force himself to go through all the reports. It would take months to understand the contents of these reports.

Lancaster and Massingham (1993) outline a means of gathering critical information quickly and in a radically simple way by having an information system that gives a manager only the information that he or she needs.

The theory

The purpose of a well-designed MKIS is to help management to make effective decisions. Teare et al (1994) and Dibb et al (1991) put it this way:

> the existence of information in a company is not enough. It must be structured and disseminated in such a way that it is possible for managers to use it to formulate policies, make decisions and resolve problems. The MKIS is focused on managing the flow of information.

> An MKIS is the framework for the day-to-day management and structuring of information gathered regularly from sources both inside and outside the organisation.

The MKIS process

The marketing audit procedures outlined in the previous chapter can easily be covered by an effective marketing information system. The character Scott in the case study faced the problem of inadequate information systems. Most times, so do the Murray brothers when they examine a potential purchase. But as Philip Murray explains:

> When we are looking at a property with a view to taking it over, or managing it perhaps, we are invariably struck by the fact that the company seldom has a regular and established means of obtaining vital information about how the operation is performing. In most cases, when we dig for data to tell us the state of the place the explanation for the company's problems becomes clear – too many wrong decisions are being made, or, alternatively, no decisions are made when a hell-of-a-number are screaming to be made. Managers like that are living in a self-imposed vacuum of information. They are either denying anything is wrong out of ignorance, or what information they are receiving is not sending them the right signals. When it becomes obvious that the operation is in trouble, frequently they still don't know why, so they react by shooting at anything that moves and usually kill off any chances they might have for survival. There are many companies which aren't up for sale that may be doing quite well without an MKIS, and I'm not saying that an MKIS is the answer to every company's problems. What I can say though, without fear of being wrong, is that an MKIS will substantially contribute towards building a successful operation and, more importantly perhaps, maintaining a strong level of growth through most economic conditions.

Philip Murray goes on to say:

> The bean counters (accountants and financial managers) are historians. They usually come into the office with a string of figures that tell you that things are going

badly when it is too late. The events that caused the problems mostly happened months before, but of course strategic and tactical mistakes aren't ever reflected in financial terms at that time.

The managing director of a leading hotel chain had this to say:

> Every day I check on how we are going, right across every property. I need this information because I don't believe I can be an effective manager without it. I can act quickly to fix things before they go too far off track. I get concise figures and reports daily, backed up on a weekly, monthly and more extensive survey results half yearly.

He recognizes the importance of accurate and timely information which helps him to do his job better.

The components of an MKIS involve setting up a regular supply of information, or data flow, for the people involved in:

- planning
- executing, and
- controlling the marketing function.

There are three types of marketing control which good management will require an MKIS to monitor:

- *strategic control,* to examine whether the planning, the strategies which have been put into place, are achieving the marketing objectives.
- *tactical control,* to examine the operational procedures and day-to-day running of the place to find out if the staff and the systems are working efficiently and effectively.
- *profitability control,* to determine if the organization is making or losing money by examining the profit contributions and the costs of each product line and item.

A marketing information system therefore has to provide data from many different sources, and the type of data has to be defined.

A large property such as a five-star hotel obviously needs a large amount of information; far more, say, than a 100-seat restaurant or a small country house hotel. But size does not diminish the need for information. The owner of a pub might argue that he and his wife run the bar and the restaurant, while a relative looks after the few bedrooms they have to let, so they store the information that they need in their heads. The trouble is, the mind is prone to have a selective memory, and what they think is happening is often far removed from what the customers know is happening. The trap for a small operator is complacency and the inaccurate reading of the customers' requirements. An MKIS for a small place does not have to be elaborate, but it should exist in some form for the owners' self-protection. Loss is far more painful for the 'little guy' than it is for investors in the corporate groups.

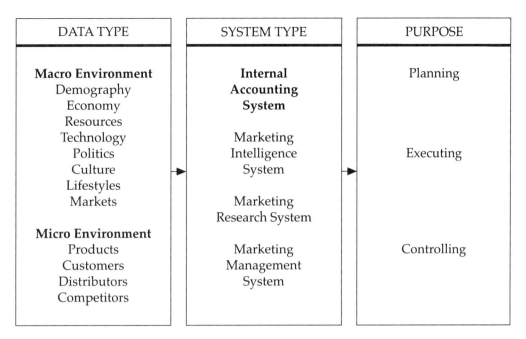

DATA TYPE	SYSTEM TYPE	PURPOSE
Macro Environment Demography Economy Resources Technology Politics Culture Lifestyles Markets **Micro Environment** Products Customers Distributors Competitors	**Internal Accounting System** Marketing Intelligence System Marketing Research System Marketing Management System	Planning Executing Controlling

Figure 14.1   *The marketing information system*

Strategic control

People, positioning, product, price, place and promotion strategies can seldom be long-term in their effects. In order to review their ability to 'keep the customers rolling in', records have to be kept of numbers of customers and their levels of satisfaction. To handle this type of situation, information about customers is required, as follows:

Internal

- Sales analysis
- Advance bookings
- Number of enquiries
- Market and customer mix information
- Customer attitude tracking.

External

- Market share comparisons
- Competitive action information
- Suppliers' information
- Channels of distribution information (intermediaries)
- Awareness and positioning information.

The information needed for strategic control can come from the following sources:

- Internal accounting and sales analysis
- Marketing management feedback, supervisor and staff comments
- Market and marketing research
- Customer attitude tracking.

Internal information should be easy to obtain with a sound record-keeping system together with reporting procedures from each product line manager. More difficult to obtain is the external information. Market share comparisons ought to be an industry task because everyone benefits from a share of information. However, some operations are not always cooperative and others tell lies to impress. Simple observation can often overcome the difficulties. Sitting in a property at random times over a few days will usually provide an experienced operator with a sound impression of the place's performance.

A marketing research system

A marketing research system is one of the most critical tools of an MKIS because it provides advance warning of change from the source of all business, the customers themselves. In short, it is a check on:

1 Customer attitudes.
2 Customer motivations and early warning of changing attitudes.
3 Advertising, sales and promotion impact reactions.
4 New product or sales change implications.
5 Market awareness and positioning information.
6 External market intelligence.

Marketing research in any organization should be conducted every six months. However, a faster use of customer reactions can be achieved by customer attitude tracking. There are several ways of doing this:

- Complaints and suggestion systems which record, analyse and respond to customers' written and oral comments.
- Customer panels, consisting of a group of selected customers who have agreed (normally for a concession or consideration) to report regularly by phone or mail questionnaire. They are sometimes referred to as 'mystery guests'.
- Customer survey, a mailed questionnaire or personal interview conducted regularly to evaluate product performances.
- Observation, which is a simple, watching brief by a trained person of what customers do, say and think.
- Pilot surveys of existing and potential customers to gauge attitudes and trends.

Tactical control

The tactical operations of a place are the day-to-day activities of the service systems, and they are the life-blood of customer satisfaction. The way to implement a tactical control system is by having a regular reporting system supervised and provided by product line managers. Their task is to measure productivity and make performance evaluations of:

- services staff and services
- sales people
- agents
- suppliers
- outside service providers
- equipment.

The information can be subjective, which is better than nothing, but it is best done by having a series of competency-based statements with required outcomes. Each outcome is then measured on a graduated scale from one to five. Over a period, a norm is established and results are compared with that norm. An unsatisfactory result is when there is a progressive tendency for results to fall below the norm. Ideally, the results should demonstrate a growing trend towards exceeding the norm.

Profitability control

The way to have profitability control is to have an accountant or financial manager draw up a reporting system which analyses expense to sales ratios of every product by:

- territory
- market segment
- client or corporate group.

This information normally comes from internal records which provide:

- sales figures and analysis
- costs
- stock inventories
- cash flows
- accounts receivable and payable.

Marketing intelligence

The purpose of marketing intelligence is to provide management with information concerning:

- developments in the market environment
- identification of social and cultural trends and opportunities
- new laws
- trade information
- technological changes.

The information sources for marketing intelligence usually come from trade reports, journals, employees, customers, suppliers' comments, agents' reports and comments, observation of competitive activity, published reports, industry conferences, staff movements, tourism reports, travel information, etc.

Some groups in the hospitality industry exchange information, either through an industry association or by arrangement. There are also trade intelligence suppliers, and the gathering of this assortment of information can be done by a clipping service. Good management keeps itself up-to-date with developments in the industry. Copying an idea that has been a success in a similar situation elsewhere makes sound sense, just as it does to avoid a problem that has occurred somewhere else.

Setting up an MKIS

An MKIS provides the information, management makes planning decisions based on that information, the planning is then implemented and the MKIS records the markets' reactions. All information supplied by an MKIS must be progressively measured and compared. It should be quantitative (numbers and percentages), qualitative (behavioural and attitudinal), evaluative (judgemental and opinionated) and exploratory (sounding out information sources).

The trend today is towards small, focused reports. Otherwise, management can be overwhelmed and confused by lengthy volumes of data. To avoid managers drowning in data, the amount of information has to be controlled. Therefore in a large organization, each manager needs to be asked:

1   What types of decisions are you required to make?
2   What information do you need to make those decisions?
3   How and when do you need it?
4   In what form do you want it?
5   How detailed does it have to be?

To make it work, a marketing management system has to provide:

• centralized reporting procedures
• a means of dissemination of information obtained to all concerned
• a regular and intelligent evaluation of the information
• a decision-making methodology.

There has to be a reason for gathering the information. By itself, information has no worth; its value comes from how it is used. Its primary use is to take advantage of situations and find solutions to problems.

Progressive comparisons are essential

The information for an MKIS should be delivered in a simple, easy-to-read and digestible form on a daily or weekly basis, so that management can maintain an on-going graph or grid. Management is then placed in a position to be able to:

- compare progressive results with goals
- conduct performance measurement
- do a performance diagnosis
- take corrective action if needed.

Solutions and decisions

The two primary concerns for management are sales and profit. These are very closely related, but are not the same, of course, and, if there are problems with either, the causes are different. An MKIS is designed to reveal the situation and the causes of the situation. But what are the solutions?

When sales are down

The natural solution for a sales decline is an intensified sales effort, but this is not as easy as turning on a tap. An increase in sales can be achieved by one or a combination of the following corrective measures:

- *An improved sales effort.* This could mean stepping up the number of client and prospective client calls, putting on more sales representatives, appointing more agents, extending into new territories, targeting different customer groups, eliminating wasteful sales calls, concentrating on more profitable customer groups, providing sales incentives and motivations, training or making staff changes.
- *Making product improvements.* This could mean adding new or different facilities to attract more of the same types of customers or entirely new types (see Chapter 21). Increasing the number of, or expanding, specific service strategies is another way of increasing sales. Add-on services or benefits is another.
- *Improved advertising or promotions.* An altered image can re-position the property (see Chapters 17, 19 and 20) and generate new customer interest. Spending more on advertising is a popular means of increasing sales, especially if research reveals that there are large numbers of people unaware of the property or uncertain about what it offers. Developing sales promotions is an excellent means of drawing attention to a property and exciting people into making a purchase, often attracting them away from their favoured establishment.
- *Pricing changes.* Most markets are price-driven unless there is an exclusive benefit advantage for the customers (see Chapter 22). Add-on value, discounts, special privileges, deals and price-geared options all bring forward prospective customers seeking value for their money.

When profits are down

When times are tough, everyone complains about the lack of profit. In the hospitality industry, it is natural for operators to look at means of 'trimming the overheads'. Unfortunately, most attempts at trimming the overheads lead to reducing services and customer comforts, which can have drastic consequences for sales numbers. In the end, a reduction in services frequently achieves the opposite of the desired effect. In the short term, profitability seems to improve, because on paper the ratio between expenses and income is greater, but as sales numbers decline the total profit gained can actually reduce. Therefore trimming measures should be aimed at eliminating waste and expensive systems rather than customer benefits.

Areas which need to be examined are:

- *Increase prices selectively.* This means raising prices where there are justifiable reasons in the customers' minds.
- *Increase sales.* Increased sales is usually the solution to most profit problems. Additional sales, which only increase the variable costs while fixed expenses remain the same, improve profit margins quite dramatically. For example, a busy bar with a rapid turnover of stock means that the bar persons are working to capacity. Bar persons are a fixed expense, whereas stock costs vary according to the number of customers.
- *Reduce staff.* If such reductions do not affect customer comfort, there is sometimes room for staff reductions in ancillary services where such reductions may be more cheaply performed by someone else or even by hiring contract services outside the organization.
- *Improve service efficiencies.* The use of labour-saving systems or careful examination by time and motion study methods of labour-intensive actions can usually lead to services being provided more easily or quickly to customers. Sometimes the solution will be a machine or some equipment such as a computer reservations programme for front office procedures or a stock control re-ordering programme.
- *Eliminate unprofitable lines.* Every property has a product line that provides a dubious return for the money invested. There is a general acceptance that certain services are expected by customers almost as a matter of tradition. However, a check with customers and the actual usage of such facilities sometimes reveals that few customers would be lost if they were not there. It is also worth considering that some facilities and services can be contracted to outside suppliers, e.g. laundry, hairdressing. On most menus and wine lists in the restaurant, there are usually items which cost money to maintain and which few customers would miss if they were not there.
- *Take on more profitable lines.* Space which is used for unprofitable lines can often be better utilized by replacing them with new products or services which can attract more use by existing and new customers. For example, a property may have a large space for functions which is only occasionally used for that purpose, whereas the space may be better utilized as a leisure centre for guests and outside members.
- *Sell additional products.* Where there is a regular customer group, there is potential for selling them additional products. This is the idea behind the hotel business, of course, but all too often the concept is forgotten, nothing new is introduced and it becomes just another place to eat and sleep. There is no point in change for change's sake, but there are definite reasons for making the best use of the property and the customer base it has by adding on to existing products, even on a trial basis.

- *Sell old stocks.* A storeroom is the best place to start for old treasures such as furniture, equipment, stock, redundant fixtures, fittings and a host of material that falls into the category of 'coming in handy one day'. Seldom does that day arrive. It is best to sell it and realize its value.
- *Reduce spoilage and eliminate waste.* Most properties keep a watchful eye on this area, but it is amazing how often an outsider can observe procedures and activities that have become the 'accepted way of doing things' which in fact cost unnecessary amounts of time and money.
- *Stop pursuing the wrong customers.* So often managers have a delusion that there are people with lots of money in the market that they should be getting. As a consequence, management builds and redecorates, provides services, advertises and creates expensive brochures and sales material to attract these people. In fact, they either do not exist or they are people who have little or no interest in ever patronizing the place. Nevertheless, many properties persist with this futile and expensive exercise of unrequited pretension. The majority of customers are simple, basic people with basic interests and requirements who have some money but not a lot.
- *Make the place a better place for the customers.* Increased numbers of happy customers who enjoy the experience of being there is probably the best solution for a reduced profit margins problem. Get the numbers up and profits follow is the axiom of Michael Hurst of the 15th Street Fisheries in Fort Lauderdale: 'The accountant's view is to bring down the product costs a few points, lift the prices a few points, and then reduce the staff numbers and cut their wages a few points. Do that, and before long you haven't got enough customers to make profits from. That's not a solution. That's going out of business in an organised way.'

Questions for discussion or revision

1   What is the difference between information obtained from the macro-environment and the task environment?
2   There are four primary marketing information systems involved. Name each one and briefly explain its purpose.
3   How does management make use of the information it obtains from an MKIS in the routine of the business?

Further reading

Dibb, S., Simkin, L., Pride, W. and Ferrell, O. (1991). *Marketing Concepts and Strategies*. London: Houghton Mifflin.
Lancaster, G. and Massingham, L. (1993). *Essentials of Marketing*. London: McGraw-Hill.
Teare, R., Calver, S. and Costa, J. (1994). *Marketing Management: A Resource-Based Approach for the Hospitality and Tourism Industry*. London: Cassell.

15 Market and marketing research

Aims of this chapter

To explain:

1 How and when to use market and marketing research
2 The various types of research methodologies
3 The basics of questionnaire design.

There is nothing more dangerous in business than an assumption or a guess. History records the brilliant and perhaps inspired successes of those who 'made it' by backing their judgement in a venture or using intuition and guessing correctly. Unfortunately, history only mentions the miserably small number of successes and seldom talks about the teeming millions of failures.

Market and marketing research has one purpose: to take as much of the guesswork and assumption out of business decisions as possible. Research is the systematic gathering of qualified information to establish facts.

A small operator in the hospitality industry may shrug and say they are too small to afford research. Rubbish! A few well-chosen questions of a random sample of twenty or so customers is often sufficient to stave off a disastrous decision, and it costs nothing. For a few pounds, a book or an industry journal can provide vital clues to profitable opportunities. Without research, a business is being run on ignorance.

Even the largest companies have to plead guilty to either not conducting research before embarking on a project or defying the research that provided a different answer to the one management wanted. There was the beer that was launched for women that research said women did not want. The research was right and the company lost millions. There was the cigarette brand that was marketed for women that research said would not work, and it did not. There was the car that was designed for everyone that research said no-one would want, and they did not.

There was a London restaurant that went through sixteen different name changes, expensive refurbishing and many different owners. None of the owners ever asked a single customer in the market what they would like, nor did they

1

What types of people use the property now?
Where do they come from?
Why did they choose this property?

2

What types of people are not
coming to the property?
Where are they going now?
Why are they going there?
What is the property doing or
not doing that makes them stay?

3

What types of people can the property get that it is not getting now?
What does the property have to do to get them?

Figure 15.1 *The reasons for market research – to find the answers to three groups of questions*

bother to research the market to see what was working and what was not. One owner went to New York, Paris and Melbourne and came back full of wonderful restaurant and nightclub ideas which he tried with a successive series of flops. Did he blame himself? No, naturally, he blamed the customers for their lack of interest in his brilliant concepts.

At the tail end of the 1980s, Ian Guthrie, proprietor of Rombald's Hotel and Restaurant, a twelve-bedroomed hotel in Ilkley, West Yorkshire, was given research from the English Tourist Board showing that 60 per cent of conferences in the UK were one-day events for fewer than thirty delegates. The research also revealed the need for greater professionalism and more sophisticated equipment in small venues. Inspired Guthrie 'invested six figures in state-of-the-art technology'.

Five years on, it was some way from realizing the projected return on his investment. Is the chastened Guthrie right to doubt whether the market is ready for high technology? Do people not expect to find sophisticated equipment in a fifteen-bedroomed hotel? Are people intimidated by Rombald's brochure extolling the technology?

The most likely explanation is that Guthrie either did not ask his potential customers the right, or any, questions before he went ahead with his investment. This example makes the point that whenever change is contemplated there is an important type of research which could have provided the answers without much pain, and that is testing the concept out with the potential users.

Market research is finding out what is happening and why it is happening.

Most hospitality managers believe that as they and their staff are in direct contact with their customers they quickly get a reading of customer attitudes. This generalized observation technique, then backed by unit sales figures, gives them a fairly accurate picture of how the operation is going. Maybe. The chances are more likely, however, that staff and management are so busy doing their job that they go through the motions of asking guests about their stay or experience. 'And how was everything?' they ask with a smile as they make up the account. 'Did you enjoy your stay? Oh, that's good. See you next time!' When staff are busy they are not really interested in the answers. Besides, at check-out the guests are in a hurry and not interested in any discussion, and often in the morning there is a queue. More than likely, any guest's comment is not recorded, accumulated or cross-analysed in any way, so management is left with asking staff for 'impressions' which are often divergent, loaded to make a point or merely the expression of a personal prejudice. Some staff use real or imagined customer attitudes to indicate how they believe the place should be managed.

A high percentage of market research involves the progressive collection of data from existing resources. A well organized MKIS, for example, ensures that this information is regularly collected, sorted and distributed. This is sometimes referred to as desk research – information that comes across the desk or can be accessed by computer records, private library or an industry library. Primary data are original data gathered for a specific project. Secondary data have already been gathered for another purpose or general usage, and come from sources such as government statistics, industry, trade, professional and business associations, private research agencies, higher education institutions, and so on.

Hotels have a large amount of information at their disposal, especially since the introduction of computerized systems which management is able to use to make marketing decisions. For instance, accommodation analysis can indicate which packages are mostly purchased and by which type of people. The geographic origins of guests can be tracked. The types and number of sales of all products can be analysed by a centralized computer network when it is programmed to collect helpful data from the various points.

For example, the data of many operations reveal that guests seldom use the establishment's restaurants and that most of their customers come from the local population. Similarly, that the fitness room, pool, spa and sauna are mostly used by outsiders and the staff. This information has made many property investors wonder why they installed and maintained such a wide range of expensive facilities for an army of guests who seldom use them.

With a planned data retrieval programme management can use the computer system to build a database of customers for direct mail and telemarketing contacts. Thus it should be possible to create a sales promotion and then ask the system to choose those customers who would be the best prospects for the promotion. The same system could be used to address letters and envelopes from its files.

However, management must decide, when the system is purchased, which information it wants and programme the system accordingly, otherwise many of the advantages of having the system are lost. Most systems are used for financial and operational purposes, and the needs of marketing are either a secondary consideration or overlooked altogether.

Once the systems are set in place to retrieve these data it is a relatively inexpensive process to maintain the flow. More expensive to do is field research, because it involves preparing a questionnaire, coding it for keying into a computer, organizing researchers to interview respondents, finding appropriate respondents, conducting the interviews (either in person, mail or by phone), collating the information, cross-tabulating it and then analysing the results.

Marketing research surveys are usually conducted sporadically on a need-to-know basis. However, a good MKIS provides for marketing field research of the hospitality market to be conducted annually so that data can be progressively measured for change and indications of market behaviour. It is an early warning system of trends and attitudes. Whereas sales analysis is historical, research will often uncover what is in people's minds before the purchase decisions are made. Marketing research takes several forms, and it is not the forbidding monster some people believe it to be, although motivation and psychological research can be complex and are best left to the experts.

The difficult part of marketing research is that often management does not want to believe the answers, preferring to persist with its delusions about how things are instead of listening to what the market is saying.

Using marketing research

There are many reasons for conducting marketing research. In each case, the information should be updated at least annually to discover whether there have been any changes. It is on the basis of research that marketing mix strategies are formulated. For example, the decision on which market segments to target (people strategies) can only come from a proper understanding of the market for a given city or region and the people who comprise that market. Product mix strategies will follow logically from the decisions on the best market segments to target. Pricing strategies will flow from the people strategies; so will product and positioning strategy decisions. Then will follow promotion strategies.

Important decisions like these have to be made on the basis of facts, not guesses or assumptions. Hence marketing research is a key factor in the marketing process because, in the formulation of strategies, questions can only be answered by marketing research of some type.

Two basic reasons for research

Customer mix research

To find out which groups of people make up the market and what percentage of each group most often use the facilities of the property. In addition, this type of research establishes where the customers are coming from and their reasons for travel. This research is designed to answer questions like:

- Where does most of the accommodation business come from? Which towns, cities, countries or regions?
- How do they arrive – by plane, car, train or ship?
- What are the reasons for each segment choosing to travel – business, meetings, conferences, holidays, personal?
- When do they mostly come?
- What types of people are they? What are their social, economic, cultural and national characteristics?
- How much does each type spend and on which products?
- How is the market shared among the various operators?

Attitude research

To find out the attitudes of each of the customer mix groups towards the property and its products compared with the competition. This research is designed to answer questions like:

- What attitudes, preferences, criticisms do potential customers have about the property and its various products?
- How well are the service systems working?
- How good are the staff at implementing the service strategies?
- Why do some groups choose the property and others do not?
- Which promotions and advertising appeal and which do not?

Corporate reasons for research

Marketing research is not only necessary to guide the marketing mix decisions and the day-to-day operations of a property. The owners and investors also have good reason for discovering information about attitudes towards the property. Apart from it being sound marketing sense to update research information regularly, events can occur in the market which need to be researched to find out the reasons for them.

The six stages of a research study

1   Define the problem or opportunity and decide what information is needed. Some research is ill-directed and lacking in purpose. It can ask the wrong questions or miss out on vital ones, and this only becomes apparent after the study is completed and the money spent.
2   Establish the research objectives. Who should be asked the questions? What questions should be asked? What will be the size and nature of the sample? How should the questionnaire be constructed?
3   Develop the research plan which will obtain the information. That means decide the sample, its size and location, the survey method that will best gather the required information and prepare the questionnaire.
4   Implement the research. Activate the research by sending the operatives into the field, mail the questionnaires or make the phone calls.
5   Collect and analyse the data. Once all the questionnaires have been completed, the next stage is to put the data into a computer and sort them into measurable quotas for cross-referencing and analysis.
6   Interpret the information and recommend a course of action. What does the information mean? Information for its own sake has no purpose. It can be misleading too, and be used to draw wrong conclusions, or ones which suit the 'tunnel vision' of some operators. The critical phase of research is the final one, the field survey.

Field surveys

The field survey – interviewing and asking questions of a number of people who are representative of the market – is one of the most common means of marketing research. Others are observation, experimentation and group discussion. Each has a reason for its use. The main use for a field survey is to interview a broad sample of the whole market. It seeks information from potential customers, customers of other establishments and the general public, not just guests of the establishment. Field surveys using a carefully planned questionnaire can be conducted by mail, media, telephone or face-to-face.

   The mailed survey is the least effective because, even with a reply-paid envelope and a very easy questionnaire, most people do not have the time to answer or cannot be bothered. Those who do answer are usually a particular type of person, unrepresentative of the whole sample, placing a bias on the results. A survey questionnaire placed in a magazine has a similar result to the mailed questionnaire for the same reason.

A telephone survey is relatively inexpensive, and more people can be interviewed in a given period of time. It is best used when the questionnaire is short and the questions require a minimum of explanation. There is some sample bias because not everyone is home to answer the phone at the same time and some have unlisted numbers. Telephone surveys are useful for testing public perceptions of a property and its products, for following up guests and getting a reaction to their experience at an establishment in hindsight, to check on the appeals of promotions and advertising.

Best of all is the personal interview, mainly because reactions can be gauged by the interviewer, with shrugs or facial expressions being indicative of the need to probe further in some instances. Longer questionnaires are also possible with a personal interview, although much depends on where the interview is conducted, with home interviews being ideal and interviews on street corners being less than ideal.

Nearly all research begins with a research proposition, a consideration that something might be so, and then the research is conducted to prove, disprove or explore the proposition. Beware of trying to find out more than is required. Retain an open mind. Always include demographics.

The bedroom or front-desk questionnaire

This is the most common means used by establishments to test the attitudes and satisfaction levels of guests. Participation is voluntary, of course, and this leads to many of the answers not being representative of all guests. Most people who respond are either very happy with their experience or very displeased. So such surveys can be inaccurate and provide a misleading appreciation of overall levels of satisfaction. However, serious problems can be revealed and provide an opportunity for a disgruntled guest to obtain a satisfying response.

A phone call to guests a few days after their stay by an independent researcher can be more revealing because the people are then away from the property and they feel they can be more honest with someone who is not a hotel employee.

Focus groups

The focus group research method, or pilot study, is an economical method of uncovering information, especially where attitudes need to be qualified rather than quantified in numbers or percentages. It involves gathering together groups of people, usually eight to twelve in number, with demographic or psychographic characteristics in common, to discuss a topic which is of interest to the researchers.

It is essentially exploratory in nature, as focus group participants give their comments, researchers observe and listen to the discussion and note their interactions. With four or five group discussions, an understanding of certain emotions, opinions and attitudes can be ascertained and this helps in the formulation of products, positioning strategies, advertising and promotion themes. Focus groups are also very useful in giving direction to field surveys by sometimes revealing surprising attitudes which need to be quantified to establish their extent.

Observation research

The simplest form of market research is to watch and record what people do, either in one's own establishment or in the competition's. A traffic count, staff attitudes and customer reactions can be gauged by observation, especially if the observer is not biased and is watching what is happening and not seeing what he or she wants to see.

For example, a coffee shop which had been doing good business for nearly two years slowly lost its business without any apparent reason until an independent observer sat in the place on and off for several days. The observer soon discovered the reasons for customer dissatisfaction: the front door screeched every time it was opened and the server doors, which were in continual use, squeaked back and forth and put everyone's teeth on edge. If that was not enough, the staff had got into the habit of shouting their orders into the kitchen to save time.

When questioned about this by the observer, the operators said that the screeching front door alerted them to the fact that a customer was either entering or leaving, which was a good system, in their opinion. If the waiters were out at the back they could rush back to the room and greet the new customer, or chase one who had not paid! As for the squeaking server doors, that was a good idea too because it signalled to the kitchen to put up the completed orders for an incoming waiter.

The independent observer carefully pointed out that, whereas the screeches and the squeaks were fine for the operators, they were terrible for the customers. The problem was, the observer said, that the screeches and the squeaks alerted the customers too. All eyes went to the screeching door every time someone came in, much to the embarrassment of the newcomer, and all eyes went to the squeaking server doors, mostly in anticipation of their order arriving. Added to the bedlam created by the waiters' shouts to the kitchen, the whole experience for the customers had become disconcerting and unnerving. A few drops of oil and a new way of getting the orders to the kitchen rescued a failing business.

Experimental research

The consequences of change can be measured by creating a temporary situation and then measuring the customers' reactions. This works, for instance, when an operation is contemplating a change to the levels of service, adding services or eliminating others, such as when making a change to a menu. Perhaps when considering redecorating, a few rooms can be done before the rest of the hotel and guests' opinions invited.

Sampling

Research draws conclusions about large groups by questioning or observing small groups. For the results to have meaning, the research sample must be representative of the whole. The underlying principles of sampling and research for marketing are the same as any scientific discipline, and are based on the laws of probability: if the sample is true of the whole, then the results will apply to the whole with an error factor which increases or decreases proportionate to the size of the sample.

The 'whole' or total market population must be defined before sampling begins. Users, purchasers or influencers? Male, female, old, young, married, left-handed, what are they? To select a probability frame, each population element must have an equal chance of selection. Accurate sampling is crucial for obtaining accurate answers to research questions. Some of the main sampling techniques used by marketing research agencies are as follows.

Probability sampling

*   *A simple random sample*, whereby every member of the population has a known and equal chance of selection. An example of a simple random sample is to choose, say, the tenth name of the second column of every page of the telephone directory and repeat the process of selection until the required sample number is achieved. This technique will yield a representative sample of the population without undue bias. There is an in-built bias if the majority of the population do not have telephones. However, in the UK around 95 per cent of homes have telephones, which makes the bias tolerable.
*   *A stratified random sample*, whereby people representing the population are divided into mutually exclusive groups (age, sex, income, etc.) from which random samples are drawn.
*   *A cluster (area) sample*, whereby people representing the population are divided into mutually exclusive groups by area from which samples are drawn.

Non-probability sampling

*   *A convenient sample*, meaning that the easiest-to-access population members are selected.
*   *A judgement sample*, meaning that people are selected who represent good prospects for information.
*   *A quota sample*, whereby researchers find and interview a prescribed number of people in each of several categories.

This latter form of sampling is one that would suit an amateur researcher best, until he or she builds up confidence and skill. Whereas the information may have a bias, it could be reliable enough for broad decision-making. Most decisions in business do not hinge on minute percentage differences, but on majority indicators of attitudes and behaviour.

If management wants real information upon which to make decisions, research must be done in a planned way with clear-cut objectives, as outlined earlier in the six stages of research, and this is best done by a competent market research firm. However, conducting a survey is not a great mystery, and an operator can gather useful information on his or her own.

Questionnaire design

Basically, a questionnaire is a series of questions designed to get answers revealing people's opinions, preferences or thoughts. To be effective, every question in a survey must be relevant, concise and easy for the respondent to understand. In addition, a questionnaire should not be put into the field that does not have the means of identifying the respondents by some form of demographic reference – in other words, what types of people are making these statements (old, young, wealthy, poor, office workers, professionals, etc.).

There are many traps in the construction of a questionnaire. Two common ones are asking an ambiguous question and asking a loaded question that leads the respondent into an obvious answer. A silly question, for example, would be: 'Do you dine out regularly?' How often is regular and what is meant by dining out? Dining out could mean having tea with the in-laws.

The purpose of the question could be achieved by a dichotomous or multi-dichotomous question (dichotomous – a question offering two alternate answers; multi-dichotomous or multiple choice – three or more answer choices). For example, the question could be asked this way:

'In a year, how often would you choose to eat in a restaurant, fast food outlet or hotel?'

- Never?
- Once or twice?
- About once a month?
- Once a week on average?
- More than once a week?

Most questions are classified as being closed, meaning that the respondent is forced into a committed response. An open-ended question means that respondents can answer in an unlimited number of ways. Simply adding 'Other' to a list of closed questions creates an open-ended question. There is also the 'unstructured question' which invites comment, such as:

'What is your opinion of the food at this restaurant?'

Closed questions are useful because the answers can be easily entered into a computer. They also define the choices that are available, prompting definite and comparable responses. Open-ended or unstructured questions are best used when the question is exploratory, when there is some uncertainty about the extent and nature of the responses.

If it is necessary to find out the strength of people's thoughts, opinions or beliefs, the Likert scale or graduated response technique is helpful. With graduated response questions you give the respondent a scale of choices to measure the extent of their answer. A common example is 0 1 2 3 4 5, ranging from never to always, when 0 is never and 5 is always. An alternative way to use the graduated response technique is to use words like never, seldom, sometimes, often, very often, always.

Some people have problems with finding the right words to describe their feelings or define their attitudes. The technique which is handy to use is called the semantic differential question, which measures the intensity of feelings towards a word or phrase. For example:

'How did you feel about dining at that particular restaurant?'

Comfortable? | | | | | | | Uncomfortable?

The respondent indicates the degree of comfort or otherwise with a tick placed between the two words.

Another open-ended type of question is word association. This involves asking the respondent for a phrase or word to gauge their reaction, such as: 'What is the word or phrase which comes to mind when I mention the following holiday destination?'

A few additional tips

- Developing a questionnaire is a bit like being a detective. It certainly requires the gift of understanding people. A good test of how a question is likely to be received is to ask oneself, 'If I was that person how would I respond to that question?' Which is why it is vital to pre-test a questionnaire with a pilot study before asking the entire sample you have chosen. Some questions can evoke a response which is quite different from the one intended.
- Do not stretch people's memories. It is unlikely that anyone will remember what they did last year.
- Lead from easy questions to more difficult ones.
- Do not ask very personal questions. For instance, people do not like being asked their income. That has to be guessed in most cases from their occupation and place of abode.
- People will try to give you an answer that makes them look honourable, wealthier than they are, younger, better educated and well-connected. In the main, they will also avoid appearing to be bigoted, silly, insular, racist or sexist. Therefore avoid questions that give them scope for too much exaggeration.

Researchers have to use a lot of charm and care to get people to relax and feel confident about answering the questions. For this reason, it is important to establish the credentials of the interviewer at the beginning to allay any fears of confidentiality, of being 'sold' or of being asked for information that can be used for other purposes.

Analysing the data

When the survey is completed, the answers can be added together and the results expressed in raw figures or percentages, and perhaps put into bar or pie-chart graphs for comparing. For an extensive survey, the figures should be entered into a computer, using a programme which is designed to cross-analyse the results.

In analysis, the demographics of the people answering have to be cross-referenced in relation to the results to determine significances. For example, let us say that a survey of a restaurant's customers to determine their levels of satisfaction with service reveals that 30 per cent of the people volunteered that they thought the service was 'too quick'. Such a result could lead the management to slow down the service, but the demographics of the people who said that might reveal that they are mainly retired people. The working customer wanted the service to remain fast and, if anything, faster than it was.

Survey results are always interesting. Sometimes they are predictable, but there are often enough surprises to make marketing research not only one of the most profitable marketing tools but also one of the most fascinating.

Trans Australia Airlines (now Quantas) commissioned a survey of air travellers in the mid-1960s, and at the time believed that most of their customers were business people. Like many operators in the hospitality industry, their close contact with their customers led them to think that they knew and understood them. The surprise was that, whereas 75 per cent of flights were for business reasons, only 25 per cent of their customers were business people. Seventy-five of their customers were flying for non-business reasons. This resulted in the airline focusing its attention on non-business customers and the promotion of reasons for flying, such as holiday travel.

Model banks

Marketing research firms utilize some sophisticated methodologies for analysis, such as regression analysis, correlation analysis, factor analysis and cluster analysis. These are used to determine significant differences between groups in terms of their attitudes, beliefs and behaviour patterns. There are also model banks available for comparative analysis, each one having a 'control' or 'norm' which are the result of long-term experience with the industry to form the basis of models, such as:

- the hotel services model
- the pricing model
- the site selection model
- the management model
- the budgeting model.

Beware of presumptions or predictions based on trends. Research does not replace common sense and sound judgement; it is a tool for providing information upon which decisions can be based.

The example of the guided missile

Marketing can be likened to the modern guided missile. This is how it works. Today's guided missile is aimed in the general direction of the target. The missile's radar searches for the target and locates it and this information is fed to the missile's computer which then adjusts the course of the missile. Every two seconds, the radar sends out a pulse to check the target's location – because most targets move – so that the computer can continue to make adjustments to the missile's speed and course until it strikes the target.

In marketing, each new strategy is like a course correction, and market research is the equivalent of the radar, feeding back information to the system telling the decision-makers of marketing not so much where the marketing effort *is* heading but where it *should* be heading.

The previous rocketry systems had gyroscopic guidance systems. They were fired at the target and could be relied upon to strike the target provided that the target didn't move. These older missiles were cheaper than today's sophisticated, computer-guided affairs but military analysts soon came to the conclusion that the expense of having cheap missiles which miss the target more often than not – because most targets move – far outweighed the cost of the more expensive but accurate missile system that always struck its target.

Marketing, which uses much of the same terminology as warfare, abounds with examples of companies that contrive to use the equivalent of old fashioned rocketry tactics. They spend huge amounts of money on implementing new marketing initiatives, and trying to hit the extremely mobile targets called customers without the feedback of marketing research. Customers, very similar to the moving targets of warfare, are surprisingly uncooperative when it comes to the approach: 'Just stay there while we take a few shots at you!'

Questions for discussion or revision

1   Why is it so important when preparing a survey to have research objectives and a research proposition?
2   What is the underlying principle of all forms of sampling which makes it possible to conduct field surveys with a reasonable degree of certainty that the results will be usable?
3   What are the most frequently used methodologies applied in marketing research?

Further reading

Hague, P. and Jackson, P. (1990). *Do Your Own Market Research*. London: Kogan Page.

16 *Achieving a sustainable competitive advantage*

Aim of this chapter

To explain that instead of competing against rivals an establishment should make comparisons almost impossible by having a value monopoly, and that the best way of achieving a sustainable competitive advantage (SCA) is by going above and beyond what others in the same line of business are doing.

The theory

The process of marketing is obsessed with competition. The terminology of the subject and the statements by grim-faced, determined people in business abound with examples of a preoccupation with beating the opposition. And yet, as de Bono (1993) contends, the notion of competition is a dangerous and seductive trap which limits and restricts business thinking.

Competition is about getting sales ahead of rival organizations. It reaches its heights in the concepts of warfare extolled by Ries and Trout (1986), with terms such as 'defence', 'attack', 'flank' and 'guerrilla', which they use to explain their considerations of marketing. They contend that marketing is a battle waged in the consumers' minds. Consequently, the 'kill or die' philosophy of modern marketing results in the desperate struggles for sales ascendancy, as exemplified by Coke and Pepsi's fight for the cola market.

If you cannot compete you cannot survive, state the leading marketing academics such as Kotler and Porter, and there is undoubted truth in their contentions. However, as de Bono points out, 'You cannot truly be competitive if you seek to be competitive. The serious mistake,' he says, 'is that many executives believe that competition is the key to success. Competition is merely part of the baseline of survival.'

The word 'competition' comes from Latin, 'seeking together'. It implies that all competitors are in the same race and that the conditions for everyone are the same. Winning is the goal and to the winner go the spoils of success for competing best.

In business, even the losers get some of the spoils. The winners only get more. However, what is the cost of winning in the death or glory battles of the beverage, food and car industries? Inevitably, the wages of war are costs which can cripple some corporations. It is more logical to avoid direct competition and, instead of running in the same race, run your own race. If you want the prizes of success do not play the same game as the competition.

De Bono's concept of 'surpetition' means surpassing the competition by being obviously different, to have a sustainable competitive advantage which does not draw an equal comparison. 'Living Benefits Assurance' is an example of what de Bono calls 'integrated values', providing something which is above competition and offers a value monopoly. With traditional life assurance, the benefits are paid out after death to the beneficiaries. Living Benefits Assurance, developed by Ron Barboro of Prudential, pays out 75 per cent of the benefits to the policy holder immediately if the policy holder is diagnosed as having a potentially fatal disease. This means that the benefits of the policy are available when they are most needed – during life. It has been copied since by rival companies, but for a while Prudential held a clear market lead.

When Nestlé's Nescafé instant coffee was introduced, it competed directly with the then accepted ways of making coffee from ground coffee beans. Today, Nescafé and its many copycats are regarded by the consumer as being in a class of their own. Nestlé has around 75 per cent of the instant coffee market and does not compete any more with coffee bean or ground coffee markets.

The story of the My Kinda Town restaurant chain, created by the highly respected entrepreneur Bob Payton, dates from Thanksgiving Day 1977. That was when the late entrepreneur opened the Chicago Pizza Pie Factory and brought American deep pan pizza to the heart of London. Over the next seventeen years, Payton developed his Pizza Pie interests and introduced a succession of sister restaurants, ranging from Rib Shack to Meatpackers to Henry J. Bean's. My Kinda Town has followed a successful international route from Argentina to Israel via such unlikely destinations as Beirut, and its ethic is to be the best restaurant in town – any town!

The key to success is not technology so much as concepts which appeal to a specific group of customers. Concepts create the added value which provides a valid SCA for the customer to consider. Cost-cutting, quality control, service, competence and efficiency by themselves will not create business. A cheap, well made and highly efficient nothing will not sell to anyone. Competitive strategies only work when there is a high demand for a product and when most competing offerings are substantially similar.

Being competitive should not mean being-the-same-and-better, but being recognizably-different-and-better. My Kinda Town introduced different, exciting new concepts clearly targeted at the 18–25 age groups and families market segment. Moreover, they were the best in town.

So many businesses, especially in the hospitality industry, are identical in most respects. The propositions of the contenders for the customers' money are really 'me too' types of strategies. To offer a difference, a comparative advantage, is an 'only me' proposition, with more appeal for the customer being targeted.

The term 'niche strategy' can be loosely applied to the concept of finding a specialized market, concentrating on it and being able to dominate it. In the case of My Kinda Town, it worked on the strategy of 'being first in, with the mostest'.

The phantom opponents

Who is the real competition? In many instances, owners of hospitality establishments are fighting phantom opponents. They think that just because other operators are doing a similar thing to themselves they must be the enemy. This is not always true. A five-star hotel fine dining restaurant may believe that it is competing with other five-star fine dining restaurants. However, how many people say to their partners, 'Which five-star, fine dining hotel restaurant shall we go to tonight?' Probably none. The selection of a place to eat does not work that way in the real world of customers.

In deciding who or what comprises the competition requires careful thought about the market being aimed at. It is not always other establishments. Most owners have an unpleasant surprise when surveys reveal that many people never think of their place when asked to list the names of places in their category. How come they were missed out? 'Surely everyone knows', they wail, 'that we are one of the best fine dining restaurants in town?'

The reason is fairly simple: customers have their own methods of labelling, cataloguing and filing places and products. Their minds do not group eateries, or anything else for that matter, into convenient business directory lists. When there is no direct conflict in the customers' minds there is no competition. Thus, by avoiding conflict or confusion with another product or place, you are creating a separate and unique category for the customer. You are achieving an identifiable difference. Ideally, this identifiable difference should equate to a recognizable advantage for the customer. This provides the customer with a reason for labelling it, categorizing it and filing it for future reference in his or her mind.

For example, a restaurant called 'Tops', which sits on a hill-top with the stars above and overlooking the brilliant lights of a city, will not be confused with any restaurant in the city. Neither is it competing with other restaurants with views (unless it is right next door) because the views are never the same. In addition, if 'Tops' has a dreamy, romantic cocktail bar with an attractive and cheerful bar person, there is an added reason for the place occupying a special place in many people's minds. That is a value monopoly.

In times of recession, the real competition for many places will be a shortage of discretionary spending power by most customers. Michael Hurst of the 15th Street Fisheries reports that when the recession bit during the early 1990s his regular customers were not as regular as before. That meant going out to find more customers to maintain the same growth pattern that the place has enjoyed. He was not losing customers to the competition of other restaurants, but to the common enemy of budget restraint.

The cure for boredom and apathy

If a hotel is not doing anything exciting it will be losing business to apathy. This is the case with some hotels in country towns or villages where there is a virtual monopoly by location. The owners stop trying because they figure they have it made. When that happens, the people do not go elsewhere; they just do not come any more or not as often.

Something new, as opposed to being drastically different, is the cure for a tired routine. For example, there was a highly successful restaurant which gained a large following by serving a free starter the moment the customer sat down and a free salad while waiting for a luscious main course. Ten years later the routine was the same and even the waiting staff had the expression on their faces of 'here we go again'. There was still a sturdy band of loyal clients attending, but the majority had moved on to new experiences. The restaurant was not defeated by any competitor; it had defeated itself by being lazy.

A small change or improvement, an exciting new way of providing a service, innovation, in other words, stimulates the management, the staff and, most importantly, the customers. However, innovation should not be confused with wholesale change. It is a matter of maintaining standards while trying a new way of doing something. Drastic change is like starting again.

A new restaurant which features dishes from another country that few people have tried may be competing with the natural reluctance of a lot of people to try something they do not understand because it is alien. During the 1980s in the UK this was the case with entrepreneurs who opened Japanese-themed restaurants. Unable to encourage people through the door, many had to shut their doors after only a short time in business. In the 1990s we are seeing a gradual growth of this style of restaurant as the market is now more willing to 'try them out'.

It was the Chinese restaurants which were the first substantial evidence of ethnic products in the UK. Twenty years ago they held a dominant position in the ethnic eating-out market. However, they are not as popular as they were, because they have been joined in the marketplace by numerous alternatives such as Indian, Vietnamese, Japanese and Thai venues in recent years. You could say that the newcomers are providing spirited competition, but the real enemy for a large number of Chinese restaurants has been customer boredom with the Chinese cuisine. It was not good enough to offer the same 'Europeanized' Chinese dishes served in the same way in the same pseudo Chinese decor that has persisted for twenty-odd years.

Michael Hurst claims that he regards every day as being like the first day of the business. Every day he wants to do something a little better or a whole lot better if he can. To maintain the customers' excitement, the thrill of dining at his place is his daily goal. You keep doing the good things, but do them better. Meanwhile, you think of new ways of doing old things or things that have never been done before but which the customer may like.

For example, Hurst has a dish called 'The Flying Fish'. Yes, it is a flying fish caught commonly in the ocean, but to make it really special for the customer the waiters bring it to the table suspended from a helium balloon. It is innovations like that which have made dining an event for the customers and given the 15th Street Fisheries restaurant a value monopoly.

The key to profitability

A lot of places strive to provide whatever the customers want, but the ones with the competitive edge do what the customers do not always expect. They go the extra bit, provide the added value and the special, memorable service to win a special reason for the customers to come back. For example, the giant Disney corporate states that at its theme parks it does not want merely to satisfy the customers, it wants them to go away 'delighted'.

An SCA must, of course, be sustained. Once others do the same it is no longer a competitive advantage and it is not special. Similarly, once it becomes a mundane event it runs the risk of becoming boring.

Competition has become a misleading aspect of marketing. In most cases, a property is not competing so much against similar establishments as competing for a piece of the customer's mind. If customers have nothing else to choose from other than a cluster of similar types and styles of hotels, then the only comparative advantage for the customer is price. Thus lowest price becomes the selection criterion and discounting or add-on values are all that matters. With this scenario, hotels start losing their profits, and before long the enemy becomes survival, as was seen during the recession of the early 1990s.

Another very real enemy for hospitality establishments is their attitude of sales-mindedness instead of customer-mindedness. It is not what you do but the way that you do it which counts with customers. An additional service becomes a 'gimmick' unless it is delivered with enthusiasm and genuine interest. A value monopoly will always be the personalized service you offer. It means special things that make customers feel special. It is customer-oriented marketing – doing something that no-one else does.

Michael Hurst says that he thinks of every customer as being worth a thousand or even a million dollars because the pass-on value of one really happy customer multiplies out until the permutations are enormous. 'Special things for special people,' he recommends. He goes to the extent of having special crockery for some customers. The cost does not warrant a gesture like that, but that is not the point. The customers with their special crockery bring in a steady stream of new customers that Hurst could not buy with advertising.

Some pubs have special beer glasses for customers with their names on them. No-one else can use that glass. Another hotel sends birthday wishes to its customers every year. The Isle of Eriskay Hotel on the west coast of Scotland sends a newsletter to all former guests. This tells them of developments at the hotel and how the family dog is doing. It also informs them of coming events in which they might be interested and gives them a reason to return. That is customizing – providing a value monopoly through personalizing the service.

At some large hotels, the manager invites new guests to a private reception to meet other guests and mingle with the staff. There are many variants of this approach, such as the Captain's table for single guests so that they will not feel alone and be more comfortable in their surroundings.

The imperative of concepts like these, however, is to make sure that the reception or the table is hosted by someone with personality who is a natural catalyst and who can bring people together and make them feel relaxed and convivial. It will not work as well if the customers believe that the management and staff are just going through the motions.

For any establishment which wants to introduce ideas like these, it must be remembered that it is not only that the hotel is prepared to do it which will impress and attract the customers. Usually it is the person who does it and the way that it is done that will mostly be remembered. A rival hotel may copy the idea, but if the personality of your catalyst is unique it is unlikely that the rival will attract any of your customers away.

Run your own race

A guest history system assists the customizing of guest services. It requires maintaining a database on the computer and it takes substantial work. But the results for the customers can be quite startling. Everyone likes to feel special. Guest histories make it possible for front desk staff, for instance, to greet people personally and provide services with the knowledge of the guest's preferences. It also makes it easier for the hotel to solicit repeat business.

An added benefit of guest histories is that over time the stored data can be cross-referenced to get profiles of customer clusters – groups of people who have things in common. Often these clusters reveal group preferences, enabling the property to amend its products and facilities so that the customers can feel more comfortable there. Some places form clubs with special privileges for members. Usually these clubs are for corporate and regular business travellers, but clubs can also be formed for sporting people and fitness enthusiasts.

Recognition of the customer as an individual and not a 'sale' which has to be processed is the simple secret of a successful establishment. When a place thinks of its guests as a number of individuals and treats them individually by name, it has a personalized monopoly of their minds as being the only place to consider. As Hurst says, 'Give them a personal experience. Customize their experience.' Instead of running in the same race as everyone else, run your own.

A lot of hospitality establishment owners are merely caretakers of their business. Everything stays the same. There is no interest, no excitement. How can you be enthusiastic if you are not building the business all the time? McDonalds is not the same as it was twenty years ago. It is not the same as it was last year. Each year it does something a little different and a little better and that is what keeps it alive, growing and competitive.

A business in the doldrums is a business which is run by management that has lost the plot because the business has become boring for them and the customers. It does not require a great deal of imagination to make improvements to a place. More than anything else it may just mean thinking for and on behalf of the customer. A value monopoly can be created overnight by customizing the service. The difference is as simple as a change of attitude. Instead of thinking, 'I am doing this because it is my job', change to 'I am doing this because I am thinking of you, the customer, and what you would like.'

When everyone in an establishment is thinking like that, from the management across the whole employee spectrum, and when everyone has the freedom to make individual gestures instead of sticking to a rigid system, there is a dramatic improvement to the business.

A gesture can be as small as this example. A guest at a hotel in Chicago left his shoes out to be cleaned. The shoes were returned, cleaned, with a new pair of laces and a note. 'One of the laces was fraying so we replaced them. Hope you don't mind. No charge.' It was not a one-off incident. The guest noticed a series of little gestures like that during his stay. He still talks about it, and guess where he stays every time he goes to Chicago?

Questions for discussion or revision

1   Explain what is meant by the term 'value monopoly'.
2   What is meant by Edward de Bono's concept of 'surpetition'? Does this concept fit into today's competitive business environment?
3   How does the concept of 'surpetition' relate to 'positioning'?
4   What are the key strategies for achieving a sustainable competitive advantage?
5   Name three situations where customers make a choice between various competitive offerings on the basis of price only. What kind of offers will feature most prominently in the advertising of companies under these circumstances? What is the long-term outlook for the profitability of these companies if they continue with this marketing approach?
6   What is a niche strategy?

Further reading

De Bono, E. (1993). *Surpetition*. London: HarperCollins.
Ries, A. and Trout, J. (1986). *Marketing Warfare*. New York: McGraw-Hill.

17 *Positioning*

Aim of this chapter

To explain how to develop a competitive position for an establishment by using information feeds to create an SCA.

The theory

Hospitality is about providing people with a place to sleep, eat and drink. The customers can do any combination of those three things, depending on what individual hospitality properties are prepared to offer. Some places offer an extensive range of additional facilities. The style of place can range from a hostel to a five-star hotel, from a little corner coffee shop to a fine dining restaurant, a country pub to a glamorous tourist resort, or a simple bed and breakfast to budget-style accommodation.

In most areas around the world customers have a wide choice of hospitality establishments. Their selection of a hospitality establishment will be based on how they feel about a particular place. Their feeling will be based on logic and knowledge, an assessment of several attributes that the place has (including price), weighted by the decision maker's perceptions of value. Perceptions are usually a stronger motivation for purchase than reality. When a significant number of people hold similar perceptions about a property, that property has what is called a market position.

Positioning takes place in people's minds. Two places can look the same and offer the same facilities, but occupy totally different positions in the market. Positioning is what people think, know, feel or believe about a place. Hence the difference between a four- and five-star hotel can often be no more than a public perception, usually a strategic position decided by the management.

In the case of many types of products, e.g. beverages and food, positioning is often the only difference between competing products. Taste tests with beers, wines, spirits and soft drinks suggest that the majority cannot discern any real differences in taste between brands. Some will stoutly defend that they can tell their favourite brand anywhere, only to be embarrassingly fooled by a blind tasting. Marketers who spend millions on brand promotion know exactly what they are doing: building a brand image which exists solely in people's minds.

Positioning is a marketing strategy. Its purpose is to provide an organization with an SCA by creating differences, advantages and benefits (DAB) which make people think about a place or a product in a certain way. Some people describe a place or property by saying it has 'a good reputation', which means in effect that it has earned a place in people's minds as a result of sound positioning. It also means that many recommend the place. Why the property has earned a good reputation is important. It may have a reputation for one or two aspects of hospitality, but may be surpassed by a place with a reputation for another aspect of hospitality. Thus, in Glasgow for example, in the early days of opening, the Hilton International Hotel had the reputation for being the only five-star hotel in the city, while the Moat House Hotel had the established reputation for offering consistently high-quality products and service.

It is one thing for a property to claim, '*We* are the best place in town', but positioning is only achieved when customers say, '*You* are the best place in town'! The name and reputation of an establishment is a business's only real asset. Upon this rock a customer base is built which represents the worth of a business. Its building, fixtures, fittings and furnishings by themselves do not create a business. Positioning does.

We all make judgements about things, unconsciously or consciously, and our judgement process is based on many factors: our social class distinctions, our needs, the benefits we want and our ability to pay. Because of these essential differences, not every place appeals to everyone, and the wide range of people's preferences and needs is the reason for the diversity of sleeping, eating and drinking options in the hospitality industry.

Furthermore, a customer's choice of place to stay may be influenced by his or her own positioning needs. A high-profile corporate executive could want to impress clients and business associates by staying at the most expensive, high-profile place available. Another executive may want to indicate cost-consciousness and choose a less flamboyant property.

To gain a position in people's minds means being known first of all and secondly, and essentially, being known for something which separates a place from the competition and provides customers with a reason for purchase. To be unknown is to be unloved.

Information feeds

Positioning is achieved by what are called 'information feeds'. These are communications which demonstrate what an organization is, says or does which leave an impression in people's minds and so create an SCA. Information feeds are statements which help to position an establishment. The main forms are:

- *The physical presence of the place*, where it is and how it looks from the outside. How it is signed, painted, decorated, where it sits in the street, the buildings or businesses which surround it, the image of the street, the town and the people who live or work in the vicinity. These are all tangible factors that contribute to the imagery which helps create a position.

First impressions are said to be lasting. Many award-winning restaurants are located in the most unassuming of buildings. On the other hand, the grandeur of some striking and highly publicized hotels masks the disappointing and sometimes over-rated service within. Nevertheless, it is easier to achieve the desired market position by looking the part.

- *The interior design layout*, fittings and decor generally are a natural follow-through of the first impressions created by the building exterior. Ideally, one should complement the other.

- *The recommendations* – the pass-on value of word-of-mouth advertising – are possibly the strongest means of gaining a hold in customers' minds. Most people listen to opinions and are considerably swayed by what they hear, generally believing the worst aspects but being heartened when they hear something good being said about a place.

  Most businesses are built on reputations. About 85 per cent of customers come from pass-on recommendations, with the remaining 15 per cent coming from other sources, including advertising. This indicates the huge reliance that must be placed on providing customers with a great experience so that they will go away with a memory of a good occasion and recommend the place to friends and acquaintances. When several people confirm that they enjoyed the experience of a place and recommend it, it has achieved a solid position in people's minds.

- *Publicity* and the public opinions generated by the publicity are another powerful means of creating a position for a property. A good review by a critic is one way, but publicity can also be generated by media reporting of events and people staying or going to a place. This is why many large properties like to have visiting celebrities stay, even offering ridiculously cheap rates for the privilege.

- *Advertising* presents the best opportunity for a property to directly convey the position it wants to occupy in people's minds. What is said can be controlled and presented in the best possible way and beamed at the target market which suits the property best. In this case, positioning can be achieved by a phrase, a pictorial image, brilliant copy and memorable music in the case of electronic media.

  But deeds are not achieved by words alone, and the property must always deliver what it has promised, otherwise the advertising is nothing more than a very expensive and useless gesture which ultimately will fool no-one. Advertising people use the term 'positioning strategy' to state that they intend to achieve their position objectives.

- *Brochures* and all the collateral material used by a property to promote its facilities are excellent means of conveying a property's position to would-be customers. The products and facilities they describe raise the hopes and anticipation of customers. They are indicators for guests and travel agents alike that comfort and service will be provided.

- *The attitudes and appearance of the staff*, the service performances and attention to detail are always the lasting means of creating an impression of a property. If nothing else, these matters are vital for achieving a position in people's minds. The edifice may be crumbling and the interior decor can be bad, but once inside and treated to an outstanding service performance the rest will be forgiven by the customers.

- *The prices and value offered* are some of the simplest ways of positioning an establishment. Both management and customers use them to position a place as being either expensive, moderate or inexpensive. Whatever the price positioning, the place must represent value for money.
- *The ambience* – music, noise, smell and generally activity of an establishment – positions it as being comfortable, popular, busy, noisy, elitist, or whatever. Care is necessary with ambience to make sure that it conveys a perception which fits with the desired positioning.
- *The people who appear to patronize the place* will contribute to its positioning. A place will invariably attract customer groups which fit with the strategic positioning provided by other information feeds. Most people like to be with, and associated with, others who are like themselves and belong to the same socio-economic class.
- *The name, slogan, symbol or logo* which represents it should be a means of summing up the desired position for a property. Designers frequently get carried away when designing a corporate logo or a symbol, depicting God-knows-what at times. If a symbol or slogan is to work for the property, it must create an image which fits with what the place actually is and does.

Take care with positioning messages

The basics of the hospitality industry are the ways in which members of the industry transform the mundane needs of eating and sleeping into pleasurably heightened experiences. The images of escape, excitement, glamour, romance, conviviality and sometimes glitz are all part of the positioning process. Information feeds position a property and indicate to prospective clients what type of place it is and what they can expect when they patronize it.

Positioning attracts and also repels certain groups of customers. An expensive property, for example, dissuades a large percentage of would-be patrons who simply cannot afford to stay there. A family-style restaurant will not appeal to a business luncheon group. An establishment cannot be all things to all people, which is why you must target the markets that have a natural affinity with each other.

Positioning is such a powerful strategy when deployed properly that care must be taken with information feeds to ensure that the right message is being communicated. It is the sum total of the information feeds which establishes a position for an establishment. One information feed will not be sufficient to establish a marketable position. Support is required by other information feeds. For instance, advertising and an impressive façade alone will not create a position that will attract customers for long. Ultimately, it is what happens to and for the customers which will achieve the strongest position.

Enhance the customer's expectations

The key to successful positioning is to provide a recognizable, measurable difference or advantage which enables customers to make a choice in favour of one property. With leading hotels, for example, it is evident from every information feed they use that the place will be impressive and expensive, that every creature comfort will be catered for and every service requirement pandered to. Customers buy the proposition in expectation of a good experience. However, in some markets there are many properties offering identical products; therefore it is one salient feature which will provide the main appeal.

For each target market in the customer mix, the position adopted by the property must elicit a predetermined desired consumer response, for example:

'The place which has bedrooms with the best views of the lake.'
'The place which appeals to the top echelon of executives and professional people because it has a fax machine in every room.'
'The place that has nannies to look after children.'
'The people who make you feel really welcome!', etc.

Do not over-sell or mislead

Good marketers build images and they use facts to support the image. Therefore do not ever try to develop an image which cannot be sustained by facts. Benefits arise from facts and support the façade of imagery.

It is a fact, for instance, that Raffles Hotel in Singapore is one of the world's most famous establishments, and that it has a long history, mostly associated with the many famous people who have stayed there over the years. The benefit for the customer of this fact is the sense of romance and being part of a bygone era while enjoying the pleasures of its modernized facilities. Raffles retains much of the memorabilia of its colourful past to sustain the imagery which strongly positions the property in people's minds.

Persistent, unilateral communications are essential to convey the image. A fudged image is a non-image. A place cannot be all things to all people and cannot have contradictory appeals.

When a customer is seeking a specific attribute, he or she will want to believe that you have what he or she wants. So do not over-sell or mislead. A property which promotes its facilities as being of 'world class standard' in so many words has to deliver a comparative level of excellence with the best in the world or else it will suffer rejection by its customers and a well-deserved reputation for being below standard. Few people believe advertising completely, but they all believe the bad word-of-mouth news about a property.

Questions for discussion or revision

1   List the main information feeds which achieve a position for an organization.
2   Explain the DAB formula and its relevance to positioning.
3   Which tangible and intangible factors would you consider in the positioning of a restaurant?

Further reading

Middleton, V. (1994). *Marketing in Travel and Tourism*. London: Butterworth-Heinemann.

18 *Local hotel strategies*

Aims of this chapter

1 To describe a range of strategies for increasing the customer base of a local hotel.
2 To explain that the foremost consideration when selecting appropriate strategies is choosing the best possible outcome for the customers.

Some background

> There is nothing yet contrived by man by which so much happiness is produced as by a good tavern or inn (Samuel Johnson).

Whether it is called the local hotel, pub, inn or guest house, this type of operation is the most widespread and most used of all hospitality establishments. I consider that they present the 'human face of hospitality' as opposed to the often inanimate, standardized product provided by the corporate groups. Within the UK hospitality industry it is estimated that 36 400 properties are owner/managed, which represents 70 per cent of the total.

Thus what is being discussed in this chapter is the small, usually unpretentious, owner/managed establishment. Mostly, such establishments are for the drinking, eating, meeting and recreational needs of a majority of local residents. Typically, it is an amalgam of hotel, restaurant cum village pub – all things to all people. In concept and cultural environment, small hotels are quite different from their glamorous and larger brothers and sisters, which cater for the sophisticated and wealthy travellers of the world.

The high proportion of small, often family-run, businesses has been traditionally explained by a number of factors.

- *Relative ease of entry.* The capital investment required is lower than in many other industries, specialist knowledge and qualifications are desirable but not a prerequisite, and there is no compulsion to join trade or professional associations or similar organizations which have codes of practice such as consumer protection schemes.
- *Market demand is highly diverse.* Market demand is highly segmented, and

many of the segments do not lend themselves to satisfaction by standardized corporate properties. As a result, this diversity of demand is often best satisfied by a wide range of small establishments offering a wide variety of locations, quality ranges, physical facilities and special interests/activities to niche markets.

- *Consumer satisfaction*. The nature of hospitality provision is such that the small establishments may be better suited to respond quickly to customer needs and expectations, in a highly personalized, flexible environment. As such, they are well positioned to provide specialist services which have the potential to add quality, variety and authenticity to the products offered to the customers.
- *Economic viability*. The small, often family-run, business can be economically viable in a limited, specialized or local marketplace, where there is often not enough profit for large businesses with their high overhead costs. As such, they have been described as the equivalent of the 'corner shop'. It occupies a niche, is convenient for the local market, is usually run by local people, offering a limited product range, but nevertheless enjoys strong customer loyalty.

However, these mainly positive factors have to be located within the realities of the 1990s. Regrettably, the viability of the small hospitality business is being threatened by operating small capacities, mainly at low market levels, resulting in relatively low turnover and profit earning potential. In addition, they are continuously struggling to attract key market segments as they lose market share to the hotel groups.

This is mainly due to corporate groups having the capacity to advertise nationally. They are capable of offering overall greater quality, consistency and value for money and ease of purchase through central reservation systems. In addition, they offer a full range of locations and invariably a wider range of products than the small operators. As such, many represent high-risk businesses unless they can recognize that customer needs have changed and that there are new and different customers entering the market. Therefore for the small hospitality business it is clear that getting the marketing approach right is crucial to survival.

Outcomes for the customers

The outcome for the customers is today's critical marketing consideration. Building a business is about developing a customer base by providing a broad range of facilities and interests for the local community. Because the majority of patrons come from an area close to the hotel, it has to be regarded by them as their 'local'. Involvement is therefore a critical issue. Furthermore, unless customers feel at ease and can identify with the establishment, they will not come back.

This approach requires owners and managers to provide these outcomes for patrons:

- the feeling of being wanted and special
- good food and drink
- a sense of belonging
- something to do and see
- something to look forward to.

There is no real order of preference because each outcome varies in significance for each customer. Nevertheless, the total experience must provide a reason for staying and returning.

The objective of modern hotel marketing is to provide a refuge for the customers and a sort of headquarters for the many things they want to do away from home. There may be no surprises in the list of outcomes because they are basic to hospitality. However, it will be the way that these outcomes are provided which will give an establishment a special place in the hearts and minds of the customers.

The first strategy to consider is the matching of each of the intended outcomes with the types of people and their lifestyles that comprise the majority of localities you target.

The feeling of being wanted

Friendly attitude

In a small establishment, the attitude of the staff and the owners is rapidly conveyed to the customers, letting them know that they are wanted and that their custom is appreciated. Warmth and friendliness is the basis of hospitality, and it is one ingredient that will make the difference every time, between one place and another and whether people will return or not.

It is emphasized over and over again in this book that hiring people who can share the gift of friendship with their customers is the first priority. And if the owners and managers do not have the right personality, patience and interest in people, they should not be in the hospitality business.

Being greeted by name

In a small community or in a close-knit town, it should not take long for management and staff to learn their regular customers' names. Nothing says 'we appreciate you' better than a friendly greeting by name.

Welcome the strangers

The person who enters the establishment for the first time may only be someone passing through, but more often he or she will be a new customer who has come to look the place over. The major fault with many local hotels and pubs with regular clientele is the suspicion and reserve which is the first impression given to the stranger. Management may not be able to change the attitudes of the locals who often give the newcomer an uncertain 'once-over', but staff and management should always counter this by an effusive welcome followed by introductions to the more loquacious regulars.

Prompt attention

Feeling wanted is about getting prompt attention. If the place is busy, there is still time for a greeting and an acknowledgement that the customer will be looked after as quickly as possible. Serving the 'usual' drink without waiting for payment until later is one way to handle a difficult busy time.

Interest and care for the customer

The majority of owners are genuinely interested in their guests and pride themselves on the warmth of welcome, interest and care for the customer. Hosts are usually local people with good knowledge of the area, so they can advise on all tourist information requirements. Furthermore, the direct contact that the owner has with the guests means that he or she can rapidly respond to the individual needs and wants of each guest. Every 'transaction' with a customer should be regarded as a unique experience.

Within a lot of large establishments, management and staff appear to go through the motions of hospitality. In the smaller establishment, providing the owner has a personality suited to the hospitality industry, it should be much easier to communicate genuine interest and care for the customer.

Customized services

The showing of interest and care for customers can be extended to another dimension, when special things are done that are personalized. This is the age of customization and individuality, and here is a good example of what is meant.

At the Grape Vine Hotel one lunchtime, a group of business people had just sat down for lunch when the owner appeared beside the table. 'Do you like mussels?' he asked. 'I've just got some delivered, they were only collected this morning. Would you like chef to cook some for you?' 'Sure!' everyone replied. 'How would you like them cooked?' he asked, and wrote down their special requirements. 'No problem,' he told them. 'Just give chef about fifteen minutes and they will be on your table.' He departed to the kitchen and appeared within the stated time with the dishes of mussels prepared to the individual preferences.

Care for children, the aged and disabled

'Look after the ones I love and I'll love you back' – that is the attitude of the majority of guests. Having high chairs for young children, cushions for the aged and infirm, child play areas, baby changing facilities, special meals for kids, diabetics, vegetarians and some religious faiths, facilities for the disabled and general concern for their well-being. There are dozens of ways of telling customers that they, their friends and family members, whatever their needs, are wanted and appreciated.

Good food and drink

In the past, the food at local hotels and pubs has sometimes been criticized for its limited choice and lack of imagination. Owners often saw food as being less important than a high volume of bar sales. However, recent years have seen the decline in the volume of beer sales in particular, and owners have recognized the value of providing a well designed menu range including traditional local specialities and dishes of mixed ethnic origins.

The growth of food sales has also been assisted by changes in legislation which have extended licensing hours and allowed children into pubs. For instance, the north-east of England is enjoying something of a gastronomic revival. Country pubs in rural areas of Durham and North Yorkshire are developing restaurants that pull in diners from miles around. The attraction is food that is both affordable and exciting. The lesson here is that if the product is right – that is, the food, the feel and the price – customers will come.

So nowadays it pays to offer a range of food throughout the day. In fact, many pubs open to capture a profitable breakfast trade, even although they cannot legally open the bar. Menu ranges should reflect the needs of the customers in terms of children and granny portions, special dietary needs and a variety of the 'safe', traditional dishes and the 'adventurous', lesser known items. Daily 'chef's specials' can help to stave off menu boredom for the most regular customers.

With the growth in consumption and knowledge of wine, it is worthwhile for even the smallest of establishments to carry a selection of wines. Wine lists can be drawn up with the help and advice of a wine supplier, who is always ready to provide the service in return for orders being placed. Interest can be raised among customers by having a 'Wine of the Month'. Similarly, the range of beers can be livened up by having a 'Guest Beer' to add variety and a discussion point.

So, like the corner shop, food and drink should be available at all legally permitted hours. In this way it is convenient, accessible and becomes established as part of the local's day-to-day routine. Quality must be consistent and variety introduced on a regular basis.

A sense of belonging

The way to success for the small hotel is not only to cater for the needs of the community, but also demonstrate that the hotel is part of the community and belongs to it. This requires involvement. Do it well, and in return the community will believe that it needs the hotel, its owners and staff. The objective has to be to make the hotel the centre of the community's activities as much as possible.

Sponsorship

Sponsoring local football, tennis, netball, cricket, bowls, car clubs – any club that requires support should be sought after and provided. Not only do sponsorships indicate involvement and interest to the local people, but from a commercially pragmatic point of view, it brings the followers and players to the hotel to socialize. For this reason, a hotel, wherever practicable, should have rooms or areas allocated for the clubs to hold meetings, or simply have an area where they can feel as though they belong. The hotel can be the venue for sponsored events, quiz nights, raffles, race nights – a whole range of activities.

Giveaways and prizes

Along similar lines to sponsorships, a hotel should always be willing to provide prizes for any worthwhile event, such as free dinners, bottles of champagne, trophies – whatever the situation merits.

Clubs

Clubs such as Rotary, Round Table, Inner Wheel, etc., which hold regular meetings are bread-and-butter functions for most hotels. They are cost-conscious organizations, and most times they break even at best for the hotel, but again it is the hotel showing its role as an important contributor to the community which is paramount.

Business clubs

Every community has groups of farmers, trades or business people, such as Young Farmers, Chambers of Commerce, etc. They meet to discuss problems and opportunities affecting them and the area. The hotel should be right behind each of these, contributing and offering facilities for business meetings and social events.

Create clubs

Smart hotel owners can use their imagination to originate social clubs, food and wine clubs, sports clubs, hunting or fishing clubs, public speaking clubs or music clubs – any type of regular activity that will bring people together on a frequent basis. Involvement for local groups with common interests is the objective.

Recognition of notable people and their achievements

A camera should be standard equipment for any hotel to take photographs of functions, interesting people and events which occur at the hotel. These photographs should be displayed on the walls. Similarly, every club or sponsorship with which the hotel is involved should be captured on film. Better still is a video camera to capture special occasions such as weddings, birthdays, anniversaries or sporting events. This provides an opportunity to replay it at an organized function for participants to bring friends and relatives.

Some form of a hall of fame is a good idea. The Inn on the Green in Glasgow has brass name plates located on the wall beside diners' seats. These record the names of famous persons who have sat in that seat over the years.

What all these activities are aiming to do is to create a sense of pride and belonging in the property. In this way, the locals will genuinely feel that it is their 'local' and will be loyal with their patronage.

Notice boards, advertising space

A notice board is always a focus of attention for locals and visitors. Again, providing this no-cost facility for the people is appreciated. It can be used for advertising local businesses, up-coming special events, local tourist attractions and activities.

Local history museum or gallery

Most districts have a history which is of interest. It is an ideal opportunity for a hotel to display old photographs of the area and any memorabilia that can be collected. The locals will bring visitors to view the displays and recount the past, and a really fine collection of historic interest will attract tourists. If a hotel is on a tourist route, a gallery or museum can provide a reason for coaches to stop and have lunch, morning or afternoon tea and a drink.

Something to do or see

There are many ways in which a hotel can provide a continuing series of activities which entertain and interest the local population. Most ideas are simple and cost little to implement, and they are proven winners. Remember, marketing is about satisfying people's needs and wants, and that does not have to require special skills, imagination or money. Just common sense and a bit of consistent hard work. Most of all, good hospitality marketing requires an interest in people and a real desire to give them a good time.

Games

The dartboard is about the oldest pub game in existence and a staple entertainer. There are also snooker tables and gaming machines. Other games to think about are indoor bowls, quoits, dominoes and board games such as chess, draughts and backgammon. The key is to encourage people to play by offering small prizes for the winners and consolation prizes for the losers so that everyone gets something. Getting the customers involved so that they find there is always something to do and see at the hotel is the objective of these strategies. It is also worthwhile considering some outdoor games, such as a mini-cricket pitch or a mini-golf putting green.

Special nights

The less frequented nights of the week for the hotel are best for the introduction of occasions that will bring people out of their homes and into the hotel for some fun. Ideas include the old favourites of quiz nights and sing-a-longs (or the modern form of karaoke). Talks by visiting celebrities are another way of filling the hotel on a quiet night, 'meet the interesting and famous' evenings. For the racing and gambling fraternity, there are also race nights where people bet on the outcomes of races which are to be shown on a video. The occasion can be tied into a well-known or local racing day. Tutored wine tasting evenings could be considered as educational entertainment, appropriate for establishments with customers who take a keen interest in wines. All special nights require to be carefully planned and publicized in advance so that the maximum numbers of people attend.

Bar promotions

'Happy hours' have been popular for years, but there is another way to achieve the same effect and that is to have a 'wheel of fortune' period. The wheel is marked off into discounted drink prices and turned every fifteen minutes. The price that comes up is the price that everyone pays for the next fifteen minutes. The owner and staff have to enter into the spirit of the occasion and moan loudly when the price is at rock bottom. Raffles, free food snacks and anything at all that can provide interest for the patrons should be used.

Restaurant promotions

In many of the smaller places, food has become the main attraction for extending the customer base beyond it just being known as the local 'boozer'. The restaurant facilities are the focus for bringing in the whole family to be entertained as well as fed. There are a number of promotions that can be run on a regular basis. Many of these are mentioned elsewhere in this book, but there are others that suit the culture of the local hotel.

An amateur night or Sunday afternoon is one that usually appeals. It is amazing how much talent can be unearthed in a small district, and the amateur night is an ideal opportunity to bring it forth. The customers are the judges, of course, and an enormous amount of fun can be had with the bad and the good acts that perform.

The mandatory occasions, such as Mothers Day, Valentines Day, Easter, Christmas and New Year's Eve should never be missed, but there are many other religious and ethnic feast days that can be turned into occasions for a special night out. They work best when everyone enters into the occasion with enthusiasm so that the room decorations and sometimes the costumes are tied to the event.

Never forget people's birthdays, wedding anniversaries or an announcement of forthcoming marriages. The simplest and most effective strategy for winning the hearts of patrons is to record people's birthdays and anniversaries in a diary. Then, a week beforehand ring them and tell them you have a bottle of champagne on ice for them, when would they like to come and celebrate the occasion and how many would they like to bring? That is a friendly, thoughtful thing to do. Yes, it is good for business too, but you will not get any complaints about that from the patrons.

Something to look forward to

Giving the customers something to do and see is a major strategy for a local hotel, and that leads to the next good strategy – to always have something for people to look forward to. Some say that is what happiness is: anticipation of a pleasant future. For the patrons, it means eagerly looking forward to what the hotel is going to do for them next.

Planning is therefore necessary. Events like the ones mentioned above will not just happen without it. Plan the occasions and promote them well in advance. Make sure they are a success by handing out leaflets and ring or write to those you think would appreciate the event most of all.

Summary

Running a local hospitality business should be fun for everyone. It is the opportunity to get to know people and build up a good rapport. When that happens, the place makes money and no-one will mind because they will be getting value. Remember, business is people.

Questions for discussion or revision

1   Involvement is a critical issue for the customers when building a local hospitality business. There are five outcomes for customers that should be provided so that customers are given reasons for staying and returning. The first one is the feeling of being wanted. How would you go about creating a feeling of being wanted for the patrons of a local pub?
2   Another vital outcome is to convey to customers a sense of belonging. How would you achieve this if you were running a country house hotel?
3   Everyone has their own ideas about what constitutes 'good' food and drink. How would you go about making sure that the food and drink you serve in your local hotel are considered 'good' by the majority of your customers?

19 *Positioning strategies*

Aim of this chapter

To create a competitive positioning strategy for an establishment by using associative imagery.

The theory

How you want a product or business to be perceived in the market's mind is a positioning strategy, and positioning strategies involve the use of information feeds to achieve the required objectives of positioning. The decisions one has to make when selecting a strategic position for an establishment require information from market research about the market's knowledge of, and attitudes towards, the place. The research should aim to discover the answers to the following questions:

- How is the establishment perceived by the market now?
- How many people can recall its name and know where it is?
- How many have used one or more of its facilities?
- How many of those who have used one or more of its facilities report favourably on their experience?
- How do the facilities rate in their minds by comparison with competing establishments?
- What is their opinion of the 'social standing' of the place?
- How many people know about its 'primary attributes'? (Primary attributes are the outstanding features of an establishment.)
- Is its present positioning competitive enough to meet the corporate objectives?
- Is it attracting a high number of people from the targeted customer mix?
- Does the establishment have the right product mix for the target markets?
- Should the positioning of the establishment or any of its products/facilities be improved, modified or changed?

The process

Successful marketers decide the position they want and fine-tune the market's perceptions to keep pace with altering market conditions, match competitive strategies and change or improve customer attitudes. To improve its position against some strong challenges thrown out by new and refurbished properties, The Sheraton, Edinburgh, upgraded itself and changed its name to the 'Sheraton Grand Hotel'. This was a positioning strategy which was planned to adopt a leadership stance within the city.

Fine-tuning of a property's positioning is accomplished by using the information feeds (see Chapter 17) to communicate the modifications and improvements when decided upon. Sheraton did not just talk about being a 'Sheraton Grand', it improved its product lines, refurbished and sharpened its service strategies with a 'commitment to excellence'. Its primary target markets, of course, were the business and high-spending foreign tourists, so appropriate special room rates and packages were on offer.

Essential to a good positioning strategy is to achieve awareness through promotion. Equally, the positioning strategy must be capable of fulfilment. Without awareness, credibility and an SCA, it is unlikely that a satisfactory position can be achieved for a property. The Sheraton Grand is a good example of how it should be done.

Terminology

The terms 'position', 'reputation' and 'image' are similar, but have minor differences.

- *Position* is a strategy.
- *Reputation* is a market opinion.
- *Image* is an emotive or pictorial perception which helps to position a product or an establishment.
- *Image association* is the use of descriptive terms which have emotive connotations, both positive and negative.

Difference, advantage and use of imagery

Imagery contributes to positioning. However, imagery is a created proposition which may be persuasive or inspiring, but images alone are not enough to motivate a customer to buy. Remember, positioning happens in people's minds and is dependent upon belief, thought, feeling and actual knowledge or experience.

This is not new thinking. Over 2000 years ago, the Greek philosopher, Aristotle, explained the three basics of persuasion: ethos (credibility), pathos (feeling or emotional appeal) and logos (logic and reasoning). He also said, 'Know your audience (target market) first.'

Lewis (1981) identified three elements of true positioning: imagery, benefits, and difference. He said that it is relatively simple to create an image of some kind, although many hotels fail to do so, but images alone do not incline the consumer to buy. The element which does influence buying behaviour is the perceived benefits of the product or service. Positioning a product or service along benefit dimensions in an attempt to reflect consumers' attitudes forms the basis of an effective strategy. Once the benefit dimensions have been defined, the marketer can isolate those target markets consisting of consumers who hold similar attitudes about a bundle of benefits as they relate to a particular hotel or hotel class. The third essential element of the positioning statement is that it differentiates the brand from the product class. In other words, it distinguishes the hotel from other hotels.

To combine these elements, the positioning statement should be designed to create an image reflecting the perception of the property that management wishes its target market to hold and reflecting promises on which the property can deliver and make good.

Finally, Lewis states that consumers do not buy products or services, they buy expectations. Statements that both promise the consumer something and give him or her a reason to believe in the promise are the most persuasive because they let the consumer know what he or she can expect and why he or she should stay at a particular hotel.

Examples of market position

The various competitors for any market can be divided into the market leader, challengers, followers and market specialists, or niche marketers. The average customer does not care about these terms, but he or she is affected by their implications. In hospitality marketing they matter a great deal to the properties involved in a particular market category, because they make a difference to how each property goes about marketing the service.

The market leader is the property which has achieved the best top-of-mind rating by customers. It is the place that most people think of first in answer to questions like: 'Where should we stay? Where should we go for a great night out? Where's a good fast food place?', etc. Because market leaders are first to come to mind they are generally the places that get the biggest share of the available business in their market category. The leaders' strategies have a broad appeal. They are probably positioned as being big, popular and extroverted.

The market challengers are the ones who want to be where the leader is, so they are constantly chasing the same markets and trying to create strategies which will shift the leader's customers over to them.

The market followers copy the leaders and challengers and offer a 'me too' alternative for customers. They follow at a distance, never promoting very hard, and are content to get the spillover from other strategies.

The market specialists and market nichers achieve a position by targeting specific groups of customers overlooked by the rest or not catered for by anyone directly. Theme and ethnic restaurants, vegetarians, art and cultural groups, music types – any strategy aimed at attracting one group by doing something special for that group is a market nicher.

The positioning statement

The positioning statement is a description of the position you want to occupy in people's minds. It involves the use of concepts expressed in adjectival terms which have emotive meanings to people with which they can associate.

For example, the Willard Inter-Continental, Washington may want to position itself as being 'an international hotel of traditional elegance at the centre of America's politics and history'. Yes, you could be dining in the same room with the President, governors and ambassadors from any country in the world. Hotels with less pretensions may simply want to be positioned as 'having the most comfortable rooms in town', or the pub that offers the 'widest range of ales in the region'.

Everyone makes experience comparisons; we describe things in much the same way as we do people, and this helps to position them not only for ourselves but also when we are describing things to other people. We are using what is called associative imagery.

Singapore's Raffles, for example, is positioned as 'the grand old dame of the East where the notables of the world have always preferred to stay'. Which means that if you stay there you could be rubbing shoulders with just about anyone who is anyone. In their advertising they use associative imagery very effectively with a campaign that draws on various distinguished guests of the past who have stayed at this historic 'shrine of mythology' – people like Somerset Maugham, Charlie Chaplin, John Wayne and the 'blue-blooded nobility'.

The following terms which can be used to position an establishment are descriptive, emotive and represent people's attitudes:

Age: Old, new, mature, experienced, traditional, updated, etc.
Size: Big, small, normal, average, huge, compact, etc.
Status: Exclusive, progressive, popular, grand, elegant, etc.
Sexuality: Masculine, feminine, alluring, seductive, etc.
Personality: Extroverted, introverted, clever, intelligent, etc.
Price: High, low, medium, budget, inexpensive, value, etc.
Place: Near, distant, close, nearby, international, global, etc.
Ability: Hi-tech, specialized, quick/easy, strong/powerful, healthy, etc.

Remember, positioning happens in people's minds. As most of us think in concepts, words are only the tools we verbalize in communication with others. Consequently, people may use different terms to describe the same feeling or belief. In advertising, terms are chosen to be evocative. The average person tends to use mundane terminology. Hence someone may use the word 'solid' to describe a property because it is old. Or it could be described as 'experienced', meaning the same thing. The Savoy Hotel in London is a classic example of a grand old establishment which is positioned by promoting the appeal of solid experience, proven elegance and dignified service.

Images change as organizations and facilities evolve, and so positioning changes, therefore strategies have to change. For example, a five-star hotel which was 'new' twenty years ago becomes 'old'. Old is OK if it means proven quality, reliable, traditional, experience, known excellence. It is not so good if it means tired, run-down and out-of-date.

What happens when a brand new hotel is built which becomes the big, smart, trendy, innovative and more fashionable establishment in the market? The 'old' hotel has to re-position itself or be down-graded to a four-star hotel. Maybe it chooses to take the lesser position but occupy the lower price end of the market and offer better value for money. Perhaps it fights the challenger and, with an up-grade of its facilities, retains the leadership position.

Advertising and various promotions do not change facts, but they are the communication means of conveying images and turning them into benefits. Each segment of the market has different reasons for purchase and seeks different benefits. For a property, a mixed image is as bad as a mixed metaphor. It should be clear to prospective purchasers exactly what is being offered by a property and in which form. Promotion can achieve a new positioning change quickly, especially if the imagery is right and it captures what the positioning will mean to the customers in the way of a DAB.

The Forte Posthouse brand positions itself to appeal to the business market: 'We're offering you a great deal for business'. A property should not attempt a positioning strategy which it is really incapable of fulfilling. Like Forte Posthouse, it should instead endeavour to adopt a positioning strategy which takes into consideration the realities of the following factors:

- Market demand
- Competitive activity
- The economics of its target market
- The economics of its own corporate resources
- Targeted customer mix
- Realizable product mix.

Most advertising does a property a grave disservice by overstating its benefits. The very nature of service makes it difficult for a customer to make a decision from the outside until the person has actually experienced it on the inside, especially as every property offers a conglomeration of products which appear to be much the same. It is argued that the excesses of advertising and brochure descriptions at least capture an enquiry. This argument is naive, though, because it is the referrals and the supporting evidence of many satisfied customers which eventually gives a place a reputation that fixes its position. A place that has won a reputation does not have to spend the same amount on promotion.

The successful operators promote differences which have advantages for the customer and support the promotion by having differences which the customer can experience. A price advantage is probably the most obvious DAB. That is believable because it is provable, but it is also the easiest for competitors to match. Nearness is believable and provable, like the Four Seasons Hotel, Tokyo, which states that it is within easy reach of both the Imperial Palace and the Shinjuku business district. Less believable is Singapore Meridien's advertisement which has the headline: 'Uncompromising service'.

The DAB formula

The steps in strategic positioning are as follows.

Target the customer mix you want

The targeted markets always drive the other strategies. When you begin any marketing assignment, always first consider the people who you intend will comprise your customer mix. It is easier to develop not only a positioning strategy but also product, price, place and promotion strategies when there is a clear idea of the groups of people you want to attract.

Find out what they expect

This is a mandatory exercise, to research customer attitudes and uncover their needs, wants, likes and dislikes, what services they are not getting, as well as those with which they are satisfied.

Decide if you have the resources to profitably satisfy what the customers expect

The product mix either has to be in place or it has to be developed to meet the requirements of the targeted markets. This may require additional financing, more people or different types of people to deliver the services. Building or re-modelling is expensive, and is often the first resort of management when change is contemplated. It is a fond belief of managers everywhere that this must be so, as if how a place looks will change how everyone feels about it. However, it is like a new hairstyle or a new outfit. It looks great to begin with, but it is still the same person inside.

Develop the services and products/facilities to meet the market's requirements

This is where all the service strategies come into effect – the procedures that will determine what will happen to and for the customers. You can throw away all your positioning concepts unless this one totally fulfils what you are striving to achieve. As Albrecht and Zemke (1990) describe it: 'This is the moment of truth'.

Decide on the key DAB which will give the organization an SCA

What you do to achieve a discernible advantage for the targeted customers will be the ultimate aim of the positioning strategy. The DAB decision will probably arise from the research into their needs and wants.

Develop a staff commitment to the positioning of the organization

Make sure that staff acknowledge and understand the modifications, changes or improvements that are being introduced to implement the strategy.

Use the information feeds to communicate the image

(The information feeds are described in Chapter 17.)

Build and sustain the strategic position with fact

The follow-through and maintenance of a positioning strategy is what will make it work long-term. Seldom does a strategy change a market situation overnight. It must be sustained by fact over a long period to reach high awareness and then conviction before a number of customers will react and favour the place with their custom.

Re-positioning

For a variety of reasons, an establishment can develop a reputation which affects its position in the market. Advertising and selling does not always help, nor does price cutting. The solution in such circumstances is to change its position. This involves a new marketing plan with specific attention to the key factors in positioning.

Case example

The Stonyfell Restaurant was originally conceived as a silver service establishment which would appeal to an up-market clientele. It was located in an old winery in the foothills next to the 'dresscircle' suburbs of Adelaide and it had the enticement of dining by candle light among vats of ageing, quality wines. Although successful at first, as dining trends moved towards more casual, lower priced eating there was a steady decline in sales.

Stonyfell was positioned as 'the restaurant in an old winery – good but upper-crust and expensive', but that wasn't working any more. So the owners decided that a change in image and positioning was urgently needed. The first step in the process was to aim at a younger age group, between 25 and 35, consisting of middle class and lower-middle class socio-economic people. The expectations of this market was for a casual eating experience in the medium price range.

Stonyfell opted for a brasserie and carvery style of presentation, they got rid of the table cloths and provided place mats on plain, roughly-hewn tables. Instead of dinner suits, the waiters wore white, polo shirts and black trousers or skirts.

The service became personalized and more relaxed with the emphasis on providing special treats separate from the carvery selection. The guests were given wine tastings so that they could make their selections. The guests could get their own food or be served at the table. It became a fun place to be.

It was a totally new experience that was being offered to a different type of market by Stonyfell. It was promoted by advertising and letter box drops around the nearby districts, and although sales didn't rocket overnight, within six months to a year it had become one of the most successful restaurants in the city. Also, as a result of its new positioning, it has since won several critics' awards.

They didn't change the name or the location. They didn't spend any money on refurbishing, except perhaps on place mats. It was still Stonyfell, and known as the restaurant in the winery, but now the positioning message was: 'it's a fun place to go that is casually elegant, friendly and not expensive'.

A new positioning strategy is not just changing the name or the messages. There have to be some palpable changes or improvements upon which to base the new positioning. Mostly it is a change in product and service strategies and a whole new experience for the customers that changes their attitudes to the place.

Questions for discussion or revision

1   What is the difference between the terms 'reputation', 'image' and 'position'?
2   If a hotel was considered a niche marketer, what would that term mean?
3   If a hotel was considered 'old' by most people in the market for hospitality, how can this be turned to advantage when it is refurbished and re-positioned?

Further reading

Lewis, R. (1981). *Cornell Hotel and Restaurant Administration Quarterly*, May.
Albrecht, K. and Zemke, R. (1990). *Service America*. New York: Warner Books.

20 *Strategic solutions*

Aim of this chapter

To explain how to deal with marketing problems and opportunities and choose a balance of strategies that will achieve an organization's corporate goals without forgetting the customer.

The theory

Problems and opportunities arise in business all the time. A market analysis or a marketing audit, any form of assessment of the market conducted on behalf of a property, usually reveals problems or opportunities.

Examples of problems

A sales decline, reduced profit margins and revenue contributions, increased competition, loss of certain types of customers, reduced market share, product failures, the property is in need of refurbishing, etc.

Examples of opportunities

New markets are emerging which present opportunities, the property has excess accommodation capacity, it has achieved its initial goals and management wants to expand, the market is changing and new products are needed to meet the demand or to replace old ones, etc.

So what do you do about these problems and opportunities? Obviously it depends on what is revealed by the analysis. Strategic solutions are the means by which an organization deals with the ever-changing circumstances of marketing an establishment. When confronted with the need for change, management cannot just sit and hope that the situation will go away. The corporate goals of sales and profit have to be satisfied.

Goals are the engine and rudder of strategic planning. Goals give an organization strategic direction. For goals to have meaning they must be timed and quantified, otherwise the strategies become well-meaning intentions as opposed to their real purpose, which is to achieve results. Most corporate goals can be classified into four broad categories:

- Expansion
- Survival
- Consolidation
- Diversification.

The trouble is, corporate goals have a tendency to make owners and managers pursue profit to the extent where they lose sight of their strategic marketing goals. It is not hard to find examples of owners who are so busy being in business that they forget that the customers are the reason why they are in business.

Choosing a strategic solution

Once a problem or an opportunity is identified and properly analysed, the answer to the question, 'What are we going to do about it?' is to make decisions about the elements of the marketing mix which need to be changed, modified or improved. These decisions will involve either one, all or a mix of:

- People strategies
- Product strategies
- Place strategies
- Pricing strategies
- Positioning strategies
- Promotion strategies.

The decisions about the marketing mix strategies then become a strategic marketing plan. To overcome a problem or capitalize on an opportunity, the strategic solutions which can be considered for each of the elements in the marketing mix are:

People

- Change or modify the customer mix.
- Target different demographic or psychographic groups.
- Target heavy, light or non-users.
- Target those markets which have certain purchase reasons or behaviour patterns (e.g. corporate meetings, conferences, tour groups, visitors/tourists, sporting groups, etc.).

Products

- Change, modify or improve products.
- Change the product mix.

- Introduce new lines or eliminate some.
- Change the service procedures.
- Change the manner or style of service.
- Change or retrain the staff.

Place or distribution

- Relocate the establishment.
- Rebuild, refurbish or redecorate.
- Change geographic sales outlets.
- Change agents.

Price

- Change the prices. Become price-competitive.
- Create value-added offers.
- Introduce price discrimination or flexible pricing.
- Use price-ranging.

Positioning

- Change, modify or improve the market's perceptions (the information feeds would involve other strategies).
- Improve or change the corporate look.
- Change internal attitudes.

Promotion

- Improve the in-reach sales techniques (the handling of customer enquiries).
- Improve sales representation (out-reach selling techniques).
- Rearrange the tactical mix.
- Introduce new promotions.
- Change the advertising approach.
- Organize better brochures and collateral material.
- Increase or decrease the budget.
- Use direct mail.
- Organize publicity.
- Change the signs.

Which strategy do you choose?

The choice is yours, and your decision will depend on the circumstances. If the decision was easy we would all be richer. Choosing a marketing strategy is about knowing the options that are available and, based on the information you have, selecting the one that will best suit the situation. That takes experience and knowledge.

As a guide to the best strategic solution to choose, always begin with a market, select a product and improve it so that it will satisfy that market's requirements. Make sure the place is right for the product, price it so that it offers value for money, position it so that it appeals to the perceptions of the market, then promote it.

The foregoing procedure sounds simple, and the basics are simple and logical. It is the agonizing over the consequences which causes most of the pain in marketing.

The effects of change

A major change to any of the marketing strategies will affect the other elements of the marketing mix. For new strategies to work effectively, there must be a measure of benefit to customers as well as the organization. Therefore new strategies must be scrutinized for their effect on other strategies and a forecast made of their impact on the whole property.

For example, by adopting a strategy which pursues a new market consisting of sporting group tours, some of whom may be rowdy, carousing footballers, it is worth considering that the strategy may drive away large numbers of quieter business meeting customers who probably constitute a large proportion of the existing customer base. If it is a restaurant, and as it is likely that the corporate goal is to increase sales, you may decide on a strategy that would allocate a large section of the building to wedding receptions and conferences. The problem with that strategy might be that groups are generally very price-sensitive. As this move will limit the place's capacity to cater for full-charge diners, that might mean a consequent drop in profits.

With every change, a marketer has to forecast its impact on:

- markets (people strategies)
- selling (promotion strategies)
- market perceptions (positioning strategies)
- pricing strategies.

In addition, the impact on profit has to be considered. What will the new strategies do to sales or market share? How will they affect existing customer perceptions or new customer perceptions? If travel agents or distributors are involved, how will they react to the change? How difficult will it be to re-educate them? A large change will be noticed by the general public who are influencers of customer perceptions. How will they perceive the change? There are also the interests of the staff to be considered. How will they react? Can they cope with the change? Will they have to be retrained or even replaced?

All these matters can present difficulties. That does not mean that a new strategic approach should be regarded with anxiety. It simply means that change can have wide implications and they should not be overlooked in the planning process.

Concepts, ideas and copying

Arriving at strategic solutions can require creative effort. Creativity is not the province of everyone. Excellence in strategic planning requires both convergent and divergent thinking:

Convergent	*Divergent*
Evaluation	Risk
Responsibility	Inspiration
Accountability	Intuition

The human brain is divided into two parts, called left and right hemispheres. The left hemisphere is responsible for convergent thinking. It is the analytical, logical part of the brain. The right side considers emotions, feelings and concepts. It is the source of creativity. To illustrate the point, the left side plays the piano, the right side experiences the music. Some people are more developed in one or other of the hemispheres. The creative people have a greater ability to use the right side to consider concepts and use their imagination. However, they are not always able to effectively evaluate their creation.

To be able to successfully weigh up the strategic options and decide on the best solution is a matter of experience and education, usually both. It is not necessary to think of good ideas. There are ample ideas that have proven to be effective which are worth copying.

The reason why so much of marketing involves lists and step procedures is because they provide the practitioner with a checklist of matters to consider, avoiding the overlooking of vital factors. In the case of responsible strategic planning, the following sequence of steps needs to be followed:

- Carry out market analysis.
- Identify problems and opportunities.
- Decide which strategies will achieve the corporate goals.
- Analyse the effects of the change on all elements of the marketing mix.
- Forecast the impact of change across all the people categories that comprise the target markets.
- Analyse the capabilities of the resources to cope with the changes.
- Set the marketing goals, finalize the strategies and set strategic objectives.
- Implement and analyse the consequences of the change.

Change usually causes disruption, varying from minor irritations to major upheavals. For this reason, it is worthwhile experimenting with change before implementing it. Alternatively, consider researching the consequences.

Case scenarios

Promotion as a strategic solution

The Pancake Place concept began in Scotland in the early 1980s. It was a novel idea for Scotland to have savoury and sweet pancakes as a meal or a snack. Previously, they had always thought of pancakes as something to have with a traditional 'high tea'. Consequently, it took time for the concept to appeal. Meanwhile, the proprietors were struggling to make enough sales to survive the consumer learning period.

The place was just off a main shopping street, and was excellently decorated with warm tones, tiled floors and country-style wooden tables and chairs. The service was fast and friendly, and prices moderate. All the ingredients for success were there.

The problem was not hard to define. People's uncertainty about savoury pancakes and their lack of awareness of the place was the main problem. The solution was promotion. All the owners had to do was increase people's awareness of the taste sensation of savoury pancakes and where to find the place. They reasoned that advertising alone was not going to be enough. In any case, advertising was expensive. Ideally, people had to experience the product to be convinced.

The strategic solution by the proprietors was to give away free pancake vouchers. They roamed the streets and offices in the immediate vicinity for weeks, giving away vouchers for a free pancake to each person they encountered, with an encouraging smile and a plea to come and try it.

Surprisingly since the Scots can seldom turn down something for nothing, not a large percentage of people actually took advantage of a free snack, but those who did enthused, and before long the magic of word-of-mouth advertising took over and the Pancake Place became a huge success. So much so, that in following years the concept was franchised and expanded nationally.

Product as a strategic solution

The owner of a successful chain of jewellery shops in Sydney was a prominent citizen who had committed himself to many community projects. Because of his large circle of acquaintances and friends, it seemed natural for him at the time to venture into the restaurant business. On a buying trip to France, he was impressed with the famous L'Entrecote restaurant and its specialty dish of steak and chips that had earned for the place its reputation. It appeared logical that Australians, being big steak eaters, would quickly adopt this style of dish, and so he purchased a tired property in a street where there were several good restaurants and opened his own cafe in the style of L'Entrecote, featuring the famous specialty.

He imported a French chef for the purpose and decorated the outside and inside to capture the atmosphere of Parisian gourmet gastronomy.

The problem was the product, together with the jeweller's lack of experience in the business. Despite a lot of publicity, thousands of advertising dollars, and his personal popularity and connections, after an initial burst of success the restaurant languished.

It wasn't that people didn't like steak and chips, the fact was Australians were used to having it as a staple diet at home – or almost anywhere. Consequently, they were singularly unimpressed by the French connection with the famous restaurant of the same name and its special dish. 'Steak n' chips? So what?' To them it simply wasn't special. What they wanted was variety, an exciting range of dishes on the menu from which they could choose. If they were going to eat in a French-sounding place they wanted French or at least continental food.

The strategic solution therefore was easy – change the menu and give the customers what they wanted, or more specifically, what they expected to have in a French style cafe. So the owner changed the chef and did what they wanted. Now, the restaurant enjoys reasonable success and he is concentrating more on his jewellery businesses.

The product, service, as a strategic solution

The proprietors who began the Italian Chef didn't lack ideas, enthusiasm, friendliness, or cooking ability. The location of the little restaurant was in a strip of shops and businesses opposite a reasonably large shopping centre. The centre had plans for expansion and they believed that as the centre grew so would their business. They worked hard over a year or two and were rewarded with enough business to provide a handy income. They had plenty of customers in those two years, and when the shopping centre went ahead with its expansion programme, it seemed that their future in the restaurant business was assured.

Things didn't work out as planned. Business dropped off and customers faded away to other places in the burgeoning shopping centre opposite. Even many of their regulars stopped coming.

The proprietors decided that they had chosen the wrong location, and that they were on the wrong side of the street. Their 'place' strategy had been their undoing. They tried to sell it but had no one interested and so reluctantly they closed the Italian Chef and went into other occupations.

A short while afterwards, the site was chosen by an experienced restaurateur and the place was reborn under a new name. Within a few months the customers were back and business was booming.

The problem was obviously not the place or the location, it was the product. The previous owners had committed the usual sin of many in the hospitality business: they had raised the prices a bit, skimped on the portions, lost their quality control, reduced the service staff numbers, and weren't doing anything new for their customers.

The incoming operators recognised the reasons for the previous owners' failure straight away. The customers know when they are not being treated properly. When the place loses interest in them they lose interest in the place.

The strategic solution was improving the product – the menu, the prices, the staff, the excitement and the experience.

Positioning and product as a strategic solution

The Duke of Wellington pub was in a suburb that served a largely working-class district with good beer and plenty of low-priced, nourishing bar food. Jack, the proprietor, was a professional operator with good staff who looked after their customers very well, calling them by name and taking an interest in them and their families. Business boomed, while many similar 'working men's pubs' were having a difficult time.

Jack saved some money and became ambitious. He wanted to capitalize on his success and expand. As a strategy, he chose product development and built a small conference facility to attract the business market which he thought would use it for meetings, training seminars and conferences – a totally new group of customers for the Duke of Wellington. There was plenty of land which at that time was being used as a car park, more than enough for his expected new clientele, and the majority of his existing clientele walked because the pub was close to where they lived.

Two years later, Jack admitted defeat. His marvellous new room, which had excellent facilities, was seldom being used for business meetings, training seminars or conferences. The problem, after careful thought and a few enquiries, was not hard to see. The corporate market could not quite come to terms with having a meeting, training session or anything else for that matter in a place which was part of a suburban, working person's pub. The problem was positioning.

The strategic solution was to re-position the facility by developing a product which did fit with the environment, and so it was turned into a games room for the locals. They appreciated it very much, especially the snooker tables, and now, although it is not making the sort of money Jack had in mind, it is helping to consolidate the market he always had.

Make sure the base strategies are in place

The basics of marketing success lie in having sound people strategies, carefully planned product and service strategies which enhance the customers' experiences and good place strategies which create comfortable environments for the customers. Then come price, positioning and promotion strategies.

You will notice in the foregoing case scenarios that the Pancake Place had a solid ground base of strategies. All that was required was promotion, leading to eventual awareness and acceptance. So did the Duke of Wellington. Not so fortunate was the Italian Chef, which eventually failed because its product strategies were flawed. The French-style café was on the verge of failure, but discovered that its error lay in an ill-conceived product strategy, and by correcting it with an appropriate strategic solution it was able to recover.

A people strategy which targets the most viable customer groups is always the first essential. Then, provided the product strategies meet the approval of the targeted customers, a satisfactory flow of sales should follow.

Large hotels depend on location and the appeal of their premises (place strategies) as essential parts of their marketing planning. The dependence of place strategies for restaurants varies. For the fast food chains place is paramount. However, some establishments are in basements of back streets with no frontage at all, doing good business on the basis of their food, ambience and service.

Pricing strategies always have an effect on the outcome of marketing, although not to the extent that many believe. Cutting prices does not necessarily bring in more sales. The product has to be in demand for a discounted price to have meaning. An up-market restaurant or hotel with a high-profile reputation can often get away with quite outrageous prices.

Most strategic solutions depend on the people who have been targeted and the fulfilment of their expectations at the time. Nightclubs, for example, are particularly vulnerable to change because of the quixotic nature of their markets, always subject to the music trends and the entertainment fashions prevailing. Theirs is a continuing quest for solutions that match their customers' needs, and choosing the right products becomes an essential ingredient of their strategic planning.

At the luxury end of the hotel and tourist resort market, strategic solutions are mostly sought in changes to product lines within the complex. The overall strategies of the properties have already been decided by long-term commitments to business travel and tourist markets, which are more consistent users of hospitality.

Large properties relying on accommodation for the bulk of their revenue contributions refer to these contributions as 'yield' – the number of rooms occupied on average over a month, season or year, and the sales value received from them. The yield figures are compared with previous periods for other years, or against sales and budget forecasts. A low yield is the stimulus for corrective action.

Most properties give priority to the most profitable market segments to maintain their yield, and top up remaining room nights with sales from less profitable segments. Some do not seek to maximize profit from ancillary outlets such as bars and restaurants. They use these facilities as a means of enticement or add-ons for their main business room hire. A Las Vegas casino, for example, which has a large accommodation and perhaps entertainment complex, makes its money from gambling, and management is sanguine about losing money from other areas.

Questions for discussion or revision

1   In which circumstances would you think a property would consider 'consolidation' as a corporate objective?
2   If a private, unlicensed hotel decided to apply for an alcohol licence, which elements of the marketing mix would the owners have to consider changing, and what would be the reasons?
3   Every change to the marketing mix has an effect on other areas of importance to the owners of a property. What would the hotel in question 2 be most concerned about?

21 *Growth strategies*

Aim of this chapter

To explain the various strategies that a hospitality establishment can deploy to achieve growth.

The theory

It is an accepted fact of business that growth is important to survival. A property cannot expect to depend on existing business indefinitely. There is always change, a turnover of customers, different trends and market conditions, so management has to consider attracting new business, even to overcome the attrition rate of customers.

Growth provides stimulus too. Michael Hurst, for instance, sets himself an annual target of $12\frac{1}{2}$ per cent growth. His strategy is to build on his existing customer base by constantly improving his products and making his place a better experience for the customers. Word-of-mouth recommendation does the rest.

Organizations grow through an increase either in sales, profit, size or diversification, or by numbers of customers or numbers of employees. One could say that only profit mattered, but there is pride and satisfaction in growth for the staff as well as the owners. In addition, size and the impetus of growth gives a place a better chance of survival in the marketplace. The sheer size and brand-name power of leading hotel chains often assures them of a sound market in any location they choose to enter.

Size through growth can also achieve economies of scale and have profit benefits for the investors and price benefits when competition becomes harder. Size also means, in the case of large hotel/tourist resort properties, a diversity of products which have the advantage of providing many profit-earning centres, and when one is down others can compensate for lost revenue.

There is a down side to size and growth, however, because unless management abilities and staff competence are adequate, size and diversity can stretch the organization's resources to the point of destruction. In fact, rapid growth places such strains on the human, physical and financial resources of an organization that it is a major cause of business failure. Many owners, somewhat unwisely, perceive that growth at any cost is the cure for every marketing ill. The takeovers of the 1980s demonstrated how disastrous this headlong pursuit of size and growth can be. Nevertheless, growth is the constant corporate goal for most organizations.

Growth: opportunities and constraints

Growth strategies should always be contemplated in terms of market demand opportunities. Such strategies should also consider the effects on the base business because the customer mix should not only dictate the product mix, but also the corporate attitude towards growth. It is not sound business practice for a property to embrace a new product opportunity unless the product has:

- a proven market
- a market which is not in conflict with existing customers.

Hotels usually offer a variety of profit-earning products, so growth can occur by adding to or improving products such as:

- accommodation
- room service
- restaurants, coffee shops, etc.
- function and conference rooms
- catering
- laundry, valet, mending and hire facilities
- business facilities
- indoor leisure facilities
- sports facilities
- more specialist facilities offered by some complexes such as casinos and boat marinas.

When an organization the size of a large hotel/tourist resort contemplates product or market growth, it should ensure that there is synergy between each of these profit-earning products. Promotion of the whole complex enables all products to benefit from the main positioning thrust of the property, and each product can feed off the customers attracted by another.

Even though a property's products are not purchased by the same people (some will use the accommodation and room service, but not eat in the restaurants; others will use the pool and the fitness centre and nothing else, etc.), nevertheless, there will be clusters of similarities among those who comprise the customer mix because the positioning of the property has attracted a particular type of person. This is the synergistic effect.

A property has to take into consideration the type of operation it is and its physical location. Sustainable growth is difficult to achieve in a finite market like a coastal village, which has a static population. Growth in that instance has to come from 'market penetration' – selling more to the existing customers

– or diversification – getting into areas of activity separate from the main business.

Some properties are also constrained in their growth ambitions by the needs of the customers and the expectations the customers have of the establishments which fall into specific hospitality categories. For example, a bed and breakfast establishment would become something else if it obtained a licence to sell alcohol. A pub would become a hotel if it accommodated guests. In these cases, it is best to do what they do best ('stick to the knitting') and grow by doing it better and more often.

Growth through positioning and service

The customer mix has to have synergy, and this synergistic relationship should dictate the product mix. Therefore customer groups mainly define a business's growth strategies. For hotel/tourist resort complexes, the perceptions of customers which management has created through positioning therefore become as important as the products themselves. Consequently, in the hospitality industry, where service is the main product, growth can be achieved through service without a penny being spent on tangible facilities or on promotion.

However, even in this day and age when service is the buzz-word, only a small percentage of management respondents to surveys really believe that service can be quantified and measured, nor do they think that service is anything more than an add-on to ambience and facilities. A prevailing belief among many operators is expressed in this quote from Lewis:

> A hotel's offerings comprise a bundle of goods and services ranging from tangible to intangible. Because the lion's share of the hotel's products – services – is at the intangible end of the continuum, it is often difficult (especially for those properties which don't have a commitment to service) to determine which attributes are most important in the consumer's purchase decision. Moreover, because every hotel property offers a heterogeneous range of services, the consumer's risk in the purchase decision is high. Finally, because service offerings are easily duplicated, the consumer cannot always draw clear distinctions among competitive offerings.

Good service, however, is a marketable difference which provides enormous potential for growth. Service is the memory taken away by satisfied customers, and good memories frequently result in the invaluable pass-on recommendation of satisfied customers to other consumers. So the soundest basis for growth is to consider service strategies which capitalize on a good image and reputation for outstanding customer satisfaction.

Intensive growth strategies

Intensive growth strategies endeavour to obtain increased sales and market share by either:

- *Market penetration*: sell more products to existing customers;
- *Marketing development*: seeking new customers for existing products;
- *Product development*: improving the existing products or developing new products to build on the customer base.

Market penetration

Market penetration is best achieved by finding new uses for existing products or by creating reasons for existing customers to use existing products. A function room, for example, can be used for many occasions, such as banquets, conferences, training seminars, trade shows and exhibitions, weddings and so on. Some of these uses may not occur to existing customers until it is drawn to their attention.

Market development

Market development can be achieved by finding new reasons to attract customers who seldom use the property's facilities, such as encouraging customers away from competing properties, either with better prices, better value or, most effectively of all, an improved customer service experience. Another strategy that can be used to achieve market development is to target new users from other locations, either through promotions, extensive advertising or sales representation.

Product development

It is through the growth of profit-earning products that large hospitality establishments can make significant gains, provided that there is an unsatisfied demand. If there is an under-supply of accommodation, add more rooms. If the restaurant is filling regularly, expand into an adjacent area. If a bar consistently overflows, extend it. This is called horizontal stretch.

If a place has earned a reputation for a product, another growth strategy is to capitalize on this reputation and attract a new group of customers by introducing a similar, but differently rated, product. If the base product is accommodation, add higher-priced luxury suites, budget family rooms or low-priced single rooms. If the base product is a European restaurant, add an Asian restaurant or an American diner. This is called vertical stretch.

Determining the opportunities for growth should be based on a careful analysis of:

- an establishment's customer base
- what it does best and better than its competitors
- how it can build on its strengths (or overcome its weaknesses)
- its primary assets, such as staff, management, location and image.

To summarize, product growth can occur through two sources:

- *Current customers*: by selling them more of the same products, offering improved products or offering new products;
- *New customers*: by increased awareness of existing products, offering improved products or attracting them with new products.

Growth through diversification

Corporate growth, as opposed to product growth, can occur by a corporate organization entering fields allied or connected with the hospitality business. These growth strategies are:

- *Horizontal diversification*, where an organization invests in new products which are allied to hospitality, or similar to their existing style of operation, but which will attract entirely new markets, such as adding a large entertainment centre, a casino or a leisure centre, etc.
- *Diversification through vertical integration*, where an organization controls or owns:
  - its suppliers (laundry, linen, butchery, flowers, etc.). This can make sense if a place has a special skill or reputation in an area and wants to maintain it, or if it has such a high turnover in its operation that it can make additional profit;
  - its source of customers (travel agent, airline, bus or coach company, etc.).
- *Horizontal integration* occurs when an organization buys out or buys an interest in its competitors. This can also entail building or acquiring another establishment and gaining a different market unavailable to the present style of operation. This move usually entails operating under a different company or brand name to avoid confusing and losing an existing customer mix.

Market expansion

An example of market expansion is when property owners decide to expand into different geographic locations and, by utilizing the same expertise, set up a chain of operations. This can be achieved by buying properties, by selling its management expertise and name, or by franchising. For instance, Forte currently has 888 hotels with 95 965 rooms in 37 countries. During the 1994/95 financial year the company acquired Meridien Hotels, a chain of international, up-market hotels, from Air France. This acquisition allows Forte to participate more fully in the strong, dynamic, long-term market growth which is emerging in Continental Europe.

The Forte company name joins those of Hilton, Sheraton, Hyatt, Inter-

Continental, Marriot, Copthorne, Queens Moat House, Friendly and Thistle and Mount Charlotte as the best known hotel chains in the UK and internationally. Many of these hotels are owned by investment groups which contract with chains for the reputation of a high-profile brand name and management expertise. One of the major advantages of chains is that members of the chain feed off each other with a reservations network, making bookings or providing referrals for travellers heading to other cities or countries. Independent hotels usually compete by belonging to a specially formed consortium to provide their own reservations network, such as Best Western and Consort Hotels.

New market assessment procedures

To enter new markets by acquisition, diversification or integration requires an assessment of the following factors:

- *Good market size.* The numbers of customers have to exist or have the potential to be developed before making the move.
- *Good market growth.* It is wise to ascertain through research and growth projections that the market is likely to get bigger.
- *Good profitability.* Whereas this seems a logical test to apply before proceeding with a new venture, management can sometimes be carried away with growth for growth's sake and not properly assess the return on investment.
- *Low competitive intensity.* A move into a new market is a risk at the best of times. It would be made more hazardous if the competition was strong and firmly entrenched.
- *Manageable volatility.* Hospitality is subjected to seasonal conditions and also fluctuations in travel and tourist activity. These factors have to be investigated and understood.
- *Economy of scale.* A new product, or the acquisition of another property, can often provide savings by avoiding duplications. It may also add to the purchasing power of the group and allow for better trading arrangements.
- *Good customer fit.* A new product should be assessed in the light of its acceptance by the existing customer mix. Old customers can often be lost if the new product conflicts with their perceptions of the property.
- *Good fit with the existing product mix.* Here again, a new product may disrupt the positioning of other products and the property's perception as a whole. It may also be such a specialized operation that specialized staff are required, making it difficult for staff to be transferred when needed.
- *The human and physical resources to handle it.* For example, for a hotel to change its restaurant from European food to Japanese teppanyaki-style food may be a good idea if the market demands it, but it would require specialized staff and equipment.
- *Market knowledge and business management experience.* As a rule, it is always best to do what one is best at doing. Diversification in particular generally requires new management skills, and these either have to be acquired or specialists appointed to handle the new situation.

Questions for discussion or revision

1 Suggest some circumstances in which different profit centres (outlets) of a big city property, such as a fine dining restaurant, leisure centre, hairdressing salon and coffee shop, can prosper even though there is no obvious synergy between them.
2 What is most likely to happen if a property decides to break with its existing customer mix and seek growth in an unrelated activity? Explain the probable outcome of a hotel with a strong market base of family holidaymakers and retired bus or coach tourists deciding to run a disco in its function room two nights a week.
3 Too much growth too soon has been identified in government statistics as being a cause of many business failures. In your opinion, why would this be so?

Further reading

Lewis, R. in *Strategic Hotel/Motel Marketing*, Educational Institute, American Hotel and Motel Association.

22 *Pricing strategies*

Aim of this chapter

To explain how to select an appropriate pricing strategy for a hotel and other hospitality establishments. Accommodation and restaurant pricing strategies are covered in this chapter.

The theory

Price is usually set by examining what the market will bear. As there are many markets, there are many opportunities for pricing strategies, and therefore many opportunities for various contenders in a market to position themselves according to price. The balance between price and value largely determines the success of an establishment. With a hotel, it is the room rate which sets the pricing levels for the rest of the hotel's products. Hence price is part of positioning. For example, one expects to pay more for a stay at a high-class, five-star hotel than at a budget lodge. Price helps to determine the customer mix and, conversely, whatever customer mix is targeted by an establishment will determine the price. Recent years have proved that the hospitality industry is a fiercely competitive one and sensitive to economic conditions; consequently the relationship between rates and occupancy has to be very finely tuned.

Hotel/Resort pricing strategies

The rack rate is the regular published room rate. In a perfect market, the rack rate is set as a result of cost-plus pricing, which is based on a simple sum:

Operating costs + Capital recovery + Profit + Forecasted number of customers = Price

Rarely is there such a thing as a perfect market. Therefore the rack rate in many instances becomes a sort of starting price for negotiation, or the price that management would like to achieve throughout the year and at all times during the week. However, the fluctuations in demand dictate that different rates apply at different times of the year, week or even day.

- *Target profit pricing* is where the hotel endeavours to determine a price based on average occupancy which will provide an adequate return.
- *Perceived-value pricing* is where an establishment sets a price based on the value or benefits being offered. This pricing strategy is generally aimed at a specific customer mix.
- *Going rate* is based on averaging, keeping pace with the competition.
- *Price ranging* is employed by nearly all hotels. It is setting a high price for the best suites or rooms ranging down to the cheapest rooms, with each drop in price representing a consequent drop in size, views, facilities and extras.
- *Value-added pricing* is where extras are discounted and coupled with a going rate to provide an attractive package offer, often referred to as a 'product'.

When customers ask the price of a room, the room rate can cover:

- room only
- room and breakfast
- room and all meals
- room plus all recreational facilities
- room plus free enticements, such as champagne, opera tickets, shopping vouchers and so on.

The purpose of a value-added pricing strategy is to make direct comparisons with competing properties difficult while making the offer appear to be worth more than is being charged.

- *Price skimming* is a strategy adopted by new properties with a well known brand name, a grand façade and a high-profile positioning. From the outset they charge a high price for their rooms and other products because they have a new, exciting, prestigious image which usually attracts a high-flying, 'nothing-but-the-best' style of customer, called in marketing the 'early adopter'. This strategy is maintained for as long as the property holds its position, and it is called 'skimming' because it is taking the cream of the market at the time. However, when other, newer properties are built, and as the facilities become less of a novelty, prices are gradually reduced.

Management usually has a policy on pricing which varies from being rigid to totally flexible. The objectives are usually survival, profit maximization, market share, quality leadership and capital recovery. However, price changes can be forced upon a property by competition. A close competitor can 'steal' guests by offering better deals. Market conditions – an economic down-turn, for instance – can force every property into a price-cutting war.

The market and demand for accommodation will set the price ceiling and an establishment's costs will set the floor for prices. The price ceiling is the maximum price people are prepared to pay in a given market environment. The price floor is the lowest price a property can charge without losing money. Somewhere in between is where competing properties struggle for market share. Price is a value-for-money equation which potential guests have to deliberate over before making a decision. In some markets, setting a rate is almost a daily decision as rivals have the option to raise or lower rates with every enquiry.

Demand differential pricing strategies

In most city markets, there is an over-supply of rooms for the majority of the year. Special events and seasonal demands are the only occasions when all rooms are filled. The marketing challenge therefore is to fill as many rooms as possible in the seasonal gaps of market demand. Price and perceived value becomes a significant strategy in this situation. On different days and at different times of the year, a room may be hired out to guests at rates which can vary considerably. Similarly, the rate will vary to attract specific customer groups, such as tour wholesalers, large companies, conference organizers and frequent travellers. This is demand differential pricing.

Holiday packages

Holiday packages are products which the property markets as its own, such as a three-day stay at the property combined with sightseeing tours or a special interest package which takes in sporting or cultural events. These are products that can be advertised, promoted to corporate clients, sold direct to customers or marketed through other tourism-related companies.

Cooperative rates for tour/travel/airline/wholesalers

These are special, discounted room rates which are negotiated with tour wholesalers so that they can market their own holiday packages. Wholesaling rates enable an airline, for instance, to market a product which entails a stay of so many nights at the property as part of a total number of benefits or events for the airline to package and offer as an attractive value-for-money holiday to their customers. Most large travel agents and transport companies package holidays in this way. From the establishment's point of view, the discount is offset by the volume of business it receives.

Weekend rates

Business people and conference organizers tend to plan their use of the property's facilities for working days. Therefore most properties find that they have excess capacity over weekends. Weekend rates are discounted offers designed to attract people to stay on over a weekend or to attract local people to indulge themselves. They can also be marketed in conjunction with transport operators to get the domestic market to have a 'short break' package enjoying the luxury of staying at the property.

Business rates

The business traveller is the most frequent user of hospitality and is therefore the target of nearly all properties. To attract their business, special incentive rates are generally negotiated. The additional attraction is usually the use of special business services such as secretarial or 'person Friday' assistance, fax facilities, computers, photocopying, meeting rooms, video-conferencing and, in some cases, language translators.

Frequent user rates

This is a strategy designed to encourage people who regularly use hospitality products to stay regularly with the property and build credit points which either reduce the rate over time or provide the recipient with a free stay after so many bookings. Usually called a 'Guest Loyalty Scheme', the rate is created mainly to attract the business person to become a loyal client. Another form of the same strategy is an offer to stay another day for free. The Hilton has an offer which is promoted as 'Another day another dollar', meaning that for just another dollar the customer can stay the extra day.

Corporate rates

Large companies, or companies with a high usage rate of hospitality facilities, are targeted and offered a low rate for continued custom, and special deals are often included for the use of other hotel services. Another variant of this strategy is to enrol them in a special club which provides not only discounted prices for every facility at the property, but also discounts with participating stores, airlines, hire cars, theatre bookings and any other attraction the property can negotiate which is likely to appeal to the corporate customer.

Family rates

'The children stay free', is one type of offer which is a strategy that many properties employ to attract family customers. Another is an offer of a free child-minding or nanny service. Special rooms arranged for the family to be together in a suite or adjoining rooms is another variation of the strategy. These types of products are frequently sold to use the excess capacity over weekends or for seasonal business periods.

Conference rates

Professional, trade, business or social groups which hold conferences, training seminars, celebrations, special sporting or cultural events hunt for the best value they can get. Most properties 'bid' for this type of business and have a negotiable rate which has a floor value to the property (which means it recovers costs and retains a bare minimum of profit). Most properties offer an all-inclusive price with meals and use of other facilities. Often the objective is to confuse the issue with add-ons so that price comparison with other properties becomes difficult. Some places negotiate with suppliers to help them with special prices to win the deal. A transport element and programme for accompanying persons in the offer is not uncommon.

Up-grading

Some high-profile hotels do not like discounting because it may harm their prestige image. Instead, when they are in a competitive situation they upgrade favoured clients from, say, a normal room to the executive floor so that they can provide added benefits at no extra charge. Or they include business facilities for free. They are, in effect, giving away some of their profits, but they are not seen to be discounting and are thereby preserving a claim that they do not have to reduce their prices to win business.

No frills rates

Another form of discounting is a published 'no frills' rate involving basic accommodation. This is a last-resort pricing strategy for large properties, but a common strategy for properties struggling to be competitive in other ways. For budget accommodation the 'no frills' approach is central to the concept and its apparent success.

There are other variations on the foregoing strategies. All of them have the same intent, which is to win business at all costs, especially during difficult times or during off-season periods.

Selling up and selling down

Various customer mixes perceive different values for different benefits they receive. Many establishments have price levels for each segment (top rates for business people, low rates for families). This can result in a disparate customer blend which harms the image of the place. A 'get-what-you-can' price strategy therefore can lead to a loss of regular patronage. However, even the best hotels sometimes resort to a sell-up, sell-down pricing approach, sometimes called an 'open-door' strategy, as opposed to the 'closed-door' strategy reflecting a policy of price rigidity.

The 'foot-in-the-door' strategy is when an enquiring customer asks about rates. The potential guest is given a number of alternatives, ranging from the very low to the highest price. The client often will choose the middle price, not wanting to look cheap or too extravagant and seeking the best value. It is then suggested to the client that for only another small amount of money he or she can get some added benefit, like a king-sized bed or a room overlooking some geographical feature. This is 'selling up'.

The 'face-in-the-door' strategy is the opposite. The price quoted is the highest. Often this will be accepted; if it is not, other alternatives are offered until a price is reached which is acceptable. This is 'selling down'.

A market penetration pricing strategy is used when a hotel sets lower than usual prices because it wants to capture market share. This is a pricing strategy that will achieve much-needed cash flow at times. It would also make sense if the establishment wants to introduce a new product and needs to gain quick recognition and win some early sales.

Pricing impacts on other products

A price strategy will impact on other elements of the marketing mix, depending on the corporate goals and the marketing objectives. Long-term discounting, for instance, must have an effect on product quality decisions. Management needs to have cost and profit predictions that will reflect the consequences of price strategy decisions. Whereas room rates set the overall position of an establishment, it can have different pricing strategies for each of its products. This approach can be used to put value back into a room rate which is perceived to be very high.

Product-line pricing can be used to offer customers a choice of values. Hence, as well as an expensive, fine dining restaurant, it has a low-priced coffee shop. Or a cocktail lounge, a medium-priced lounge and a public bar. This way, everyone can find their own price level without feeling that they are being 'bled'.

The other strategy is to maintain a high value-for-money room rate and recover profits from its other products and services. Incentives can be offered, such as off-season rates, early booking discounts, preferred customer discounts, or special offers tied with a sales promotion.

Restaurant pricing strategies

A hospitality establishment is no different from a retailer when it comes to making offers. Everyone likes a bargain, which is why sales promotions and premium offers usually attract additional customers, or bring regular customers into the establishment more often. Therefore the same types of strategies used by the large properties can be adapted by other hospitality businesses. The principles do not vary, but some businesses are perceived in a certain way by their consumers and therefore sensitivity to market demand has to be recognized.

For example, a restaurant which has the same prices for dinner, lunch and weekends is being a bit hopeful, and certainly inflexible. At different times of the day customers want different types of eating experiences. The luncheon period is normally patronized by business people who want a quick, light meal with a minimal amount of alcohol. A restaurateur could stipulate that his or her kind of place does not cater for the crowd, which is fine, but he or she could be missing out on business. More importantly, he or she might be forgetting that the same luncheon customer is also a potential dinner, snack or even breakfast customer.

Michael Hurst, the guru of the restaurant business, changes menu and price structures according to the demands of various customer needs. Hence there is a lower-priced lunch menu and an 'early birds' menu (which is half of the dinner price) which caters for those who want to eat before going on to a function, party or the theatre. It also appeals to retired people looking for a cheap, good-value meal. During the dinner session, full prices apply because this is the time of greatest demand. Then he has a supper menu for late eaters or those who have come from their evening's entertainment. A varying level of prices and menus makes sense because it is maximizing the use of the staff and the premises. This variable pricing strategy helps Hurst at his Fort Lauderdale property to turn over the tables several times in the course of a day.

Questions for discussion or revision

1   What is the likely long-term outcome for a property which consistently reduces its rack rate in order to fill unused room capacity?
2   There are many different pricing strategies. List the five main types and explain what they mean.
3   Would you advise a new tourist resort on an island to offer special discounts to fill the place and make a good opening impression, especially with the media and travel trade? Or would you price it at the normal rate and hope that extensive promotion and advertising will achieve a 'full house' by the time it opens?

Further reading

Buttle, F. (1994). *Hotel and Food Service Marketing*. London: Holt, Rinehart and Winston.

23 Promotion strategies: sales and the tactical mix

Aim of this chapter

To explain how to use the tactical mix to expose target markets to the selling messages of a property and achieve promotion objectives.

The theory

There is a firmly held belief in the hospitality industry that selling is the most important function in the marketing mix. Some may disagree. Certainly Drucker disagrees. He claims, 'Good marketing makes selling unnecessary.'

Michael Hurst is adamant that getting the product and service quality right comes before anything, and he points to a run of successes that have been achieved without a penny being spent on advertising. In Hurst's opinion, word-of-mouth – the referrals from satisfied customers – provides at least 85 per cent of the business. The place, and what happens to the customers in the place, has to be right, otherwise no amount of selling will bring customers in the long term. True, but despite these valid points, customers will be few and far between unless a property's management gets off its posterior and starts to tell a lot of potential customers about how good the place is to stay at and eat at.

Communication is the life-blood of the hospitality business, and there are many markets that have to be reached and told the good news about the place. They have to get the message and get it often.

Promotion is the communication process that uses information persuasively presented to achieve a positive customer response. It is divided into a number of functions, called tactics, embracing advertising, selling, publicity, brochures and sales aids (called collateral by the Americans), direct mail and sales promotions. How much is spent on each tactic, and the degree of emphasis on each one to achieve strategic marketing objectives, is called the tactical mix. The best promotion tactic, or message delivery system, is the personal, one-to-one contact of selling.

Out-reach and in-reach selling

The two main sales functions can be termed 'out-reach' selling and 'in-reach' selling. Out-reach selling refers to the communications going out to existing and potential customers. In-reach selling refers to inward-coming enquiries from interested customers. They are different in the way in which the selling function works, but both have the same intent – to secure business.

For some strange reason, many establishments have experienced and accomplished sales people handling out-reach selling, but inexperienced and often disagreeable receptionists handling in-reach selling. The handling of clients in both functions is equally important.

Out-reach selling encompasses promotion as well as selling. It utilizes both direct and indirect contact. The differences are: advertising, publicity, displays and signs and brochures are indirect contact with the market, because in most cases the people being addressed are unknown; personal contact, direct mail and telephone contact are direct out-reach selling contacts, because in most instances the people are known.

In-reach selling is the handling of people who have made enquiries via the telephone, correspondence or have personally attended the property.

The tactical mix is a sequence of message delivery systems

Each of the communication processes is a message delivery system because promotion strategies are messages about places and products. Thus information is concerned with differences, advantages and benefits, which need to be communicated to the target market.

The intent of a promotion strategy is to use tactics to achieve a desired consumer result – a sale, in other words – either in the short or long term. The tactical mix is a combination of the following message delivery systems. They can be categorized as being directly, or indirectly, in contact with the customer.

Direct

* Personal selling – out-reach and in-reach
* Direct mail
* Sales promotion
* Product presentation
* Point-of-sale activity.

Indirect

* Advertising
* Brochures
* Publicity
* Signs and displays.

Advantages of direct contact

- Physical presence – the dynamics of face-to-face confrontation and adaptability to individual behaviour
- Sales can be clinched on the spot
- Cost-efficient when targeting is used.

Disadvantages of direct contact

- The high cost of employing people
- Buyer resistance – feeling of pressure
- The impracticality of reaching large numbers quickly.

Advantages of indirect contact

- The message can be communicated to a broad audience
- An image can be conveyed
- Costs per contact can be small because of volume provided that a high rate of return is received.

Disadvantages of indirect contact

- Impersonal
- No need to react to message
- Advertising in particular is very expensive.

The task for management is to decide which mix of these tactics will be employed to make their promotion strategies work and achieve message comprehension. Message comprehension can be slow or fast, depending on which message delivery systems are utilized, for how long and to what extent. With a large budget, the combination of advertising, publicity, direct mail and selling can get a message to a large number of people, and if the message is clear and contains an obvious benefit for customers, large-scale comprehension can be achieved quickly. The consumer's message comprehension works on a graduated scale:

- Nil awareness
- Awareness
- Interest
- Desire
- Conviction
- Desired consumer response – Action.

Several things happen in communicating:

- There is the sender of the message, usually the property.
- There is the message, which contains favourable information about the property or its products.

- There is the symbolic form of the message; the spoken word, the written word, the pictures and text of a brochure or an advertisement, or the moving pictures, sounds and words of a television or radio commercial.
- There is the message vehicle which takes the message to the receiver, and that can be a person, a letter, fax, phone or advertising medium.
- There is the receiver, the person or people for whom the message is intended.
- There is the interpretation placed on the message by the receiver. What message did he or she actually get?
- There is the response by the receiver to the message. Is the message ignored or understood?
- There is the feedback, either in the form of a sale, a changed attitude, or nothing.

This communication process makes it obvious that much depends on the clarity of the message and the effectiveness of the message delivery system. It demonstrates the need for good sales people, soundly conceived advertising and brochures, and proper identification of the best people to receive the message.

Target markets

Every property has a wide range of people to contact in a number of specific market segments. There are therefore many segments to target, with each one requiring a different promotion strategy.

Corporate and professional clients

For this segment, personal contact is the most effective, supported by direct mail and brochures. Domestic and overseas contacts should be mailed unless there is some representation in the area, such as a sales office of a member of the hotel chain. Corporate clients will not necessarily react to image advertising. However, for the launch of a property, or a significant refurbishing which re-positions the property, advertising can set the scene and establish a climate of interest for the sales representatives to open dialogue with prospective clients.

Social clubs, business and professional associations, sporting clubs

The main ones, or those most likely to use a property's services, should be contacted in person, with regular mail follow-ups. Most corporate and professional clients of the property belong to an association, and these contacts offer an ideal opportunity for an introduction or referral to their association executives. This is called using a 'networking' strategy.

Government departments and education institutions

The strategy for this segment is to identify and make personal contact with the decision makers and those who organize conferences, travel and training seminars. The departmental heads are not always the people who do the organizing and the selection of the venues. Sorting through the labyrinth of the bureaucratic process is not easy at times.

Fraternal, ethnic, religious organizations

Use the same approach as for government departments.

Travel agents

This group of prospects poses a geographic problem because they are scattered all over the world. For the local ones, particularly those which package their own travel products, it is obviously best to maintain regular and personal contact supported by mailing and brochures. For national agents, it is essential to select the main ones and have area representation if possible, otherwise mail regularly and fax them. Overseas agents have to be selected for their viability as an influencer of travel to your region, and it may only be possible to regularly update their files.

Tour operators and wholesalers, bus, train and airline companies

These segments are significant creators of business for a property, especially if the property is targeting holidaymakers. The development of offers and attractive packages for them to use, and the negotiation of mutually suitable arrangements, can be an involving and profitable exercise for the sales department.

Suppliers of goods and services to the property

For this segment, personal contact is best.

Media

This segment is usually the province of the public relations department, depending on how the property has structured its marketing division. Personal contact and mailing is mostly used to establish good rapport with each medium.

Individual business and holiday travellers

Advertising is the only way to reach these segments because they are mostly unknown to the property until they become customers. It then becomes the task of direct mail and the use of offers to stimulate return business.

Products to be sold

Communication and promotion is a multi-directional effort requiring constant contact with existing and potential customers for a property to convey the benefits of its products. These include its function and convention facilities, accommodation, business facilities, meeting and conference rooms, dining and restaurant facilities, sporting amenities, holiday packages and special deals.

A large property usually divides the selling function into market segments rather than products. This means that department personnel who concentrate on, say, corporate accounts can communicate all the products and services and be in a position to respond to any type of enquiry. The reason for this is that the corporate customer who uses accommodation one day can hire a conference room on another, be a diner the next, organize a convention another day and be a holidaymaker in a few months' time.

With this division of tasks by market segmentation, the dissemination of brochure material and direct mail has to be coordinated with the product line managers. Market segmentation is more successful than the division of task by products, with each person making his or her own contacts. The duplication of effort and confusion for the property and the customer caused by segmenting the sales effort by products can make it an inefficient method of working.

However, small properties do not have the luxury of a sales team to whom they can allocate market segments to individual sales people, in which case the product line managers may have to wear the sales responsibility for their product line.

An example of promotion, a strategy, a message, and the use of tactics

Tough competition forces many hoteliers to find innovative sources of revenue. Few have gone as far as the Novotel in Birmingham city centre. Rather than simply watch as his guests eat and drink in nearby pubs, the general manager fought back by building a pub, called the Canal Boat, in the 148-bedroom property. 'Birmingham is known for its pubs. We were losing out because we were not supplying a pub atmosphere or real ale,' said the general manager.

To create the right atmosphere, a former pub manager was recruited, who in turn recruited his own team of staff. It is estimated that the bar takings have doubled since the opening of the pub. The message being sent out by the Novotel has been clear: 'Novotel offers you a great pub, in the heart of Birmingham, without even having to leave the hotel. Come and try it.'

Novotel has a sustainable competitive advantage, and the promotion strategy was a tactical mix which was aimed at delivering the message to specific target markets:

- a range of clients who were, or had been, their clients;
- a number of social groups, many of whom had never been their clients;
- locals and visitors to the city.

The customer mix was selective to those who enjoy an authentic pub atmosphere and good real ale.

The tactical mix was:

- flyers and a discount voucher in all bedrooms encouraging residents to pay the Canal Boat a visit;
- flyer and discount voucher distribution around the city centre;
- publicity in the Birmingham branch newsletter of the Campaign for Real Ale;
- a mailing to past customers telling them about the new facility they can enjoy on their next visit;
- a general information colour leaflet to travel agents and sister hotels in the chain;
- media coverage of the opening and promotional events.

Novotel hoped that those who responded to the flyers and discount vouchers would pass the word on to others. The publicity, mailing, leaflet and general media coverage were more long-term tactics. Their job was to create awareness and arouse interest.

The response to the flyers and leaflets was good, and for the opening night the pub was packed. There were two slower weeks after that, but the word had gone out that the Canal Boat was fun and the beer was good, and thereafter the Novotel management patted themselves on the back for achieving a successful promotional outcome.

Measuring feedback

Tactics are major expense items, therefore they must be result-orientated and measurable. The amount of money allocated to each message delivery system, and in total, has to be budgeted to meet forecasts of sales. For example, the tactical mix for telling existing customers about a special one-off rate offer may only involve some calls on large corporate customers and letters to all other regular clients. A major initiative affecting all levels in the customer mix would involve most of the tactics and be expensive.

After a tactical campaign has been running for a while, the communication effects must be analysed to measure their impact on the target markets. The objective is to find out the level of message awareness and message comprehension, how many reacted favourably and unfavourably to the message, how many intend to purchase and how many did purchase.

Choosing the best tactical mix

The choice of message delivery systems is the tactical mix, and how it is utilized will be dictated by the following considerations.

The promotion objective

What does the promotion have to achieve? In the case example of the Canal Boat, it was to create awareness of the existence of the pub in the Novotel, and selected people (target markets) were targeted as potential patrons. In this case, a moderate budget was needed and not all tactics were employed. If the whole property had to be promoted to form an umbrella positioning for the sale of all of the Novotel's products, the budget would have to be large, and most tactics utilized.

The targeted customer mix

The target markets and the sales objectives, either for the property or individual products, determine budgets and message delivery systems. Corporate markets, for instance, will always require personal contact, but may not need specific product advertising. Image and positioning advertising is a more likely tactic. When the general business and professional markets are targeted, it would be more efficient to use business magazines and the business press because their numbers would be too large for all but the biggest to be contacted efficiently by sales staff. In this case, it may make sense to promote individual product lines, such as accommodation or meeting room facilities.

Catering for target market needs

Markets can be segmented by their needs for certain facilities, such as for weddings, birthdays, celebrations, meetings, conferences, entertainment, etc., in which case a property can promote its facilities by advertising in local, regional, national and international media as appropriate.

Market locations

For one property to mount a campaign to other countries by advertising or direct contact is almost impossible because of cost. Large hotel chains can use this tactic more effectively because there will be a synergistic effect on their other properties. There are examples of this approach in the chapter on advertising strategy.

Buying behaviour and patterns of purchase

There are many markets for hospitality. Each market has its own ideas about the type and style of establishment it prefers. Understanding the differences in market behaviour and choosing the right benefits to present to each market is critical in the formation of promotion messages. It is important to use a message delivery system that suits the pattern of purchase of each market.

Evaluation of the budget and the message delivery systems to use becomes a question of numbers. How many people can be attracted by a specific occasion or situation, what will be the likely sales return and how much can be afforded to promote it? A large amount of free publicity by media in conjunction with advertising is often the only way to justify the promotional effort.

The product mix

Which products need to be promoted? A property like a restaurant may have only two products: its main dining area and a function room. A large hotel or resort has many products. Advertising a mass of products usually fails to impress anyone in particular because it is general information and many customers do not think the promotion is meant for them. A property can group some of its products and promote them efficiently to selected target markets. For the corporate market, for example, business facilities, conference and meeting rooms, transport, banquet and exclusive entertaining areas, etc., can be packaged for a promotion, using advertising, sales contact and direct mail in the tactical mix.

The marketing mix strategies

A promotion strategy generally emerges as a result of a marketing plan involving all the elements of the marketing mix. A one-off promotion should never conflict with the main thrust of other strategies. For example, if the positioning of the property and its pricing strategy are to protect the image of its products by not discounting, it would be sheer folly for the accommodation manager to take it into his or her head to advertise a floor of rooms at 'bargain basement prices' just to fix a short-term occupancy problem.

Budgets based on sales and profit forecasts

All promotions should be considered for their ability to produce sales and profit from an investment. An advertising campaign for a restaurant costing £5000 which produces only ten more customers is a dead loss.

Timing

People mostly plan their main holiday for seasonal times, travel for business more often at certain times and seek some products more often than others at various times during the year, causing well-known fluctuations in demand. When should promotions be run? The answer is, when the targeted markets are mostly available and when they are in the most susceptible frame of mind.

Promoting other products to customers during and just after a purchase is one good time. Promoting holidays during holiday seasons is another good time. Research shows that most people plan other holidays when they are having them.

Distribution: selling by intermediaries

Most establishments which provide accommodation acquire their customers from a wide number of geographic sources because in most instances a travel component is involved. To secure business or make contact with people from other towns, regions or countries requires a network of agents who can 'distribute' information about the place. This service is mostly provided by travel agents. It is only when there is a large volume of business or demand from a location that it is worthwhile having one's own representation there.

The benefits of belonging to a chain come from the fact that statistically a network provides a high percentage of a property's reservations. Those people who have obtained a satisfactory experience with a property in one location believe that they can be assured of at least duplicating it with another property in the chain.

Both in-reach and out-reach functions can be handled by intermediaries such as travel agents, tour wholesalers and through cooperation deals with associated or related businesses of the industry. Travel agents can be businesses in their own right or be departments of other operations. Banks, building societies, airlines, train and bus companies, department stores, etc., have travel departments which capitalize on the lucrative business of securing travel and accommodation bookings for a commission. Non-competitive hotel chains will also take bookings for a commission in many instances. Tour wholesalers who put together holiday and travel packages and include accommodation as part of the package are an important source of business for a hotel. Cooperative deals involve organizations which, in the process of selling entertainment, conventions, sporting events and various festivals, will do a deal with a hotel to have a travel and accommodation component included in their arrangements.

All large establishments depend on intermediaries. The disadvantages are:

- Margins have to be allowed, and in the case of some 'deals' the profit is minimal.
- Sometimes there are advertising subsidies involved.
- A huge amount of expensive literature is required.
- Often the representation by intermediaries is poor and can even be misleading.
- Intermediaries have to be constantly 'sold' on the product and serviced with information and inspiration.
- The control of the selling process is passed over to the intermediary.

In-reach selling

Usually as a result of out-reach strategies and referrals from satisfied customers, potential new clients conduct their own out-reach and make an enquiry or want to make a booking. A substantial amount of money has been invested in achieving these contacts, so the handling procedures are critical. The objective of out-reach and in-reach selling are the same – to achieve a satisfied customer who becomes a client and who will tell others how good it is.

Questions for discussion or revision

1   Which tactical mix would you recommend for communicating with customers in the event of: a complete reorganization of the style of decor; a new menu for the restaurant of a hotel; and the provision of four more 'presidential suites'?
2   The hotel you work for has built a casino attached to the main building. How would you handle the selling of this new facility?
3   Sales from travel agents have been slowly falling over a period of six months. Some agents claim that many customers regard the service as 'not being as good as it used to be'. What steps would you take to change their attitude?

Further reading

Christie Mill, R. and Morrison, A. (1992). *The Tourism System*. New Jersey: Prentice-Hall International.

24 *In-reach sales tactics*

Aim of this chapter

To outline the procedures to use when guests make their first contact with the property, how to handle their enquiries from the front desk or telephone and turn them into clients.

The theory

Managing in-reach selling

The front desk or the telephone enquiry is the moment of truth for the customer and the property. Here is a 'live' prospect who is offering him or herself up to the establishment for help. Whether he or she is seeking a place to sleep, to eat, to be entertained, to hold a banquet, conference or seminar, what happens next is often critical.

Customers come in all shapes and sizes, from many countries with differing nationalities, sometimes strange languages, contrasting backgrounds, little or plenty of money and all with varying needs. Will they be 'processed' as one of many to be 'dealt with', or welcomed as individuals? Will they be treated with respect, concern and genuine interest, or will they be judged by their appearance, labelled and relegated to pejorative anonymity? Will they ring first and wait while they listen to the 'burr-burr, burr-burr' for an interminable number of minutes, and then, when the phone is eventually answered, be told to 'hold' for another five or ten minutes? If they come to the reception point, will they wait and watch with growing irritation as other people query, complain, enquire and chatter until it is their turn? How they are treated will determine the future of the property and its success as a member of a historical élite of hospitaliers stretching back for over 3000 years.

There are two critical factors to the management of in-reach selling:

- Have a service strategy with operating procedures in place so that the sales person has support from all departments to effectively serve the customer.
- Have people in sales reception with the ability to handle the prospects and the product knowledge to assist them and sell to them.

Every prospect who makes an enquiry, either by phone, by mail or in person, has opened the dialogue either as a result of out-reach selling or because they have been influenced by a third party. Invariably they are half sold, and what they want is reassurance to make the final decision to purchase, or be given more information with which to make their decision. The 'front-of-house' is where it all happens. Perhaps it is not quite the place where the deal is made or broken, but it is very close to it.

A property, whether it be a hotel, resort or restaurant, has to convert enquiries into customers, so we term their function accordingly – in this case, in-reach sales. Whether it be the receptionist or the telephonist who deals with an enquiry, management should recognize the important status of their function. Once this is conveyed to the staff concerned there will be a vast difference in attitude, and therefore effect on the customer, between being regarded as an unimportant, routine function and being exalted into occupying about the most important position in the establishment.

The five principles of front-of-house management

Anyone on the reception desk who calls out, 'Next please!' to waiting guests should be frog-marched out of the foyer. Does the host of a party greet the guests with 'Next please!' at the front door? The principles of in-reach selling are as follows:

- Appoint staff to guest reception positions who like and respond well to people. They should be the epitome of charm, grace and manners, efficient, intelligent, patient, knowledgeable, multi-lingual if possible, and well presented. For the patrons, they are the property and everything it stands for.
- Have a measurable set of procedures for the sales staff to follow. They need all the back-up that can be provided.
- Make sure that there is an immediate implementation of any action affecting a customer or prospect. Operational procedures need to be in place to support the sales person with a minimum of delay.
- Establish follow-through procedures – a traffic-flow system which monitors every action by the property to ensure that it provides the best outcome for the customers. That means logging the enquiry into the system for other sales people to take the enquiry through the various stages.
- Maintain contact with the customer after the sale is made. Once a service is provided, a customer exists, and that customer can either be nurtured into being a long-term friend or allowed to become another entry in the computer under 'past sales'.

Management styles

Wherever one goes in the world, various hospitality establishments have a different approach to front-of-house procedures. Most will say that they follow all the following styles. They do not. Each one places a different emphasis on style, and that emphasis will dictate their attitude to customers, and it will show. Therefore it will affect how the operation goes about handling the customer and, in the long term, that will largely determine the property's perceptions in the customers' minds.

- *Sectionalized* – front desk, sales, marketing, advertising, publicity and promotions perform separately. However, customers can come from a variety of sources, and no-one, except maybe the general manager, is actually in charge of the smooth transfer of information about a customer from one section to another, so that what happens to the customer is coordinated.
- *Product-orientated* – each product is a profit centre, and all enquiries are sought by, and therefore steered towards, the managers in charge of each product. If the enquiry is about a conference, it goes to the conference manager. If it is to make a restaurant reservation, it is transferred there.
- *Market-orientated* – business people, group bookings, conferences, functions, etc., are markets that are handled separately by different departments.

All of these management styles are OK, but they have an in-built problem that needs to be recognized. Let us take an example.

Bill Williams, who is head of the Ports Authority (fictitious), wants to have a conference at the property as a result of an advertisement. After his initial enquiry he is put through to the property's conference organizer. Several conversations and an inspection of the property later, he decides to proceed. A sale now exists. Who tells the front desk, sales, marketing, advertising or publicity departments? In some properties, they will not know Bill Williams exists. Sure, the word goes out that the Ports Authority is in conference room number 4, but who knows Bill in the other departments? Who talks to Bill after the conference about trying some of the other products the property offers? The answer is, probably no-one.

For these styles to work effectively, a traffic department is required. Someone has to recognize Bill as a customer who can be developed into a friendly client whose pass-on value, let alone the business he can generate from his own position, could be worth tens of thousands of pounds to the property.

The best, but seldom used, style is marketing-orientated – out-reach and in-reach are coordinated under the marketing manager, sales people handle all clients as account customers and maintain contact from beginning to end. Bill is a person, not just the chap from the Ports Authority. Remember what has been said – a hotel client can be a business person one day, a family on holiday another time, a convention organizer on another occasion, and maybe eventually a wealthy, retired visitor. The value of loyal, regular clients and their pass-on recommendations cannot be over-estimated.

As the sales person is the original contact with the customer, it pays to facilitate the development of a personal bond. The departmentalizing of many establishments makes continuing contact and after-sales service difficult. At best, customers' details go into a database and they are written to or phoned once in a while. The sales person is in the best position to maintain the client relationship and to recommend other products to the client. If someone else does it, the client thinks it is selling. If the person who helped him or her in the first place does it, the client is being given good advice.

Here is a quick test for those people who now work in the sales or marketing area. Pick a regular customer's name at random from the files and ask around whether anyone knows or remembers the person. James Murray, the doorman of the Park Royal would remember! Business is people. If you do not know your customers, why should they bother to know you, and how long do you think you will keep them?

'Whatever it takes'

The following procedures are divided into principles. They are not just nice things that should happen if 'everything goes right', or 'when we're not too busy'. They should be standard operating procedures for handling customers at any reception point. However, there are always exceptions. And this is why management should allow the staff, and have sufficient confidence for them, to depart from procedures and do whatever it takes to satisfy the customer.

There is the story about the porter of a New York hotel who noticed that a customer, Mr Schuster, had left his briefcase behind at the front desk. He had just put Mr Schuster into a taxi for the La Guardia Airport, so it was too late to catch him unless....

The porter had been trained by management in the service principles espoused by Albrecht and Zemke, essentially the one which said, do whatever it takes. Not only that, but management had told him he had the freedom to depart from procedures if necessary to keep a satisfied customer. So the porter grabbed the briefcase, hailed a taxi and followed Mr Schuster to the airport. He arrived just as the Chicago plane left. The porter considered the situation for a moment, shrugged his shoulders, checked with his hotel to find out which hotel Mr Schuster would be staying at in Chicago and then followed on the next flight.

Two hours later, as the amazed Mr Schuster was booking into his Chicago hotel, the New York porter arrived and handed him his briefcase. 'You left this behind, sir,' said the porter. He then turned and left, leaving Mr Schuster with the impression that it was the type of service the New York hotel always provided.

When the porter returned to New York he wondered if he would still have a job. The story goes that not only did he keep his job, he was thanked, congratulated and promoted to duty manager. Today, so the legend goes, he is the manager of a five-star hotel!

In-reach sales procedures

- Greet the customer immediately.
  Make eye contact.
  If busy, acknowledge the customer, indicate interest and say: 'Be with you as soon as I can'.
  If it is a phone contact, answer within three rings.
  Do not use 'hold'. Answer and ask him or her to wait or ring back. 'Hold' with recorded music and taped sales messages is now a 'put-off'.

There should always be a back-up for unexpectedly busy periods.
- Give the customer undivided attention.
  Never act disinterested or bored.
  Show that you consider him or her special.
  Get his or her name and get it right. Put it down on paper. Get a contact address or phone number. Pass the customer's name on. From then on, the customer should only be addressed by name.
  Do not try to handle two customers at once.
  Concentrate on key points.
  Demonstrate efficiency.
- Make the first contact count.
  Listen carefully to the person. Make sure you understand exactly what he or she wants.
  Do not put customers into a single mould. Treat every customer with uniform respect and friendliness.
  Talk to him or her as you would a friend, mother, father, uncle, aunt, brother or sister.
  Do not have standard answers. Treat each person as a unique individual and each situation as a new event.
- To the person standing in front of you, you are the hotel, representing everything it stands for. Accept the responsibility with pride, interest and enthusiasm.
  Your role is sales person, but you act as an adviser and problem solver.
  You are the liaison with other sections. Smooth the transitions. Hand over your valued customer to the next person as if you are handing over the crown jewels.
- Never ridicule the opposition. Convey the impression that they are friends, not enemies.
  Never blame others for any mistakes which you or they make.
  Take responsibility for others' errors. Remember, you are the hotel.
  Assume that he or she will always be a customer and that you will be seeing him or her many times in the future.
- The job is to sell by solving.
  Understand the customer's needs.
  Provide factual information. Never lie.
  Present benefits, and support the benefits with facts.
  Create awareness, create interest, create desire, provide conviction, cause action.
  Always seek a decision. Try to close the sale.
  Use 'dual choice', 'assumptive', 'recapitulation', 'benefit in reserve', closes (explained in the next chapter).
  Always try to sell up, but remember, the customer's interests and the hotel's objectives must coincide. The best deal is the one that makes both parties happy.
  Do not argue. When you have a difficult and rude customer, seek the help of someone in higher authority and let the disagreement happen away from other customers.
- Use common sense. If it is not in the manual, take the initiative or check with your superior.
  Try to avoid acting out a service ritual, as though you are doing everything

by the book. Rules do exist to make procedures work efficiently, but if the rules get in the way of solving a customer's problem, bend them if necessary.
- Make the last contact count. The last impression is just as important as the first.
  Always leave an opening to make contact again. Never close the door.
- Let the customer know that the establishment appreciates the enquiry even though he or she may not purchase. When customers place an order, thank them for their business and be genuine about it because if they were not there you would not have a job.
  Check to make sure that all the things that were supposed to happen for the customer did happen.

The seven deadly sins of sales and service

1 Apathy (insensibility, indifference, laziness, indolence).
2 Condescension (racism, sexism, patronizing to peripheral or poorer clients).
3 The brush-off (haven't time, can't be bothered, not important enough).
4 Coldness (being aloof, superior, unfriendly).
5 Robotic (going through the motions. It's only a job).
6 Run around (someone else can do it, it's their problem, not my department, you'll have to speak to . . .).
7 Rulebook-bound (we can't do that, it's not our policy, we're not allowed to . . . , we don't accept . . .).

The seven deadly sins infect most places, and their evil can spread. The hospitality business is service. The people who understand what service means succeed and enjoy what they do, and, most of all of course, so does the customer enjoy what they do. The seven deadly sins are the real competition for every hospitality property and a very nasty enemy. Not the hotel or restaurant down the street.

A good manager of a property needs people who believe in what they do and who are thinking all the time about how they can give the customer a really fantastic time. Selling is a bad term. Guests resist people who sell. It is friendly interest and enthusiasm which should be offered to the guests.

Questions for discussion or revision

1 What are the five principles of in-reach selling?
2 Explain the four management styles you would favour for a tourist resort hotel.
3 List and describe the principal sales front-desk handling procedures.

Further reading

Albrecht, K. and Zemke, R. (1990). *Service America*. New York: Warner Books.

25 Out-reach sales tactics

Aim of this chapter

To outline the procedures used for out-reach selling, involving contact with new customers, developing existing customers and building a customer base.

The theory

Out-reach selling has one initial purpose, and that is to open the door for a prospective customer to step through so that he or she can experience the property and become a client. Once the client has tried one of the property's facilities, and provided that the experience was enjoyable and represented value for money, the selling approach enters another dimension. From then on, it is no longer a cold call. It is a follow-up to the beginning of an established relationship whereby the client is entreated to either repeat the experience or try other products offered by the property. Out-reach selling faces a daunting task if the property fails to live up to expectations. Hence selling cannot replace the interest and excitement of a well-organized property which treats its customers like welcome guests.

The tourist industry sells dreams of journeys to faraway places, of scenery, service, fun, relaxation, sport, sex, excitement and escape. The hard-nosed executive wants speed, efficiency and convenience first, but the extras usually make the difference when choosing an establishment.

All prospects are only interested in one thing: what is in it for them? To open the door therefore requires an enticing offer, an irresistible appeal which will cause the prospect to take the first step over the property's threshold. A general presentation which merely outlines a string of the property's attributes is as boring as it sounds. Finding the benefit that will appeal most to a prospect is the skill that has to be developed in selling.

Some properties try to get prospective clients to join a club which has benefits for the members, such as a free introductory meal, a night's accommodation, an interesting speaker. There are many ways of creating an offer that will break the ice with the prospective customer.

Most big hospitality establishments employ sales representatives to handle large account customers such as companies, professional groups, government departments, sporting bodies, institutions, etc. In addition, sales people are required to liaise with travel agents, airlines, bus companies, tourist offices, convention bureaux, tour wholesalers and other organizations connected with the tourism/hospitality industry likely to produce business. In all cases, it is the deal which is usually the justification for the guest to purchase, and the add-on benefits which count most. Usually in selling, especially hospitality, one has to give to get.

The role of sales representatives

The job of out-reach selling is to persuade prospects or existing clients to use the establishment's services instead of those of rival establishments. The way sales staff go about doing this can vary depending on the buying readiness of the contact. The most common tasks are:

- cold call to initiate new business
- follow-up to a lead
- regular customer contact
- tender for a conference or seminar
- trouble-shooting.

Sales people can be called 'marketing executives', 'account executives', even 'public relations executives'. In order to be effective in their work, sales representatives need:

- *Company knowledge.* They must have a full understanding of the establishment's objectives, strategies and policies.
- *Product knowledge.* How do you sell if you do not know what you are talking about?
- *Market and industry knowledge.* They must understand the tourism and hospitality business.
- *Competitor knowledge.* They must know and understand the activities of competitors so that they can respond to property and product comparisons.

What types of people make good representatives?

The ideal person needs to be able to: plan, prospect, manage time, speak fluently, keep basic records, be attentive to detail, be likeable, confident, persistent and have people skills.

The selling process

A sales plan follows the same principles as a marketing plan. It requires an analysis of the market, an identification of opportunities, the setting of sales objectives, a series of strategies for winning the maximum number of clients and some detailed tactics that will achieve the strategies.

There are two ways of getting to a prospective client: one is to write and give a reason for the prospect to call you for more information; the second is to speak to the prospect with a reason for calling him or her. This is called a 'cold call' and is usually the most difficult. The planning procedures are:

- Start with prospecting and choose those organizations suspected of having a need (target marketing).
- Make initial enquiries and narrow suspects into prospects (research).
- Find out who has the authority to decide and who influences the decision maker (research).
- Establish who they used in the past, in what circumstances and find out as much as you can about the organization and the contact (market analysis).
- Develop your offer (strategies).
- Write beforehand and establish the reason for your call.
- Phone for an appointment or discuss your offer on the spot.

Organizing the sales approach.

The target markets for hospitality are reasonably obvious. In the main they are business and professional people and government departments of all descriptions. The larger companies are easy to identify and they make the best targets. The problem is, everyone else thinks so too and therefore the competition is tough.

If the property has been established for a while, it probably has a sales history consisting of several successes and a litany of dashed opportunities. A lot of companies will have tried the place but remain loyal to other properties, others will have had bad experiences and are currently hostile, and there will be those who are regular users of the property.

The task of the sales department is a continuing one – to:

- develop the present users and sell them more products;
- convert the indifferent ones from another property to yours;
- try to overcome the disastrous ones and bring them back;
- turn new, uncommitted ones into regular clients.

This is where having an attractive offer as a means of getting the prospect's attention is vital.

Good sales strategies consider the best outcomes for the clients

Sales is a maligned occupation in some ways. There seems to be an attitude among us all that sales people will make us do what we do not want to do, and we feel threatened. Greene (1987) advises that the way for the seller to overcome this natural worry by the prospect is to be a solver, not a seller, and be consumer-orientated, not product-orientated. The two are interrelated.

For instance, Greene relates the story about an occasion when he wanted to book a place for a seminar. One hotel manager was thrilled and proud of his new hotel and showed Greene around with considerable enthusiasm for the product. 'At the end he thanked me for my time and was absolutely charming,' said Greene. 'But he never asked me about my problems or my needs (even the size of the seminar). His sales approach was totally product-orientated.'

Everyone has a problem about making a purchase, otherwise they would just waltz in and buy without asking a question. The problem with most selling is that the poor customer often never gets an opportunity to ask a question.

The best selling strategies are always those that provide the best outcomes for the clients. Success will be determined by the sales person achieving the following points:

- matching products and services with the client's expectations that will satisfy their needs and wants;
- calling frequently and constantly exposing the property's advantages to clients;
- strong personal credibility;
- making value-for-money offers to attract the clients so that they can experience the property.

Roger Blades, a sales manager with an internationally renowned hotel chain, cites several problem areas which affect a new client's choice of establishment. Feeling strange in a new environment is the most common, he believes. Most people like to be in familiar surroundings, which is why they repeatedly go back to the same place, even though they complain about things all the time. Roger asks a prospective new client to 'come and see some of the rooms', and while they are walking together he gets the person to talk and hopefully reveal some of his or her main concerns about hotels in general and his place in particular.

Value for money is another worry for prospective clients, according to Blades. 'That is the easiest to overcome,' he says. 'You throw in some extra value for nothing. That's a bottle of champagne, a free breakfast, or a taxi to the airport. A few pounds and you've got a customer who, with luck, you've got for a repeat visit.' He says, 'The places that go out for every penny they can get from the customer shoot themselves in the foot. For example, I give people asking about a banquet or wedding a free meal and a taste of what they can expect. That's why I don't miss out on too many deals.'

A property is selling an experience, a bundle of benefits which add up to customer satisfaction. How can you sell satisfaction in advance of the customer getting it?

Referrals from other satisfied customers are persuasive. Giving away some services is convincing for the nervous newcomer. It overcomes his or her fears of making a bad decision.

Conferences, seminars and meetings are wonderful opportunities for collecting a large number of people together at one time and making a big impression of the property's benefits. The trouble is, a lot of properties blow this opportunity. Having secured the conference for a special, no-frills price, they pay back the organizers by treating attendees like no-frills citizens. That is not very bright, and definitely not the way to make friends and influence prospective customers.

A conference is the organizer's big nightmare. The eternal fear is that something will go wrong. Here is the ideal opportunity to win a customer for the next time and make a big impression on a lot of the delegates, who may well be planning one of their own sometime in the future. The smart operator therefore goes all out to make sure that nothing goes wrong from beginning to end, irrespective of the price that was paid for the occasion. That means covering every detail and contingency, little things like spare bulbs for overhead projectors, the coffee arriving just when it is needed, deferring to every guest's requests, triple-checking the sound system, keeping outside noise to a minimum – in other words, thinking ahead all the time on behalf of the organizers and attendees.

The accountant's view of life

'The accountant's view of life', said Michael Hurst in one of his training sessions, 'is that everything goes in a straight line.' The point he was making was that the accounting approach to hospitality dictates that every unit of an employee's time, every morsel of food and the use of any item of equipment not only has to be accounted for by the property, but somehow it also has to be paid for by the customer.

A miserly approach to hospitality makes everyone miserable. It is the antithesis of the generous and nothing-is-too-much-trouble style of operation that attracts and keeps customers. The bottom line is not two straight lines under the final balance in a ledger, but the customer base.

With the current staff costs running at 25 to 35 per cent of sales, and competitive pricing squeezing profit margins, management cannot afford to be silly about cost controls. However, financial controls are matters which happen in the office, out of sight and kept well away from the customer's eyes. If the budget has to be trimmed it has to be anywhere except the areas that directly affect the customers' experiences. Otherwise the sales staff will have to sell in a climate of 'making a quid at every opportunity', in which case they will be fighting a losing battle against a sequence of rapidly disinterested and disappearing customers.

The sales presentation

Various ways of setting up the appointment

Breaking the ice is the first part of the sales approach, and there are several ways of doing this. For instance:

- Introduction approach – 'You don't know me, but . . .'
- The letter in advance – 'The letter I sent contained a . . .'
- Referral approach – 'Jack Smith suggested I call you . . .'

- Question approach – 'Are you planning to go to . . . ?'
- Benefit approach – 'We've cut the cost of . . .'
- New product approach – 'We have just added on a . . .'
- Free gift or sample approach – 'We thought you might like to be our guest for . . .'.

The best one, of course, is the referral approach if it can be arranged. This is the basis of 'networking', moving from one contact to the next by using the previous contacts as a lead-in.

How to go about selling the property

Having made the appointment, the sales presentation is a series of steps which are not in any special order; everyone has their own style. But the essentials are:

- Involve the client. Talk in terms of his or her interests.
- Keep the initial statements short and simple.
- Do not use superior jargon.
- Explain the features and sell the benefits.
- Listen to the customer. What does he or she want?
- Ask leading questions. Probe. Suggest. Advise. Listen.
- Find the key benefits and prospect wants.
- Keep emphasizing the benefits.
- Support what is said by demonstration. Show pictures, slides, videos.
- Talk about satisfied customers.
- Watch for verbal clues and body language for signs of conviction.
- Back-track if there is any misunderstanding.
- Summarize the main points.
- Give the prospect a chance to buy.
- Ask for the booking.

Handling objections

Objections usually demonstrate interest and present an opportunity to establish conviction. They are not necessarily a rejection of what is being said or of the person saying it. The techniques are:

- *Listen to the objection.* Sometimes it is a real difficulty the prospect has with some aspect of the property or product – in which case, reply with a fact or feature which presents a benefit that overcomes the difficulty. On many occasions, it is a 'fob-off' and the real objection is hidden, so ask 'What makes you say that?' to find the real reason for the objection.
- *Avoid arguing.* Even if you win the argument, the chances are you will lose. No-one likes to be proven wrong. And the prospect has the last say. Instead of defending, say, 'I can understand your concern, but I think you will find that . . .'

- *Defer an objection.* 'Can I come back to that?' Often the objection will be forgotten. If is not, you have time to consider your reply.
- *Sweep aside the objection.* 'That's not a problem. Let me show you this . . .', and present more features and benefits.
- *Present additional information to counter the objections.* 'Of course, I haven't told you about this yet . . .'
- *Good sales people plan for objections and anticipate them.* An objection should seldom come as a surprise. Some raise them and use them as a way of getting across a benefit. 'I guess you are concerned about this?' 'Well, that's not a problem, because it has this . . .'.

Closing the sale

Closing the sale is the reason in most instances why the representative is there. And yet there are sales people who are frightened to ask for the booking in case the prospect says, 'No', so they do not ask. If a prospect says 'No', it means that he or she has not been convinced, so you simply treat it as an objection and endeavour to find out why he or she remains unconvinced. 'No' does not necessarily mean that the prospect disapproves of you or your property. Some proven closing techniques are:

- The simple, direct close. 'Can we have your OK?'
- Recapitulate the main benefits and then close.
- The assumptive close. 'If you wouldn't mind just signing here.'
- The benefit-in-reserve close. 'What I haven't mentioned is this . . . Can I have your OK now?'
- Dual choice close. 'There is this one or that one. Which one would you like?'
- Last chance close. 'I don't know if there is one left, but if there is, would you like it?'
- Balance sheet close. 'If we add up the positives and the negatives, it is clear that . . .'.
- Trial order close. 'Book for one session and if you are happy after that we can extend the agreement.'
- Impending event close. 'The price goes up next month. If you say yes now . . .'.

Selling aids and sales support

Out-reach requires selling support, especially if the prospect has never seen the facilities. Therefore videos, slides, colour pictures, brochures and advertising are really mandatory. The out-reach functions of selling, advertising, publicity, sales promotion, brochures, travel agents, any form of contact via a message delivery system, are not separate functions, but have to be coordinated activities which impact on prospects. In selling, no-one should ever feel alone. For a very large sale, other people may be required, for example, the food and beverage manager, the conference and banqueting manager and the rooms division manager. Invite the prospects to the establishment to see and experience it.

Develop the long-term relationship

A sale should not be perceived as having a beginning and an end. It is the foundation for a continuing relationship with mutual advantages. Therefore follow through and provide constant contact – reinforcing the relationship is vital. Building a customer base is the name of the game.

As the client will come into contact with most of the facilities and the staff, everyone contributes to the experience. When every person from the pot washer along the chain to the chief executive realizes that he or she is contributing to the selling effort, the property becomes a customer-driven organization and success is reasonably assured.

Networking

Your present customers are the means to more customers. Their recommendations, referrals, influence and contacts are the soil into which you plant the future of the property. It is far easier to keep your existing customers than it is to replace them with new ones. Furthermore, it is easier to get new customers when you have an introduction or recommendations provided by a happy client. Moving from and through the help of existing customers to secure new customers is called networking.

The value of an offer

The room that is not being used by a paying guest does not cost much to give away. The table that is not being occupied takes a bit of extra service time and some food and wine costs, but it is not a big deal. Sure, a property will go broke if it gives too much away, but we are not talking about that. 'Giving to get' and building a customer base is the principle involved. Making offers, allocating money so that prospective customers experience the property, should be regarded and be costed into the promotion or marketing budget. It is an investment in the future, not an expense that comes out of profit.

Do not over-sell

There is a tendency for most sales people to get carried away at times with their own enthusiasm and make promises that are difficult to honour or, worse still, protect the prospective customer from the truth (tell lies, in other words). This is a highly dangerous and short-term approach and must never be contemplated. Over-stating the case with adjectives is understandable. 'We'll give you the time of your life!' is a gross exaggeration, for instance, but not reprehensible. It is when the offer is made and the deal is being finalized that the delivery of products and services must be absolutely precise and leave no room for argument or error.

What the customer buys is the expectation of a need or want of his or hers being satisfied. For holidaymakers and tourists as an example, the value of the understated suggestion, leaving the prospect to imagine the experiences that he or she will have, is often a more powerful sales tool than the over-stated claims. In selling, the absolute truth is the only sensible, and, in the long term, profitable course of action to pursue.

Questions for discussion or revision

1 Imagine that you have made a successful contact with a corporate prospect who has exhibited a strong interest in opening an account for the company's business users. However, the person is hesitating. How would you go about securing the business and close the sale? Consider first the reasons why the person is delaying the decision.
2 Let us assume that you have a tip from a friend that a top of the league football team is unhappy about its accommodation arrangements for a start of the season training session. They have used the same place each year for a long time. What are some of the means you would use to make contact, and how would you plan your presentation?
3 When talking to a good prospect for a corporate account the person is taking exception to the hotel's rack rates. How would you handle the situation and secure the business without giving too much away?

Futher reading

Greene, M. (1987). *Marketing Hotels and Restaurants into the '90s*. London: Heinemann.

26 *Advertising strategies*

Aim of this chapter

To explain how advertising strategies are used to achieve awareness of a property and its products and convey messages that will create a competitive position.

The theory

Advertising is one of the main message delivery systems used in promotion. It is not just paid space or time in media. Advertising is also signs, brochures, leaflets, tent cards and an array of name reminders on sold merchandise or giveaways. It is also 'signature' items which feature the name of the property, such as towels, linen, crockery or glassware. Any opportunity to get the name of the property or a message about it to people can be described as advertising. It can be general or specific. It can send a message about a whole hotel complex or concentrate on individual products.

There are four broad classifications of advertising:

- *Reach advertising*. Selling a promotion or product when immediate results are the objective and advertising is probably the main tactic (for example: an announcement about a restaurant price offer (two-for-one meal offer), a cut-price weekend accommodation rate). In these cases, the advertising is expected to generate enquiries from interested customers. Reach advertising is 'retail' in its approach and a price offer is often an essential component of the message. It can achieve its aim through paid media, brochures mailed or delivered in person to a prospect, or be simply a tent card or flyer distributed around the property. It can also be in the form of a banner across the façade, a sign in the window, a voice over a public address system or a recorded phone message while enquirers are waiting on hold on the telephone.
- *Teach advertising*. Telling a specific segment of the market about the benefits of the place or one of its products, with medium-term results being the objective. Advertising in this instance, for example, may be providing a

support role for a telephone canvass for special leisure club membership, a new holiday package, or to announce the opening of a new facility. Price is seldom mentioned because teach advertising is not meant to make offers but to assist in securing the final sale.

- *Preach advertising.* This is meant to achieve a position in the market for the property and makes general statements about the attractions of a place. Such advertising creates an image or an ambience about a property. It can also be used to re-position a property which has undergone considerable refurbishing. It can remind would-be customers by re-stating the key benefits of a property which many have overlooked. The intention of preach advertising (dubbed corporate advertising by the advertising industry) is to present the establishment in an appealing, favourable way to attract enquiries by positioning it as offering better value than the opposition. For existing customers, it reaffirms their opinion that they are making the right choice in continuing to use the establishment.
- *Reminder advertising.* This is simply keeping the name of the property foremost in people's minds so that it will be remembered when an occasion arises for the use of one of its facilities. Reminder advertising is similar to preach advertising except that it is passive, mostly achieving the objective of maintaining awareness by the use of corporate advertising signs, giveaways and signature items.

The shortcomings of advertising

Services are easily duplicated. The customers cannot always draw clear conclusions from competitive offerings, so advertising fills the breach by conveying the messages about differences, advantages and benefits. However, it is not a panacea for poor marketing in other areas of the marketing mix, especially product strategies. Wild claims are not convincing. It is tangible evidence cleverly communicated that is most likely to attract attention.

Too much is usually expected of advertising. It is simply public communication. It cannot make a sale on its own, it can only generate an enquiry and someone still has to physically close the sale. It will not work if the message is wrong, the product is wrong or if there are no people in the market who want what the advertising is offering.

A major shortcoming of advertising in the 1990s is its limited ability to communicate with the main business markets, essentially the largest users of hospitality. By the nature of their occupations, business and professional people are light watchers of television, indifferent commercial radio listeners, scanners of newspapers and only read magazines which apply to specific areas of interest to them. To make matters worse for communicators (the message originators), there is a plethora of communications aimed at business people through every medium, especially direct mail. They are being submerged in information and, as a consequence, they have to be very selective about what messages they want to take in. Unless the communication has immediate relevance and a benefit or offer, it is ignored.

The other major difficulty for advertisers is the high cost of advertising – not only the cost of buying the space or the time, but in the preparation of the communication. Colour photography, type, copy writing, finished art and colour separation work used in print magazines and brochures is a very expensive process. Even more expensive is the filming or videotaping of television commercials, with actors, sound effects, music, graphics and editing running the costs into four figures or more.

Cut-through

With so much advertising bombarding the population, the majority of people switch off mentally and do not notice the advertising unless it obviously applies to them. Cut-through is a term which describes getting through the clutter of messages and being noticed and understood. Most marketers attempt to achieve cut-through by clever advertising or by volume advertising. The problem with creativity is that it can be so obsessed with achieving cut-through that it can lead to a very expensive production which sells the ad but not the message. Segmentation and careful strategic positioning of the advertising message and a cleanly executed creative approach is the way to achieve cut-through.

Too many hospitality advertisements are 'me toos'. They look the same as everyone else's adverts. They end up selling travel, holidays and luxury accommodation, but fall short of selling one place in particular, or providing competitive reasons for using a property's facilities. How to get the best advertisements is discussed in Chapter 27.

Who does the advertising?

Most large properties use the services of an advertising agency, some do it themselves and others leave it to the medium to prepare the advertisement, based on a brief and rough outline of what is required by the property.

Clearly the best way is to employ an advertising agency because they have the expertise and the experience. A good agency also has the discipline to coordinate several advertising thrusts and maintain consistency of the look and presentation of the client's messages. However, few of the smaller properties can afford to have their own advertising specialists for the creation of advertising. Those which allow the media to do the work usually get the worst adverts simply because the various advertising media seldom employ people with specialist expertise for the purpose. For most media, it is an add-on facility which is provided at the cheapest price or free.

For a large property which has many products to promote, the advertising has to be coordinated by one person whose function is to sift through the various requests and needs for advertising so that the promotions of the property are efficient and cost-effective. This can be a specialist position or be part of a sales and marketing executive's job specification.

The three essential elements of advertising

Determining the best use of advertising requires an analysis of:

Target markets

As in every aspect of marketing, it is the people who form the most viable customer-mix groups which have to be targeted. Aiming the advertising at target markets and selecting media which mainly reach them avoids wastage of 'impacts' (the number of people reached by the advertisement). Given the high cost of advertising, this makes obvious sense.

Having specific target groups also gives the advertising direction. It is like writing a letter; if you know to whom you are addressing your message the composition is easier and more telling because you know the person and have a good idea of how he or she will react. If you do not know the person, even the beginning presents a problem – 'Dear Sir, Ms, Miss or Madam' you might say, and you are in trouble already.

That is the problem with much advertising – it talks to people who are stereotypes which exist in some creative person's mind but are hard to find in the real world. As a consequence, the message misses the market and the tens of thousands of pounds spent in buying space or time, let alone the production costs, go down the drain.

Competitive positioning

Chapter 19 on positioning explains how important it is to position a property so that it gains the competitive edge and has at least one reason for being considered and remembered. With so much hospitality advertising already looking the same, having a clear-cut difference in positioning is an added reason for advertising that expresses the difference. However, that does not mean going mad with a bizarre-looking advertisement.

Positioning is a whole-property marketing strategy. Having an advertisement which is different for the sake of being different is a creative strategy. Advertising is the method of publicly proclaiming how the property wants to be perceived in people's minds. It is an expression of the property's personality, referred to by advertising people as the brand personality.

The advertised positioning of a property has to be consistent and persistent. Therefore, individual promotions which concentrate on products and special package offers must support the basic positioning of the property, even though each of the promotional messages will have separate marketing intentions. Sheraton and Inter-Continental advertising always maintain a consistent profile and present their respective properties as members of an exclusive group at the top end of the market. This positioning strategy is maintained by every piece of literature and communication item used by their properties.

The main benefits of the establishment to be portrayed (the message)

All advertising communicates best if the message it delivers has an offer and strategically positions the property with a sustainable competitive advantage. This can be a price, product or service difference which few others have, or a seeming benefit from a special feature of the property. This is why 'the message comes before design', meaning that it is the message which is more important than how the advert looks. In a nutshell: if the market aimed at by the advertising does not receive (wrong media) or does not understand the message (poor copy), the advertising fails. Therefore the success of advertising depends on:

* knowing who to talk to (the target markets);
* knowing what to say (the message);
* knowing where to say it (the medium);
* knowing how to say it (the creative approach).

Communication objectives

Communication objectives have to be set for advertising and used as a means of measuring its effectiveness. Like all marketing objectives, they are the driving force for tactical messages. Communication objectives read like this:

* 'To increase the awareness of lawyers, accountants, architects, medical practitioners, dentists and other professional people that our property has a closed-circuit video-conferencing facility which is ideal for training seminars.'
* 'To communicate to couples with children in the middle to upper income groups that the property has full-time child-minding facilities to enable them to have a carefree weekend at a very attractive weekend package rate.'

These objectives make it clear what is required from the advertising and, if advertising is the main message delivery system, it is possible to measure the sales and therefore the cost-efficiency of the media and the creative approach used.

Teach advertising communicates the benefits of an establishment in a general way. Over a period of time, this has a cumulative effect and builds an impression of the establishment which at some time leads to an enquiry and then to a sale. The selling 'load' in this instance is not as heavy. It is also difficult to establish whether the advertising worked or the enquiry came from a referral. Few people will ever admit that they were 'sold' by advertising.

Segmentation of markets for advertising

Advertising can be utilized for a number of communication jobs. Segmentation avoids talking to people as 'think-alikes' and sends a message to a specific group of people who have been defined as having a need or preference for a product or service. Some of the primary segments that advertising is aimed at are:

- existing patrons of the establishment or its profit-earning products;
- travel agents, tourist offices, convention and visitor bureaux and tour wholesalers;
- allied business operators such as airlines, railways, bus companies, tourist resorts and facilities, etc.;
- professional and trade organizations;
- suppliers and service providers;
- customers of other hotels, restaurants, etc.;
- the business, leisure, entertaining, sporting and holiday population;
- prospective customers in specific geographic locations which offer potential for market penetration.

Positioning advertising steps

When preparing an advertising campaign, assume that the reader or viewer knows nothing. No-one can talk back to an advertisement and ask it questions. Therefore the advertisement has to say enough to interest the audience and provide enough information to answer the most pertinent questions without stuffing the communication with an overload of detail.

The steps to consider

- Occupy a geographical and physical place in the target market's minds. Where is it? On an island? In the middle of the city? By the sea?
- Communicate a clearly defined benefit or reason for the establishment's existence. Does it have a golf course, ten different themed restaurants, 4000 rooms, a butler for every room?
- Indicate who mainly goes to the place. Are they business and professional people, film stars, sports personalities, young, mature, families?
- What else is special about the place? What is so different in the way of facilities, surroundings, ambience and features that no-one else has?

Differences, advantages and benefits (DAB) are the promises of a better value experience for the customers that a property has to sell.

The value of persistence

Few people keep a file of advertisements. Advertising works by attrition and constant repetition. You have to sustain awareness of the message. If you do not, in three months the advertising will probably be forgotten.

Communications should also be consistent. Frequent changes of image present a confusing picture to the market.

Positioning can be achieved by an image which could be a picture and a phrase that tells the market: 'Hey! This is what we are on about. Come and experience it!' Some of the best advertising for the hospitality and tourism industries utilizes simple imagery to capture people's emotions and is repeated again and again. Some properties present a different aspect of the same message, but always the same message comes through. The Sheraton and Inter-Continental advertising demonstrates a commitment to a brand personality for their properties which is consistent in every advertisement.

Sales promotion campaigns

Short-term tactical objectives will give direction to much of the advertising required for a property, such as a special event, a sales promotion, a product promotion, to take advantage of a change in the market, or to offset a competitor's move. Sales promotions have become a way of life for many establishments. They provide immediate reasons for customers to come and use the facilities.

Giving a reason to 'act now' is the best use of the advertising pound these days because it is immediately productive. Sales promotions, special offers, rewards for sending a coupon, discounts, early booking reductions, off-peak specials, weekend rates, etc., work best with a jaded public which has become used to the glossy hype associated with the industry. 'What's new?' is the question that has to be answered if advertising is to achieve 'cut-through'.

The large, successful establishments use advertising in a support role for a concentrated sales promotion, and they have the money to involve all the promotion tactics in the mix.

As opposed to image advertising, where results are almost impossible to assess with certainty, sales promotion advertising is more an investment in future sales, and the results are measurable. This is why sales promotion advertising overcomes many owners' fears of spending a pound and not seeing a return for it.

Supplementary advertising

Making the ad-pound go further can be accomplished in several ways. Some of the options are:

- *Contra-advertising*. This is when a medium commits to use the facilities of an establishment and repays it with an equivalent pound value of advertising.

- *Cooperative advertising.* This is when the establishment and another company combine their advertising as part of a joint marketing arrangement. The partnership could include a casino, bank, airline, tour wholesaler, tourism operator, festival organizer, etc.
- *Region or industry advertising.* This is when all the establishments in a geographic area combine to conduct a large campaign to attract a market to the area that will benefit all the participants. This is the purpose of a city's visitor and convention bureau, for example, or an area tourist board.

Collateral

Collateral or below-line advertising is brochures, factsheets, tent cards, signs, posters, flyers and folders. Even a menu is an advertising item that can be classified as 'collateral'. It is the foundation of most of the advertising effort and arguably the most effective for the majority of properties.

Small properties can use collateral without resorting to main media advertising and its associated expenses. Some can do just as well as the larger properties. Much depends, however, on the quality of the collateral material – not its gloss or cost, but on the distinctive messages, the use of pictures, clever imagery and the offers which are relevant to the markets being aimed at.

Let us not forget either that some of the simplest and least expensive advertising mediums are giveaways, such as pens, pads, notebooks, baseball hats, diaries, etc., all of which carry the name and maybe a simple message about the property's DAB. There are also the reminders in the form of take-away menus, brochures, calendars of events, recipes, signature items such as ashtrays, coasters, spoons, glasses, towels, soaps, toiletries, all featuring the hotel's logo and messages. Some places sell novelties that pay for themselves, such as postcards, maps, gifts, toys, local crafts and sold through the property's shops. These are called 'self-liquidating advertising mediums or premiums'.

Questions for discussion or revision

1 Name four of the essential factors that have to be considered in the preparation of an advertising campaign.
2 Explain what 'cut-through' means in advertising parlance and give an example.
3 What is 'contra-advertising', and in what circumstances is it ideal for a property to use?

Further reading

Buttle, F. (1994). *Hotel and Food Service Marketing.* London: Holt, Rinehart and Winston.

27 Advertising: creative strategies

Aim of this chapter

To explain how to assess good creativity in advertising and promotion literature.

The theory and how it works

The intention of most commercial advertising activity for hospitality is to communicate benefits and values and invoke a favourable response from people in the market. The response will vary from group to group, depending on the message and the needs and wants of the individuals in each market group targeted. Therefore, just as it has to be certain about its target markets, the property has to be clear about the type of response it wants. When the advert is being created, the writers have to consider the answers to the silent questions from the readers or listeners who may be interested but will want to know, 'What sort of place is yours? What are you offering me? If I stayed (or ate) at your establishment, what would I get for my time and money?'

In answer to these questions, many of the larger hotel and resort properties present an array of breast-beating self-indulgence. Their adverts boast about their gloss, glitz, marble, silver, brass and crystal. How do people react to breast-beating propositions? Some might say: 'If I stayed at the hotel I think I would be treated very well.' Others might think: 'Looks good, but I know it will cost a lot of money and I doubt whether I need to spend that much.' Most will say: 'It's very impressive and I believe it would be lovely, but I can never afford to stay there. It is out of my league.' The rest may be singularly unimpressed. For them, it will be just another hotel advertisement.

The basis of effective advertising is to know in advance what the target markets are likely to think, feel, believe or know as a result of being exposed to the messages in the advertising. Thinking ahead, putting one self in the minds of the target market is part of the preparation of advertising. It is called formulating the consumer action proposition and means predetermining the reaction to the message and its presentation. Its purpose is to answer the question: 'Will the advert deliver the message to the people we want and will they react the way we expect?'

Messages, objectives and media

Creating an advertisement for mass media or other message delivery systems has to be driven by the communication objectives. In addition, the creative solution, which is the way that the message is presented, has to be encoded into words and pictures so that the markets it is aimed at get the message quickly and easily. The creative solution must also suit the message delivery system.

Let us use, for example, the strategic message for a family-style restaurant, which we will call 'Family Fare'. The message that has to be delivered is 'At Family Fare children under 12 eat free, and there is a special supervised activity centre for them to play in while the parents finish a leisurely meal.' This attractive offer, which has a good DAB in comparison with other places in the vicinity, would result in a communication objective which might read like this: 'To make people with children aware of the offer and achieve a 40 per cent penetration level of the message within a month.' Notice that the objective has a target market, a measurable level of awareness and a time criterion.

To achieve the objective, the media chosen to deliver the message might be a mail drop to all the homes in the area, supported by a weekly press advertisement in the local newspaper. In an area with a statistical population of around 5000 homes with children, 40 per cent awareness would mean that 2000 homes should get the message and understand the offer. It can be assumed that the other 3000 would not get the message either because they do not read brochures, they missed the advert in the paper, or the offer did not register in their minds.

The response to the advertising will depend on how enticing the offer was perceived to be, how many people were actually interested in eating out with their children and the success of the creative approach. Experience suggests that a 5 per cent response would be good, that is, about 100 couples and their children over the period of the campaign would respond to the message and take the action of coming to the restaurant. At least forty of those, hopefully, would become regulars. Then maybe, with the help of word-of-mouth after that, and perhaps some reminder advertising there would be continued growth for Family Fare to make its advertising expenditure justifiable.

The creative solution: the KISS principle

The purpose of a creative approach is to use a message delivery system, such as a newspaper, to its best advantage by drawing attention to the message and making it easy to read and understand. Good creativity should considerably enhance the possibilities of readership. Creativity on its own though, will seldom save a poorly conceived or uninteresting message.

Any advertisement, for any medium, which obscures the message is a foolish waste of money. In print media, it is the opening headline that has the main job of conveying the words that spell out the key points of the proposition. At all times it must be assumed that the readers are largely disinterested in reading advertisements, so the headline is no place for subtlety.

Here are three creative alternatives for the headline in the Family Fare brochure and press advertisement. That attention-grabber has to be the headline if the rest of the advertisements is going to be read:

1   'We'll mind the kids while you eat.'
2   'Kids eat free and run free at Family Fare.'
3   'Supervised activity area provided for children.'

Which one do you prefer? Which one do you think would work best? The first headline is misleading even though the copy explains the offer in full. It takes a single benefit approach and latches onto the belief that most parents want the kids taken off their hands while they eat. A dubious assumption because many parents would not trust others to look after their children. The second headline is a clever play on words but it is still reliant on the copy to explain the offer. The third headline is dull creatively but gets the message across without the reader having to get the details from the copy.

Adverts work better by using an illustration. Remember the adage, 'a picture is worth a thousand words'? In today's picture thinking world and lowered literacy standards, the value of a picture has increased to around five thousand words! The Family Fare advert could show two children in the foreground playing in the activity centre, while through a picture window in the background we see a typical restaurant scene with the parents relaxing, enjoying their meal. We now have the readers' attention and a communication which is appealing and hard to misunderstand.

One of the most common mistakes in advertising creativity is being too clever. Puns are clever but use a double meaning to say something in a round about way. Many people miss the meaning. Advertising is too expensive to waste it on being clever at the expense of message clarity. Every so often, a headline with a pun will emerge that is stunning in its creativity, such as 'Go to work on an egg', or more recently BT's 'It's good to talk'. Even they are rare – the world's advertising copywriters spend their working lives dreaming of emulating those winning statements. The trouble is, most of them die with little more to show than a handful of poor substitutes.

A recent country house hotel advertisement, for example, has the pun headline: 'Meet in a historical setting and go back to the future'. The writer was trying to say that the hotel was built in 1777, presenting a Georgian elegance but combining modern technology to create an outstanding conference environment. However, you had to read the copy to find that out.

If you want to make sure that you get your message across, one of the first rules of creativity is the KISS principle – Keep It Simple Stupid.

A general checklist

Here is a simple advertising copy checklist which applies to most advertising and brochures:

- *Know the target markets* at which the advert is aimed. Try to understand the people and how they are most likely to respond to the message and the presentation of the message contrived by the creative approach.
- *Get attention*, usually with an interesting picture. If the picture can deliver the message on its own, the words only have to confirm and add to what the reader sees. Use colour if you can; it provides warmth and feeling to the message.
- *Build interest.* Have a headline that ties in with the picture and delivers the main benefit of the message. The copy provides the details; it should never have to solve the riddle of the illustration and the headline, as is the case with so many adverts.
- *Create desire.* Write copy that points up the benefits and confirms the facts for readers. Spell out the reasons why they should purchase.
- *Be credible.* Prove the point with testimonials. Endeavour to reassure the readers that they will get what is promised.
- *Make it easy to get.* Provide the reader with enough information to find the place and make the purchase. For some silly reason, in many adverts the purchase details are contained in type so tiny that it is hard to read.

Some basic creative rules

For any form of message presentation in an advertisement there are a number of basic rules to follow which will make the communication more effective.

- Keep the communication very simple. Do not try to communicate too much. Advertising should be single-minded.
- Whereas there may be several salient facts or features to present, highlight the main ones. Memories are short. No-one gets all the information. Make sure that one or two benefits stand out.
- Use pictures to tell the story. They are worth 5000 words these days.
- Present the message in a friendly, pleasant way. Shock has its place, usually in a horror film.
- Utilize emotion wherever you can. We are emotional creatures and respond to it.
- Do not introduce sex, nudity, religion, racism, sexism or violence into the advertising unless it is directly related to the advertising objective. It may achieve 'cut-through', but cut out a large percentage of your audience.
- Do not be a copy-cat. You run the risk of being confused with another advertisement.
- Knocking the opposition is dangerous. You may invoke the underdog syndrome, but, more importantly, you are drawing attention to the opposition

for free. The best examples of this are political campaigns. Slinging matches can help to elect an opposing candidate.

- Reinforce the message at every opportunity. Coordinate the creative approach throughout the tactical mix if more than one message delivery system is used. One helps the other by reminding them of what they have seen or heard before. This also helps to build trust and conviction.
- Use advertising to position the property or product. The tone and manner of the advertising should reflect the personality of the property. Run 'theme' advertising. Even though you may have several campaigns running concurrently, each one aimed at different markets, one can support the others as a member of a 'family' of advertisements.
- Avoid making introverted statements like 'We have . . .' Involve the customer and make what you say beneficial: 'You can have. . . .'.
- 'Humanize' the advertising by portraying one or more people. Advertising and media research over the years has proven conclusively that a voice or picture of a person draws the attention of the listener, viewer or reader more effectively than objects or just words.

TV recommendations

In these days of high costs, it is mainly the large hotel chains who can afford to use TV advertising. When it is used, they make sure that it works by following these principles:

- Too many commercials attempt to be mini feature films. Have one central core of action.
- Avoid telling stories to make a point. An entertaining commercial entertains, but frequently the audience forgets the message. Often people remember the commercial but cannot say whose commercial it was.
- What is seen and heard must work together. No-one can read one thing while watching something else.
- Utilize music which sets a mood. Music is one of the greatest communicators and sets a scene quickly.
- Be original and believable. Be informative and interesting.
- Casting is critical in a TV commercial. The target market must be able to identify with the people portrayed. People will see themselves as they would like to be, not how they are.
- It is moving, colour pictures you have at your disposal, and they are strong communicators. Use them to send the message. Words are used to reinforce what people see.
- Maintain the action but avoid visual clutter. Do not cram the time available with too many scenes.

Radio creative rules

- Do not raise the volume because it is a commercial. It annoys listeners. Radio is an intimate medium.

- Use the theatre of the mind. Listeners imagine what they cannot see, and it is often more impressive than reality.
- Do not cram the time available with words. It is not a word race and you will get less value for your money, not more. Allow no more than fifty words for every thirty seconds.
- Construct the commercial like a melody, with a beginning, a middle development and a recapitulated close. Make a statement about the benefits, explain the facts, repeat the statement.
- Make one point per commercial stand out.
- Set the mood with music. A few bars of evocative music carefully chosen can transport the listener to anywhere in the world, or even deep into space! The same applies to sound effects.
- Radio responds well to humour, as long as the joke does not overwhelm the message.

Print media creative rules

- Always use an illustration. Most people are picture thinkers.
- Have a person or people in the picture.
- The headline must support the picture. They work together.
- Use the headline to present your basic message.
- Do not puzzle the reader with the picture or the headline. 'Clever' adverts mostly fail.
- Restrict the headline to fewer than seventeen words.
- Use a typeface that is big enough to read and easy to read. Serif faces are best. Never use less than 10 point type for copy. People over 40 have trouble reading small print.
- Do not put type on an angle to make people turn their heads to read it. They will not.
- Avoid 'widows' – a word which is turned over to the next line and sits there on its own. One thought one line is the rule. Readability is essential.
- Do not use white type on black (reverse) background except for special-effect headings. It is difficult for some people to read.
- Keep the advert clean and open with white space.
- 'All display – no display' is the old rule of layout. Do not try to attract the readers' attention to everything.
- Lead the reader through the advert from top to bottom, just like reading a book.
- Maintain one typestyle throughout. Adopt a typeface which becomes part of the advertising's corporate 'look'.
- Use enough copy to make your point. When readers are interested they want information. There is a silly belief that people do not read long copy. Disinterested people will not. Interested people do.
- Do not stint on the size of the advert. The smaller the advert the less chance it has of being read. There is an exception – when you are really interested in finding something.

About advertising agencies

Most large establishments employ advertising agencies whose task is to plan the media, create the advertising, produce it and place it in the media. Some agencies offer additional services, such as marketing planning, public relations, brochure preparation, print and design work. They generally retain a commission from the media (usually 10 per cent) in which the advertising is placed and add a service fee of around 7.5 per cent. Others work on a flat fee for services.

Creativity is the main benefit derived from having an agency. Equally as important is the ability of the agency to interpret the brief and choose the best media to effectively present the message. Do not let them run away with creative flamboyance. Pull them back to the brief and quote the rules mentioned before.

Marketing is the client's responsibility. The client should set the communication goals and give the agency the task of achieving those goals. The communication goals should have measurable criteria so that the work of the agency can be measured.

Points to use when checking an agency's work

- Is the advert according to the brief?
- Is the advert aimed at the right target markets?
- Will the media reach the target market?
- Does the advert 'talk' to the target market?
- Is the message clear and simply stated? Is it easy to understand?
- Is it offensive in any way?
- Does it achieve cut-through?
- Does it achieve attention, interest, desire, conviction?
- Does it call for some action by the respondent, and is that action obviously stated?
- Is the establishment positioned correctly by the advert?
- How will the target market react to the consumer action proposition?
- Will it achieve the communication objectives?
- Will the costs of producing the advertising be excessive and reduce the number of media exposures as a consequence? As a rule of thumb measure, product costs should not be more than around 10 to 15 per cent of the amount spent on media exposure.

Choosing an agency

- Do not call for creative submissions. Look at the work they have done for other clients. Ask other clients for a reference. Check with the media. The majority of clients report that the exciting creative submissions by agencies are seldom backed up by good service and a long-term understanding of their requirements.

- Choose people to whom you can relate.
- Do not be bemused by hyperbole.
- The biggest are not necessarily the best.

Examples and comments

Here are a number of advertisements chosen at random from colour magazines to illustrate some of the points made in the print creative rules. On the whole, the adverts are good; therefore criticisms merely serve as guidelines for learning purposes.

- The illustration of the Beijing Palace Hotel is creative as well as intriguing. Then there is disappointment. The follow-through is both a headline and copy about 'sophistication' and 'exquisite serenity'. And it does not send any message about the place or what one can have there.
- The Four Seasons Hotel advert is not bad, but it is one of many examples around the world of advertising that makes a point in a clever way. So clever at times that no-one knows what they mean.
- The Sheraton Towers advertising campaign is a series of elegant advertisements which promote the chain as well as individual properties. There is a benefit in each advert treated with subtlety. Good positioning is achieved too.
- The Inter-Continental Hotels advertising approach cleverly emphasizes the uniqueness of each of their properties at international locations, while reinforcing brand identity. The adverts are well themed and introduce their range of products.
- Raffles is positioned by its history and 'the mythology of this Grand Old Dame of the East'. There are benefits for readers who like romance, gin slings and sleeping with ghosts. The creative approach, an old-fashioned layout and typestyle, focuses on the establishment's SCA. A good message convincingly communicated.
- Someone could have tried harder with the illustration for the Singapore Meridien; it would not be very appealing to many people. The headline 'Uncompromising service' does not mean much either. It is, after all, what one expects at a hotel.

Questions for discussion or revision

1 List seven basic creative rules for advertising.
2 Imagine you have employed an advertising agency to build awareness of your hotel. The agency puts forward some press advertisements for you to consider. What criteria would you use to evaluate their creativity and potential effectiveness?
3 Explain how an advertising agency is remunerated.

Figure 27.1 *The Palace Hotel*

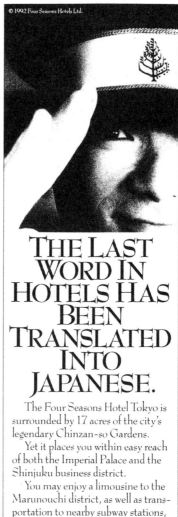

Figure 27.2   *The Four Seasons Hotel*

The Individual

One of the greatest pleasures in life is simply to be treated as an individual. To speak and be heard. To ask and be helped.

That's why we created Sheraton Towers. To offer you what you want, when you want it.

Like much of life, it's just that simple and just that difficult. But we like the challenge. Because meeting it makes life that much more satisfying for all of us.

Sheraton Towers

WHERE SERVICE IS ANYTHING
YOU WANT IT TO BE

FOR BOOKINGS WORLDWIDE, CALL SHERATON RESERVATIONS (008) 07 3535 OR YOUR TRAVEL AGENT

AUCKLAND • BANGKOK • BRISBANE • HONG KONG • MELBOURNE • NEW DELHI • SEOUL • SINGAPORE

ITT SHERATON

SPH 1067 C

Figure 27.3 *The Sheraton Towers (1)*

The Timing

Long before you arrive, we'll be expecting you. We'll know your flight or your car or your footsteps and we'll welcome you at the door.

From the door, we'll take you directly to your room. For if we know one thing, it's that we'll both be truly comfortable only when you're in your room and you've been introduced to your personal butler.

Then it's time for us both to relax . . . and let him, or her, take care of everything.

Sheraton Towers

WHERE SERVICE IS ANYTHING
YOU WANT IT TO BE

FOR BOOKINGS WORLDWIDE CALL SHERATON RESERVATIONS (0081) 07 3535 OR YOUR TRAVEL AGENT

AUCKLAND • BANGKOK • BRISBANE • HONG KONG • MELBOURNE • NEW DELHI • SEOUL • SINGAPORE

ITT SHERATON

SPH 1057 T

Figure 27.4 *The Sheraton Towers (2)*

Individually
Distinguished.

Uniquely
Inter·Continental.

To fully appreciate the world, one must honour its differences. The subtleties of its peoples and places, its cultures and customs. Inter-Continental Hotels does just that. With historic landmark hotels that are as much a part of a city's present as its glorious past. With striking, contemporary hotels that are reflections of the vibrant cultures they represent. And with luxurious resorts that are both a tribute and an attribute to the natural beauty surrounding them. On six continents, in 53 countries and more than 100 cities, all of our hotels share this intrinsic value. And each is uniquely Inter-Continental.

For reservations and information, call the Inter-Continental Hotel nearest you.

INTER·CONTINENTAL HOTELS

Europe • The Americas • Pacific Asia • The Middle East • Africa

Figure 27.5 *Inter-Continental Hotels (1)*

Distinctively Washington.

Uniquely Inter·Continental.

Washington, D.C. is the heartbeat and the pulse of a great nation. The capital of the United States and the home of the powerful and the celebrated. And in the heart of it all, amidst its monuments to presidents past and two blocks from the home of the current president, stands the Willard Inter-Continental. Here, in this meticulously restored landmark, 150 years of American heritage have been brought to life with contemporary comfort and style. From the moment you enter the lobby, you know you have entered a world synonymous with distinguished guests, important events and glittering galas. The Willard is, indeed, a reflection of the nation's capital.

For reservations, contact your travel agent or call (202) 628-9100, toll-free 800-327-0200.

WILLARD
INTER·CONTINENTAL
WASHINGTON

Other locations in North America: Chicago • Los Angeles • Maui • Miami • Montreal • New Orleans • New York • San Francisco • Toronto
And over 125 hotels throughout Europe, Latin America, The Middle East, Africa and Pacific Asia.
Global Partner hotels: Atlanta • Boston • Cambridge • Dallas • Ft. Myers • Garden City • Palm Beach County • Pebble Beach • Redondo Beach • Seattle

Figure 27.6 *Inter-Continental Hotels (2)*

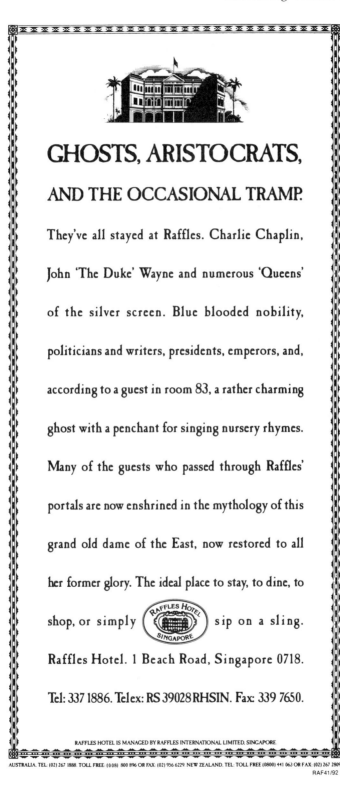

Figure 27.7 *Raffles Hotel*

Uncompromising service.
One of our finest ingredients.

You'll find something infinitely welcoming about Le Méridien Singapore, at 100 Orchard Road.

Maybe it's because we've recently refurbished our hotel rooms. Maybe it's because we're right at the heart of the shopping, business and nightlife downtown.

Maybe it's because our staff strive to be just that little bit more attentive. Creating a perfect blend of local efficiency and charm with more than a hint of typical French flair.

Or perhaps it's because we've all the business and leisure facilities anyone could ask for (including a fully equipped business centre and overnight pressing service).

Then again, could it simply be that our cuisine in the renowned Restaurant de France is simply superb? Of course, you may never be able to truly define what makes our *savoir faire* so different from other hotels.

But you'll enjoy yourself trying to find out.

For more details about Le Méridien Singapore, please contact Méridien Sales Office in Sydney, at telephone (61-2) 235-1311, (008) 221-307 (toll free), or fax (61-2) 223-1351.

Le
MERIDIEN
SINGAPORE
Travel Companion of Air France

Melbourne. Jakarta. Singapore Changi. Bangkok. Phuket. The Golden Triangle. Colombo. New Delhi. Tokyo.

Figure 27.8 *Le Meridien, Singapore*

28 Advertising: media and budgets

Aim of this chapter

To explain how to select the most appropriate advertising media for promoting a property and how to budget for the advertising campaigns.

The theory

Promoting an establishment can be one of the most expensive parts of running a business. There is no doubt that promotion, using a mix of message delivery systems, is essential to assist in the development of a customer base and retain existing patrons.

Before money is spent, each campaign has to be carefully assessed for its ability to contribute to sales and profit. Promotion is goal-driven; therefore the sales objectives, the markets to be targeted and the time frame have to be compared against the costs of communication. Large hotels, for example, even though they are mainly targeting travellers for accommodation, must still consider promotions for the local market. The local market is the major user of food and beverage products, for instance. In addition, local people are an important source of recommendations for visitors.

These days there is some doubt about the value obtained from large-scale mass media advertising as a primary means of securing new business because of its high cost and low efficiency. Mass media advertising is more often used in a supporting role for sales promotions. The questions that have to be answered before proceeding with an advertising campaign concern the selling load that has to be carried by advertising. Is it:

- as a support role for a sales promotion?
- the sole communication vehicle to promote a product?
- to position the hotel by creating an image that sets the stage for other selling activities in the tactical mix?

How much should be spent compared with the anticipated sales return may be difficult to calculate accurately in the case of the third option because there is no way of knowing how much advertising contributed to the securing of a customer. A person or a corporation may have been influenced to come to the property by information obtained from several sources: a referral from a satisfied friend or business acquaintance; a travel agent; a sales presentation; a price promotion; or from simply passing by the property.

Much advertising to which people are exposed merely establishes a favourable impression of the property, or provides name memorability. Asking respondents questions like: 'Did you decide to come to us after seeing our advertisement?' seldom provide a true indication of advertising effectiveness because most people do not like to admit that they have been influenced by advertising. Indeed, they may be unaware of whether they were influenced by advertising or not.

The effectiveness of the contribution made by image or positioning advertising can only be measured by research which reveals how many people are: a) aware of the establishment; b) know where it is; c) recall its chief attributes; or d) hold favourable attitudes towards it. When research is conducted every six months, it is possible to identify a change in people's awareness and attitude, and it may then be concluded that advertising contributed towards the change. With direct response advertising, the ensuing sales can be attributed more accurately to the part played by advertising.

Budgeting

There are three basic budgeting approaches which can be used to estimate the amount to be spent on advertising when preparing a realistic budget:

The retail approach (how much can the property justify spending?)

- Allocate an amount of money for each anticipated sale.
- Estimate the number of sales, then multiply the estimated number of sales by the amount allocated to each sale to arrive at the budget.

The market approach (how much does the property need to spend?)

- Fix on a market and estimate the numbers of prospects it contains.
- Forecast the likely return from advertising in money terms.
- Decide which mediums will reach the market.
- Estimate the number of times the message will have to be exposed.
- Cost the schedule according to the amount of money required to meet the communication objectives to arrive at the budget.

The corporate approach (how much can it afford to spend?)

From the establishment's anticipated gross income for the year, arrive at a budget by allocating a percentage for advertising. Divide that percentage into two parts: image or positioning advertising, and promotional support and direct response advertising campaigns to arrive at the budget. The percentage to use in this approach can be arrived at by checking the industry average. Although this is a broad, yardstick approach, it is not uncommon among all industries to do it this way, with some exceeding and others spending less than the industry average.

The large hotel chains allocate a higher percentage of their gross income to advertising because the cost burden can be shared by many properties, such as the Inter-Continental, Sheraton, Hilton and Hyatt chains, for example. Individual properties find it difficult to justify large advertising budgets, even though it can be argued that they need the exposure more. To overcome this problem, many individual properties belong to a marketing group which pools the advertising and provides an international reservations service.

General advertising principles

Here are some general advertising principles to remember before embarking on a mass media advertising campaign:

- Always try to have an offer in your advertisement. Even if the advertisement is carrying a positioning message, it will work better if the reader is given something to do or given information which enables him or her to make a decision. For example, the Uniquely Inter-Continental advertisements suggest the reader calls to discuss holding a business function and be sent a copy of the Global Meeting Portfolio.
- The message of the advertisement must be clear and has to be the most interesting and compelling purchase reason for people to consider. The Sheraton Towers advert, for example, offers people a convincing promise about the types of experiences they can expect.
- Have a distinctive style to every advertisement. So many adverts for hotels look the same. The Sheraton Towers advert provides an example of an individual style which separates them from other property advertising.
- Good advertising is noticed, but good messages are remembered! The content, the offer, the reason for being considered will usually override poor layout or small size. The Raffles advert has a good message for those interested in romance and history.
- Give advertising time to work. It takes time for a message to get through, especially image advertising. Therefore do not go in for large-scale advertising unless it can be sustained over a period. 'Surge and saturate' advertising – that is, two weeks on and two weeks off – has been proven to not only extend the life of a campaign but actually improve its performance in awareness and retention of the message.

- Timing. It is always best to cue advertising bursts to the seasons or times when travel is being considered. It makes sense, for instance, to tie in with special events which bring large volumes of traffic to the city.
- People will only respond if they are in the market. Advertising does not have the power to suddenly put several thousand pounds into someone's pocket so that he or she goes on a holiday any more than it can influence a business person to take a trip and do a deal simply because you want him or her to stay at your hotel.
- Do not expect miracles. There is so much noise and clutter to get through. The world is saturated with information and advertising. Restaurants in the doldrums are the chief culprits in trying to reverse poor sales by advertising, and invariably they throw good money after bad. Advertising can only support sound product strategies. It cannot change poor perceptions unless the reality is changed.
- Follow through your advertising at point of sale. It reminds people that they have seen the message elsewhere. Good packaged goods marketers use the technique of having a memory 'trigger' at point of sale, either through the label or a display card. Such companies recognize that they are still competing with other brands being displayed. In your own property your competitors are down the road, but just the same a memory 'trigger' is reassuring for the new patrons.
- Use supporting media. Two media are more effective than one because they reinforce each other. It can be two radio stations, for example, a radio station and a newspaper or a radio station and a mail drop. It is the same with recommendations. If one person tells you some place is 'great' you may be interested, but when two or three say the same thing you are convinced.
- Remember, most advertising only serves to reinforce existing knowledge, social values and habits.
- All establishments require below-the-line advertising material. This is any promotional expenditure that is not main media, such as brochures, leaflets, flyers, folders, catalogues, etc. The Americans call it collateral. In every case, media advertising and collateral must be coordinated so that it has a corporate 'look' that presents the same image or personality of the property. To be effective, collateral has to be informative and persuasive, but with the emphasis on informative. Information 'sells as it tells'. Flowery phrases and adjectival claims are puffery that do not fool anyone any more.
- Some places do not spend money on mainstream advertising, they only produce collateral material. In fact, the trend in the industry worldwide is for less to be spent on media advertising in favour of direct response marketing. Experience says it is more cost-effective, although it is limited in its reach of a broad market.
- Creating awareness and providing information is what advertising is best at doing for hospitality properties. However, it takes a lot of it to make an enduring impression. This is not said to decry advertising, but to put its use into perspective so that its true worth as a communication vehicle can be realistically assessed.

Choosing media

Advertising in mass media is more obvious to the general public than other forms of advertising, and it can work very well provided that it is selectively chosen. The most appropriate and efficient medium to use is influenced by the intention of the message, the type of message to be delivered and the market to which it is to be delivered. Here is an assessment of each of the main mass media vehicles.

Print media

Newspaper advertising refers to daily, weekly, national, local and regional newspapers. With most of the population preferring to get their news in short bites from broadcast media, newspaper circulations around the world generally are not keeping pace with population increases and in many cases are static or falling. Many afternoon newspapers are closing down, while morning newspapers with large classified sections are surviving because they continue to satisfy a need for certain types of information such as a summary and commentary on events for the serious-minded, a guide to financial markets, share trading, births, deaths, marriages, weather, shopping, sporting events, etc. Crosswords, brain teasers, cartoons and public services information also help to sustain circulations.

With this preferred reader-use of newspapers in mind, hospitality advertising objectives would be better served by using newspapers for retail-type announcements and customer information rather than the long-term intentions of image building. If the advertising does not contain news and an offer, it probably will not be suitable in most cases for placement in a newspaper.

Magazine advertising as a category includes glossy publications such as women's and men's magazines business periodicals, holiday and travel magazines and special interest publications on subjects such as boating, fishing, golf, rock climbing and so on. Magazines generally represent good value for the hospitality advertiser because they are bought by people with specific interests, enabling the advertiser to reach particular markets which have high sales potential for their products. Provided the advertising refers to the market's interests it has a good chance of being noticed.

In addition, quality magazines provide a prestige environment for a hospitality establishment. Colour is virtually essential. The drawback to magazines is the long lead time required to meet most magazines' publishing deadlines. Special price offers or deals therefore have to be planned well in advance and have a long life. Magazines are expensive, but ideal for long-term positioning.

Cheap publications suggest cheap products, and should be avoided because products are judged by the company they keep.

Trade publications means those magazines or journals which are distributed primarily to the hospitality and tourism industries and associated industries such as wine, beer, provisioning, food, etc. These publications can be used to good effect to reach the important group of 'influencers', those whose opinions are sought and respected by some markets, especially the corporate sector.

Marketing messages need to be carefully handled when placed in trade publications, a medium which is often overlooked because it does not reach the general public as a rule. However, it has the benefit of being relatively inexpensive. The circulations are seldom large, but respected industry publications, such as the *Caterer and Hotelkeeper*, are widely read.

Placement of advertising in print media

With all print media, page positioning is relevant. There is no conclusive evidence that left and right pages are any better than each other. However, some pages, such as front, back and early pages, are read far more than others. It is worth paying the extra. Do not be lost among a lot of other adverts. For this reason also, as a general rule avoid industry features in newspapers or magazines. You will be one of the mob.

Broadcast media

Broadcast media refers to television and radio. They are also referred to as 'electronic' media.

Television is the most popular media for consumer products because it has all the communication advantages of sight, movement, sound and colour. It is an excellent means of building a position through imagery. However, it can also be terrifyingly expensive, and for this reason it is not favoured by the hospitality industry in general, nervous as it is about getting a return on its investment from advertising pounds.

In many Western countries, 'free-to-air' television is losing its audiences to home video, pay-TV and narrow interest cable, plus an assortment of new forms of entertainment.

The all-important corporate and professional customers and the wealthier holidaymakers are not by nature large watchers of television, and given its expense it has to be purchased with care. Selected programmes which have proven ratings against the markets being targeted is the only way to buy TV. Packages of spots which are exposed to a general market may appear cheaper, but very often most of the viewers are never likely to be prime candidates for customers at a restaurant, an expensive hotel or resort. The use of TV or radio also needs to be consistent. If a continuing schedule cannot be maintained it is unwise to consider it.

Radio can be used for image positioning, but it probably works best as a retail medium, communicating new developments, special offers and price deals. Again, run-of-station spot packages which can be aired by the station over 24 hours of transmission are not recommended unless the station chosen has a consistent audience type throughout all sessions.

Radio stations are proliferating, with AM and FM licences being handed out in many countries to almost anyone with a case. The stations to choose are those which have captured a market that suits the establishment's communication objectives. The commercials are better placed in sessions where the major proportion of the audience represents the property's target markets. Announcers and music styles, for instance, build loyal listeners of audience types.

Most people listen to radio as a background to what they are doing. They do not listen intently unless something is being discussed which is of interest. Cut-through is sought by radio advertisers. However, all too often cut-through is attempted by silly gimmicks which lose the message. The announcer who has already captured the audience is the best presenter of a message, provided that he or she does not suddenly put on a false 'selling voice' to 'sell' the commercial and turn off the audience.

Buying media

The way to evaluate one medium's cost against another is to compare their unit cost-per-impact for the same sized advertisement or length of commercial and find out how many impacts can be obtained in each medium for the same cost. Here is a simple example comparing an '9 × 7' press advertisement appearing in three different newspapers circulating in the same market:

Cost	Readership	Unit cost-per-impact	
Newspaper A	£2000	150 000 daily	.013p
Newspaper B	£2500	170 000 daily	.014p
Newspaper C	£1500	120 000 daily	.012p

On a cost-per-impact basis, Newspaper C appears to represent the best value provided that it reaches the target markets the property wants. It is false economy to buy on price alone. Media know this so they conduct research and maintain a vast amount of statistical data to help advertisers make their choice of medium. Care has to be taken when analysing statistics, though, because they can be used by a medium to prove almost anything.

Television and radio stations use a ratings formula to assist buyers in their choice. Television sets which are switched on at any given hour of the day are called 'sets-in-use' and expressed as a percentage of all homes with TV sets. Thus, in a city with 500 000 homes with TV sets, 50 per cent sets-in-use means that 250 000 homes are watching TV at a particular time.

A rating is a percentage of TV sets which are switched on to a particular station and programme. Thus a programme which has attracted 22 per cent of all homes with TV sets has a rating of 22. When television commercials are purchased in several programmes, the percentage ratings obtained each time are added together into GRPs (Gross Rating Points) as a means of determining the total 'reach' of the commercials.

Ratings can also be measured by target audience segments, such as 'men aged 18 to 39'. These are called TARPs (Target Audience Rating Points). Costs-per-impact of each station can be compared by using either GRPS or TARPs, TARPs being the better means of comparison because the advertiser normally has an interest in reaching a defined audience.

Radio stations use a similar rating formula, but also employ the term

'CUMES', meaning the number of listeners which have been 'accumulated' every quarter of an hour in the same session.

Miscellaneous media

Catalogue, directory and diary advertising can be good value because such media contain information such as where to stay or dine, which is sought by the readers. Some of them have a long life and will be around for years. Therefore make sure that the message will last for years.

Outdoor advertising, the oldest of all media, remains one of the most effective. Visibility is the key. Outdoor advertising is excellent for creating awareness and acting as a brand name reminder. There is a broad range of outlets which can be classified as outdoor advertising.

The key is simplicity and impact. The message has to be shortened to the number of words that can be read and absorbed in two or three seconds, essentially no more than ten words at the most. Pictures therefore have to carry the main impact load.

The first sites to consider should be the property's building itself and its vehicles. They are obviously cheap sites, apart from the cost of creating and producing the signs or displays used. However, for aesthetic reasons, the temptation to splatter signs and posters all over a building has to be resisted. In any case, most councils restrict the use of signs to prevent visual pollution.

All forms of public transport should be considered for advertising for their relatively low cost and high visibility. They are noticed more if the creative approach makes good use of the area hired.

For properties wanting to reach inward-bound customers, consider the purchase of carefully located sites on major roads, near airports, large sporting venues and conference and exhibition centres. Many people who have not made bookings will be influenced by these signs, and even those who have already made their decision will have their decision reaffirmed.

The clue to the use of outdoor advertising is to change the posters and displays regularly. Do not let them get stale. Outdoor advertising works best on initial impact and subsequent sightings for about a month. By the time most people who have passed by have seen them several times, they lose impact and become part of the scenery.

Point-of-interest advertising

It is becoming apparent to many advertisers that 'point-of-interest' advertising is the most effective in achieving high awareness and interest in the message. When people are at a place or doing something connected with the advertiser's interest they are more susceptible to receiving allied messages. Thus airlines, airports, restaurants, buses, trains, bars, travel agencies, fashion dress shops – wherever people are in a spending or recreational mood, it is easier to divert them into considering like interests of places to go and stay. The people who go to such places are generally the types the hospitality industry wants as customers. This point-of-interest approach is particularly true of theme resorts and hotels. A place which has a golf course, for example, would be advised to expose its messages wherever golfers are likely to be – pro shops, other golf courses, golfing publications, golfing programmes, etc.

Similarly, there are many opportunities on the property for conveying important items of promotional information to existing and potential customers at the points and moments of greatest interest. Good examples are tent cards on counters, brochures on restaurant tables, in the guests' rooms and in the bars. Also consider signs, information boards and displays in foyers. Strategically placed window displays, especially if you can tie in with a retail promotion, represent good value at relatively low cost.

Questions for discussion or revision

1 Before you spend money on advertising you need a budget. What are two of the procedures you would use in its preparation?
2 Explain what 'surge and saturate' means when buying media.
3 What do the terms GRPs and TARPs mean?

29 *Sales promotion and publicity strategies*

Aim of this chapter

To explain the purpose of sales promotions, the staging of promotional events and how they can be effective in generating sales.

The theory

Sales promotions are special selling efforts for boosting sales or introducing new products. They are usually short-term projects. While they can be repeated at a later date, they can seldom be extended for long. Promotions should be thought of as a means of providing immediate reasons for customers to use the establishment's services. In this instance, we are talking about promotion events rather than sales drives such as discounted packages, club membership and special deals which are covered in previous chapters.

Surveys of customers reveal that one of the main reasons for people to use an establishment's facilities is for 'special occasions'. Special occasions also mean special reasons. Instead of waiting for the customers to find a reason for coming to the place, promotions offer the reasons. For well-marketed hotels, promotions have become a way of life.

The benefits of sales promotions

- *They address specific needs and opportunities.* Promotions can fill low-occupancy periods by attracting guests who may have had no intention of staying or eating at the property. If a property is having an awareness problem, a sales promotion can draw attention to it and renew interest in the property. Staging an international cookery competition which attracts media attention and public interest is one type of promotion that can be considered.

    There are thousands of ideas for promotion that can be copied or originated. One does not have to wait for some event to happen. Most promotion concepts are generated by the property. The intention always is to solve a business problem or exploit a market opportunity by bringing together a number of unrelated elements by the use of a central theme. The more outside business people can be involved the better because it spreads the interest and often spreads the costs.

- *They establish relationships with customers and the public.* Strong promotions can indicate to the public that the property is a 'good citizen' by organizing events which involve the physical and cultural environment of the city. They also enable the management to come into contact with executives and public figures at a personal level. Most of all, promotions stimulate existing customers and bring them closer to the property and its staff.
- *They appeal to basic human motivations.* Promotions often have a cost advantage for customers, and this in itself is appealing. More importantly, the public loves being involved in a special occasion which offers excitement, interest or a chance to be part of a 'happening'.
- *They involve people who may not otherwise be customers.* Regular customers can be targeted for promotions as a means of bringing in others. Promotions do not always have to make money for the property. Whereas the intention is not to make a loss, a promotion which brings in new customers who become regular patrons has been successful.
- *They generate word-of-mouth advertising.* People talk about good promotions. They can also create media interest and coverage. Essential to a property's future is its ability to keep expanding the customer base, and the best way to do this is to have many, many people passing on the good times they have had at the place.
- *They can show the place in a different light.* Attention can be focused on products and facilities that people do not know much about or about which they have a misguided concept – a promotion around a themed bar, for example, or a function room that many customers did not know existed. The whole property can be given a lift by good promotion which helps to re-position it in people's minds.
- *They can solve weekly and seasonal down periods.* Nearly every property has trouble filling at weekends. The time-honoured solution is to run special weekend packages and 'theme' weekends involving special events or staged attractions such as murder mystery, music, personalities, games, food and wine fairs, national celebrations.
- *Prices can be submerged into add-on value products.* Most promotions involve a package of events or situations which are offered at an attractive all-inclusive price representing good value for the participants. For those properties, conscious of their image, and not wanting to appear to be discounting their room rates, promotions are ideal.
- *They raise staff morale.* Properties which are seen as being promotion-minded find it easier to attract good, talented staff because it is more fun to work there.

Promotions can be used to tie in with:

- visiting celebrities
- seasons

- festivals
- exhibitions
- trade shows and demonstrations
- historic occasions
- national events and calendar days
- international events and celebrations
- food and wine events
- sporting carnivals
- holidays and holiday packages
- openings
- parties
- training programmes
- value for money packages.

Promotions offer an ideal opportunity for joint promotions with other businesses. Used this way, they can spread the promotional pound further – a special travel package involving an airline, casino, bus or coach company, a distillery and shops, for example. Everyone contributes financially to the staging costs, including the advertising. Moreover, each plays a part in using its own customer base to make it a success. Merchandise can also be sold with promotions, thereby providing additional opportunities for profit.

Sales promotions add fun, excitement and value to the establishment. They offer something special, over and above what normally happens.

Promotions are for people

Michael Hurst advises everyone in the business to run promotions because they are vital in gaining and keeping customers and for giving people something to talk about. 'The challenge is in coming up with interesting things that make your place distinctive, unusual and exciting.' 'The object is not to sell, but to fill the place with people,' says Hurst. 'Generating word-of-mouth advertising.' 'People are looking for a social experience,' he says. 'They don't go to a bar because they are thirsty, but because people are in the bar. Promotions are for people, not profit. At a more elevated level, we have beer tasting. Imported beer, that is. We keep fifteen imported beers in stock. We say to the customers, "Taste a little of this, a little of that. Tell me your opinion. Vote on what imported beers you like and which ones you want." Get the idea? Taste testing. Involvement. Conversation pieces. Word-of-mouth advertising.'

One of Hurst's favourite promotions was a Halloween party. It proved to be the best costume party of all time because he had people come in pyjamas. It took three years to build up, but by the third year it was a sell-out.

He brought in the Oklahoma Marching Band to a tent party and it caused a sensation. He had elephants attend a New Year's Eve party. They arrived unannounced, and people were saying, 'Do you know what's over in the corner? Mary, you've just been seeing pink elephants!' He has staged 'cocktails from the sky', chicken flying contests, you name it and he has done it. As he says: 'The possibilities are endless. Stage a happening. Give people something to talk about.'

Marketing promotions

Objectives for promotions must be set so that it is clearly established what is required of the promotion in monetary terms, numbers of customers and the customers' reactions to the propositions. Remember, promotions are for people, not for profit. Be greedy and you will ruin the event. There are three basic types of promotions:

1 *Price* promotions, which give people some extra value.
2 *Party* promotions, which offer people an exciting different experience of the same property or one of its products.
3 *New product* promotions, which introduce people to something completely new and different.

It is even better when all three are combined.

All promotions must contain an offer of some type, either a price advantage, some special value not normally available and essentially a sense of excitement. Promotions need to be targeted at specific groups, and these are usually the people who best suit the place's customer mix. For example, where an establishment finds that it is not gaining enough customers from a desired market, promotions can be devised to attract them. However, do not aim at customers who will only come for the promotion because of the value that is being offered. They are unlikely to return. Aim at those whom you believe you can keep as clients and help to build the customer base.

When new people are pulled in by a promotion, get their names and add them to your mailing list. As one of the aims of every promotion is to gather new customers, find a reason for the customers to give you their names and addresses, either by a competition, raffle or a small giveaway which has to be posted to them.

Care is necessary to make sure that the promotions are within the establishment's resources, both human and physical. Nothing will be gained by an event which overwhelms the place and leaves many patrons disgruntled because they could not get in, were not served properly or missed out because some of the benefits they came for could not be provided.

The staff must enter into the spirit of the promotion. There is nothing worse than a badly run promotion without 'fizz'; it ruins a hard-won reputation. Therefore never stint on the budget and the preparations.

Promoting sales promotions

Ascertaining the target market is just as important for promotions as it is for any other tactical effort by the property because the knowledge helps to refine the message delivery systems to be used.

Here are some message vehicles to be considered:

- Direct mail to potential customers.
- Send leaflets to everyone who attends the place from six weeks to a month beforehand.

- Tell the regular customers in person if possible.
- Advertise in selected media which reach large numbers of the target market.
- Involve media and get publicity.
- Network through organizations which are connected with the promotion and use their customer database.
- Use the property's outlets for cards, signs, posters, window displays and notices to spread the word.

Use enticements

A promotion is a special event, and it should offer value not normally attainable for it to work well. To add to the attraction of a promotion, offers and enticements are nearly always necessary in some form, as follows:

- Redeemable vouchers handed out liberally to customers and outsiders, perhaps posted to prospective customers, is one way of getting a reasonably sure return. Coupons in advertisements is another way.
- Gifts and give-aways are hard to refuse, especially when people know that they can get them free as well as the benefits of the promotion. Reduced price merchandise is in the same category. The world is full of bargain-hunters.
- Raffles and prizes are probably over-worked because everyone does it, but they will always appeal. So will quizzes and contests.
- Value-added products and bonus packages included with the price of the promotion are excellent enticements. A promotion combined with a casino, for example, with chips to the value of £50, plus champagne and a free meal, could be part of a 'wild gambling spree weekend' promotion that 'will cost nothing to get started'.
- Free samples are the most neglected but easily one of the best means of enticing new customers or for selling something new to existing customers. A cultural event, such as a small orchestra or dance night with a special band, can be enhanced as a proposition if the customers either get a sample CD or tape beforehand or the offer of a free one on the night.
- The opening of a new accommodation wing can be promoted by giving away free bed-night samples to selected corporate customers. Another way is to hold a function with a lucky draw for the rooms plus consolation prizes for the unlucky ones so that no-one goes away empty-handed.

Publicity and public relations

An organization which is as publicly exposed as a hotel depends heavily upon its reputation and the goodwill of the many publics that can affect its future viability. Public relations is about the management of public attitudes, or the attitudes of those publics which are important to an organization. In other words, mostly the customers and future customers, but also political, business, financial and hospitality trade publics. Therefore the function of public relations can embrace all marketing functions because public relations is concerned with image and positioning.

In a hospitality establishment, the role of a public relations person is often more concerned with using sales promotions to gain media exposure. As a consequence, the two roles are often combined, and it can fall on the shoulders of the PR person to do much of the organizing of a promotion. The name of the position does not always reflect the function that the incumbent has to perform.

Every establishment likes to get some favourable and free exposure to the media. Promotions provide this opportunity in many instances, especially when the promotion is newsworthy. And this is the clue to obtaining free mention in media, i.e. making news. Gearing a promotion which gets publicity has a twofold advantage: it achieves the objectives of communicating the occasion to a broad audience; and gives the promotion added impetus and stature.

As well as gaining public mention through its own promotions, a hotel can also get a mention by having someone else's event staged at the establishment. It can be worthwhile in these instances to offer a special deal and win the business just to achieve the media mention. Internationally acclaimed visitors and entertainers are chased by media, and an astute PR person can capitalize on this, sometimes by merely arranging for TV cameras to include the hotel's name in the background.

Summary

Promotions can be business saviours. The sequence of steps to follow are:

- Set the customer and product objectives.
- Fix on a sales target and prepare a budget.
- Get the idea right.
- Sell the staff.
- Organize it down to the last detail.
- Promote it.
- Turn it on and make it happen.
- Do it again next year if it works really well.

The risk with sales promotions is the tendency to extend them indefinitely, particularly if they are successful. It is a bit like repeating a joke many times over. There is also the possibility that customers will think that a product is not good enough to be purchased on its own merits and that some form of inducement has to be offered to compensate. However, this usually only applies with a property which has to continually resort to hype to survive, a bit like a run-down second-hand car business which has a sale every week. It does not apply to a property with a strong position.

Questions for discussion or revision

1 Explain the difference between public relations, publicity and sales promotion.
2 Name five of the inducements you would consider for a sales promotion to increase the trade of a property's American theme cocktail bar.
3 If you were the manager of a 200-seat restaurant and decided to mount a sales promotion campaign to increase customer sales, with whom would you communicate and how would you send them a message about your promotion?

Further reading

Buttle, F. (1994). *Hotel and Food Service Marketing*. London: Holt, Rinehart & Winston.

30 *Direct marketing strategies*

Aim of this chapter

To outline the main direct mail marketing techniques used in promotions and to describe how they can be used effectively to build and maintain a customer base.

The theory

Direct marketing for hospitality establishments means marketing directly to existing and prospective customers either through the mail or by personal representation and customer contact. Direct marketing has become an important source of business for hospitality establishments, especially as the cost of advertising increases. Some places exist solely by this means of promotion. This chapter concentrates on direct mail, sending letters with various enclosures, such as brochures, samples, incentives, reply-paid cards, invitations, etc., to sell a property's outlets, products and facilities.

There are many advantages to direct mail. One is that it can reduce selling, advertising and distribution costs and so reduces many traditional marketing expenses. However, it incurs new costs in the production of mailing material and postage. In addition, essential to its success is the creation and maintenance of a database of customers, which takes time and money to develop. So direct mail does not necessarily represent a cheap alternative.

The simplest letter, when the costs of labour, paper, envelope and postage are added together, is far more expensive per impact (people reached) than media advertising, which can be less than a penny per impact. When enclosures such as multi-coloured brochures are added, plus reply-paid envelopes, cards, vouchers, menus and even samples of products, the mailing costs can soar to several pounds per impact. Each mailing impact therefore must count, and to be effective and cost-efficient it needs to be personal.

Unlike advertising which, although it may have a defined target market, reaches unknown and unnamed people, direct mail has to be mailed to someone, identified by occupation at least, with an address for the post office to deliver it. When it is used in an impersonal, general way, like sending a large number of letters to companies or homes simply addressed 'to The Manager' or 'The Householder', it ceases to have much advantage over advertising. It is also doubtful whether, without a person's name, direct mail has any advantage by being a letter. A general communication in an envelope with a continuous adhesive label has only a marginally better chance of being read than an advert.

Some markets consider a letter to have an advantage over print media because they can send 'kits' of collateral material, but most print media will allow enclosures in their newspapers or magazines, and often the costs of insertion or 'stuffing' are comparable with postage costs. It is just that mass media reaches a large audience, many of whom are of no interest or value to a hospitality establishment.

So direct mail's main advantage is its ability to deliver a personalized message to people known by their name and address, with the effectiveness of the communications being considerably increased when details of the receivers' relevance to the sender are known. Therefore the more that is known about the customer the more personal the letter and its contents can become and the more direct and effective is the market.

Mailing lists (which become databases when put into the computer) usually originate from the establishment's own records, together with lists of people obtained from outside sources. There are brokers who sell lists of names, and some organizations will sell or exchange their customer lists.

Database marketing is a buzz word at the moment. It simply means maintaining a list of people on computer files. To have value, databases need to be constantly updated with information about customers' purchases and any other facts relevant to their habits and preferences that can be used to influence a sale. The benefits from having customer information stored in a computer are that it can be easily cross-indexed to cluster and highlight various customer combinations by demographics, psychographics, buying behaviour and purchase histories. By having accessible, historical information on file, an establishment can choose the most likely customers to mail with information about an offer or impending event. In addition, because direct mail works best as a personalized message delivery system, a good database provides customized information enabling the writer to refer to that person's interests.

The reasons for using direct mail

The reason why most establishments use direct mail is to inform people about special offers, value-added packages, sales promotions, forthcoming events and new developments. They choose the people to whom they mail by their status. Status refers to their being either a regular customer, an infrequent customer, a new customer, an old customer who has not used any of the facilities for a while or a potential customer.

The intention of the message may be different in each case. It can be employed to attract new customers, maintain contact with existing customers and perhaps sell them more facilities or get them to use the facilities more often.

It can also be applied to bring back customers who may have drifted away. However, working through existing customers to keep them, and hopefully to get them to bring in others, is often the most rewarding use of direct mail.

Direct mail is a more controlled diffusion of messages than advertising, and the message will not conflict with whatever the competition is saying. You have the recipients' undivided attention provided that you match the message with their interests. Remember, each category of customer has varied reasons for considering a property's facilities. The classic mistake is to send the same mailing piece to everyone and not distinguish between types of customers. People are not think-alikes. They usually seek benefits associated with their occupations, age/stage in life and their desired lifestyles. Even if the offer is the same, it should be customized to suit the situation of the recipient.

There is also the added advantage of direct mail not being inhibited by space or time. A mailing piece can range from being a parcel of promotion materials, including gifts and novelties, down to a single sheet of paper. Anything that will go through the mail (or be delivered by courier) is possible. There is therefore considerable scope for ingenuity and creativity.

The main uses of direct mail

- *As an adjunct to an existing marketing plan*. The combination of advertising, direct mail and sales calls is a very effective strategy to employ when making a push for new customers, and one of the truisms of marketing is like the cat said in *Alice in Wonderland*: 'Anything I say three times is true!'
- *To sell new products*. Direct mail works well when a new outlet has been created, a new menu introduced, or some important changes have been made which are newsworthy. News is interesting. It is far better if an offer is made around the new item to encourage the recipients to respond in some way.
- *To sell promotions*. Similarly, for inviting customers to become involved in a sales promotion, a letter which details the features and the benefits often works better than advertising.
- *To maintain confidentiality*. Some new products and sales promotions apply only to selected people, and a mailing can do that. In addition, sometimes a property may not want to telegraph its intentions to competing establishments.
- *To reduce old stocks*. Some establishments find themselves over-stocked from time to time, with wines for instance. Limited offers on a 'privileged customer' basis can not only shift these items but develop a loyalty to the establishment.
- *To generate new customers*. This is the most common use of direct mail.
- *To retain customers*. Keeping in touch with regular clients is one of the best reasons for using direct mail. They are the chief assets of the business and have to be treasured.
- *To reactivate old or lost customers*. A friendly overture with an interesting offer from the property can work wonders with people who have drifted away over a period of time.

- *To up-grade some existing customers*. This is a common technique of banks, credit providers and retail stores. For a hospitality establishment, up-grading entails offering customers a series of special privileges not available to most people and may include a club membership, extended credit and access to certain 'private' facilities.

The newsletter or house magazine

Newsletters and house magazines are really in a category of their own. Their intention is to build rapport with customers by keeping them informed of the property's people, its products, new developments and news about its performance as a hospitality establishment such as promotions, awards, happenings and visits by famous personalities.

Newsletters and house magazines have to contain news and items of interest to the receivers, otherwise they will work no better than a brochure. When they are publicity organs full of self-interest publicity and sales messages, they will end up in a place where all indulgent mailing pieces go – in the waste-paper bin.

Everyone is interested in news, pictures and people. Long, boring pages of type will not enjoy readership. Some of the best examples of house magazines are often published by airlines. Whereas this type of material is beyond the budgets of most properties, even a four-page, photocopied black and white leaflet with several pictures can be very effective.

The intention of newsletters and house publications is to assume friendship, to involve the customers and give them a sense of belonging to the establishment. They work well, especially when used in conjunction with enclosures about special offers or appealing new developments.

Building a database

Direct mail is a dynamic marketing tool when used properly. When it is employed merely as a broadcast medium it becomes an expensive communication with dubious sales value. Having a sound list of customers and prospects is the clue to effective direct mailing.

When selecting a mailing list of potential customers, the rules of targeting apply. Search for people who match the desired customer mix. As the database grows, there will be a need to constantly update the list from guest records. The term 'merge/purge' used in direct mail refers to merging one list with another and purging, or getting rid of names that are not responding, do not apply any more, or are duplicated.

A good database is programmed for correlations which are cross-indexed into categories that sort people by their demographic, psychographic, buying recency, frequency, product type and size of purchase. The source and date of names on the list should also be noted on the files, for instance sales records by outlet, mail, passing by, referral, advertising, promotion, etc., so that their relevance and recency can be checked.

New lists of prospects can be obtained by searching company shareholders' records, club memberships, various government registrations, electoral rolls, etc. But the best source of leads often comes from existing customers, and some organizations offer them incentives for recommending names. A low-cost source of names can be achieved by exchanging lists with other businesses associated with hospitality.

When buying or exchanging lists, evaluate their worth by using the 'recency/frequency/money spent' test. That means a check on how recently the people purchased, how often they have purchased and how much they spent each time. Make sure that they are active lists and avoid old lists. After two years most lists are worthless. The best ones are those compiled in-house from one's own customers.

Make an offer

Obviously direct mail works best when there is a specific offer. A mailing which does no more than inform the recipient is impossible to measure in terms of effect. Whereas it is an excellent idea to keep in touch with both existing and prospective customers, the point of the exercise is to obtain a response or a sale. Both objectives are better achieved when an offer or a benefit is the reason for the mailing.

Each mailing therefore should seek a response, and the type of response required has to be clearly identified from the start. Then you have measurement and accountability – feedback from the mailing that can be evaluated by numbers, sales and cost so that responses can be tested and adjustments made to the approach.

A message about the right product effectively communicated to the right people should elicit a response, but with even the best offers there is the human inertia syndrome to overcome. Response rates will vary depending on the appeal of the offer, but anything over 3 per cent can be considered good, and anything over 7 per cent outstanding. Different creative approaches and variations to the offer can be tried to test the best response rate.

Various offers that can be made

- A *free trial* or *demonstration offer* is one of the best because it asks the recipients to do something without conditions attached. They simply have to try the meal, the drink or the facility. This trial offer approach suits the service products of hospitality because they can seldom be seen, felt, handled or experienced in advance.
- The *conditional sale offer* means offering the use of a facility at a special rate provided that, if satisfied, the recipient will continue to purchase.
- The *positive option offer* means that by paying a fee and joining a club the customer can buy a range of goods or products at very reduced prices.
- A *'your choice' offer* is when customers are offered a range of specially discounted products from which they can choose one or two. It is a good way of determining the popularity of various hospitality products by measuring the responses to each one.

- *Discount offers* are straight money-off propositions. No mystery about these, and they can be offered to attract customers during a down period, such as for a business traveller's hotel like the Hyatt Regency, Adelaide (Figure 30.1).
- A *'refund-if-not-satisfied offer'* is a good way to introduce a new product such as a special food item, business facility or even a small item like a new beer.
- There are also *'you-can-win offers'*, which are always popular with customers. They can be used as an inducement to try a facility, or simply to respond by sending back a coupon or token. The responses will often reveal the degree of interest by customers in a product, which can be used for a follow-up call by a sales person.
- *Limited time offers* are added motivations for customers to respond to any offer, and they often overcome people's natural inertia.

Direct mail strategic development

In the preparation of any promotion it is necessary to have defined and measurable strategic objectives. The choice of the right mix of message delivery systems will be determined by the markets to be targeted and their accessibility.

Direct mail is very popular in the hospitality industry, perhaps in the mistaken belief that it is relatively inexpensive. However, it has to be borne in mind that direct mail is really only cost-effective when it makes an offer and when the people to be targeted can be named so that the mailing can be personalized. Some messages are not suitable for direct mail. Simply using it to build an image, for instance, does not suit direct mail as well as advertising, which is more cost-effective and reaches a larger audience.

Direct mail, like all correspondence, is a more subtle medium than most users realize. Think of direct mail in the same way as you would correspondence with a pen-friend or acquaintance some distance away. One letter does not bond you to the writer, but consistent letters tell you that the person cares for you and eventually you warm to the writer. You want to meet the person after a while and cement the friendship. For the hospitality industry, this is the subtlety that has to be conjured by direct mail, which is quite unlike some of the obtrusive uses made of the medium by other industries.

This is how the property is customized so that the gift of friendship has meaning for customers. Customizing should not be an act or gesture. The more authentic the offer and the way it is presented the more effective it will become. Do not say, 'This is a genuine offer'. Does that mean that previous offers were not? Few people are fooled by trite statements like: 'Yes, that's right! For only £1 you will get . . .'. It follows that, with direct mail, the products will be promoted and the offer have to suit not only the customer mix of the property, but the individuals who comprise the mix.

When it is decided that direct mail suits the product and the customer mix to be targeted, you have to develop a proposition that has a distinct price benefit or immediate advantage for the recipient. 'What's in it for me?' is the question that has to be answered by the proposition in the mailing piece. Then comes the creative part – working the offer into a communication which tells

There are many ways to go to a show at the new Entertainment Centre - but none compare with the 'Great Stretch' package offered by Hyatt Regency Adelaide.

'Great Stretch' starts with secure valet parking at Hyatt - well away from the congestion around the Entertainment Centre.

A complimentary glass of Hardys Sir James champagne and a delicious pre-show cold buffet in Riverside follows.

Your chauffeur driven Hughes limousine then takes you from Hyatt to the Entertainment Centre and, of course, back to the hotel.

Finally, it's up to Shiki for a supper of salmon and steak with dessert and coffee.

Available Tues-Thurs for $63, or Fri-Sat for $65 per person,'Great Stretch' is the only way to go to and from a show at the Entertainment Centre. Enquiries and bookings, telephone (08) 231 1234.

SIR JAMES

VISA
WEEKEND

Celebrating an anniversary? Having a night on the town? Need a blissfully undisturbed weekend away from the kids? No excuses necessary, you deserve the pampered pleasures of a 'Visa weekend'! This top value package includes valet parking, champagne on arrival, a deluxe room, two complimentary drinks at The Atrium Lounge and Continental breakfast. Only $175 per room per night.

Offer valid at time of printing.

WINNERS
WEEKEND

Bring your lucky horse shoe along to this one! Our 'Winners Weekend' offers champagne on arrival, two complimentary drinks in The Atrium Lounge, priority access to the Casino, a $20 discount voucher for the Pullman restaurant, Five Lucky Dollars and the chance to win back the price of one night's accommodation on the Lucky Wheel. At $169 per room per night, 'Winners Weekend' is the best deal in town — apart from a Royal Flush that is!

Offer valid at time of printing.

Figure 30.1 *The Hyatt Regency, Adelaide*

the recipients what they will get in the clearest terms and which overcomes the natural worry of making a decision. Essential to the composition of the direct mailing piece is to provide easy response methods, such as a reply-paid envelope, a freephone number, a gift voucher or coupon that can only be redeemed by personal attendance at the property.

Direct mail should never be considered a one-off attempt to win customers. It works as a planned series of communications which are scheduled in with carefully timed intervals between them.

Direct mail creative tips

Organizations such as *Time* and *Readers' Digest* have built up a formidable business around direct mail which most people in business have experienced at some time. Even though it can be a bit annoying to be constantly addressed personally when you know they do not know you from a bar of soap, it is still preferable to being addressed as 'Dear reader' or 'Dear customer'.

Direct mail does not have to be in the form of a letter – it can be a leaflet, postcard or brochure, and yet it will always be better received if it is written as a letter and there is some reference made to the receiver as an individual. For example, it is better to start with a statement that recognizes who or what they are. If you know nothing else, this can be achieved by acknowledging the profession, interest or occupation of the person. Let us assume that the recipient is an accountant:

'In your day-to-day occupation, you have to constantly assess the relevance and accuracy of the figures put before you. Would you mind pausing for a moment or two to add up the financial benefits that will accrue to you if . . .'

In this example, you do not know any more about the person other than that he or she is an accountant, but at least you are writing in a way that gives you some affinity with the recipient.

It would be better still if you have more information about the person. Let us take the example of a letter written to the accountant who has dined three times at a restaurant, and you also know that she is married:

'Dear Mrs Williams, You have dined at our establishment several times in a professional capacity, and we would like you to experience our services in a social way. May we express our appreciation of your patronage by offering you . . .'

Some hints are as follows:

- There is no need to grovel when you write a business letter. You must keep your dignity, but endeavour to express warmth and friendship while remaining businesslike. The analogy of the distant pen-friend is a good way of thinking about how you should express your message.
- Always get to the point in the first or second sentence. Make your offer early and be quite clear about what you are saying.

- Support what you say if you like with a leaflet or brochure with a reply-paid envelope, telephone number, or even a promise to call for the person's response.
- Talk in terms of benefits to the customer. Not 'What we have is. . .', but rather, 'What you will get is . . .' Talk to the customer. Court him or her. Do not 'hard sell'. You want to be their long-serving friend.
- Do not stint on quality. Use colour and lots of pictures in your collateral material if you can afford it. Excite and enthuse, but do not make the message flowery and full of adjectives. In the main you will be writing to business people. Economy of words is what they are used to and want. However, do not be so brief as to leave out vital information.
- Good letter writing is a carefully developed skill. If you feel uncertain, employ the services of an expert.

Remember, your image, and therefore the position of your property, is on show when you write, so do not think of direct mail as being a separate part of your promotion strategies. However, do consider the medium and its ability to be personal and have the capacity to reach out to the heart and mind of your receiver with the offer of friendship and interest.

Questions for discussion or revision

1 A three-star hotel of 200 rooms is located in a city which is a major tourist destination for overseas visitors. The competition is intense and there are numerous hotels competing for the tourist pound and thousands of travel agencies around the world which can recommend clients. The hotel features two good restaurants: one is fine dining and the other is a brasserie for the casual diner. In the way of recreational facilities, it has a swimming pool, spa, sauna, well equipped fitness centre and four squash courts. The sustainable competitive advantage of the hotel is its massive five-storey car park which can accommodate 400 cars. Your task is to plan a direct mail campaign which will economically produce awareness of the property and increase its share of the tourist market. You will need to decide to whom the mailing will be sent (target markets), what the main message will be, how many prices will be involved in the package and which inducements you would use to interest the travel agents.
2 List the chief advantages of direct mail.
3 Your tennis club is fifty years old, but due to increased competition from new clubs, membership has been steadily falling. You have changed and up-graded the courts and the clubhouse facilities. The next task is to increase membership. What direct mail strategies would you use to communicate the changes to members and potential members?

Further reading

Middleton, V. (1994). *Marketing in Travel and Tourism*. Oxford: Butterworth-Heinemann.

31 *Product development strategies*

Aim of this chapter

To explain how to develop new products and improve existing products, and how product development can rejuvenate an establishment by giving the customers a better experience.

The theory

Marketing students at a well-known hotel school are asked each semester to do an exercise on product development. Their task is to think of new ways of doing the ordinary things of hospitality like serving a beer or serving soups. Each semester it is the same – the students overwhelm the lecturers with great new ways of doing things that make commercial sense – that is to say, ideas that would work in the marketplace, please the customers and make money.

The trouble is, you will probably never see any of their ideas used by a commercial operator. Why? Because hospitality is one of the most traditional and conservative industries in the world. It should not be. Entertaining, giving people good food and wine and providing pleasant places to sleep is fun, and for the customers it is one of the most consistent and enjoyable features of life on this planet. And yet, from one side of the world to the other there is a dreary sameness about the way things are done in too many restaurants and hotels. Some owners are wary and frightened of innovation, of daring to be too different. Others are too stubborn. They do not listen to their customers and believe that they know best. Most owners worry about how much it will cost to change or improve things. The funny part about that is that the improvements which are appreciated most by customers are simply in the way things are done, and those sorts of improvements cost nothing.

The world is full of property owners who start out with the premise that it is theirs to do what they like with it, and they do, irrespective of the customers' preferences and needs. They overlook the point that the customers think that it is their place and that is the reason why they keep coming back. All that sensible owners have to do is to capitalize on that innate sense of proprietary interest and encourage the customers to involve themselves in the property and they will always have loyal, and mostly forgiving, clients.

The American situation comedy, 'Cheers', was a classic portrayal of the comradeship that should be part of an integrated relationship between customers, staff and management. Human beings are prone to adopt a confrontation situation, an 'us or them' attitude. Owners and managers who think like that try to get all they can, and go for every penny that can be extracted from the customer. They are traders, and trade is not the way to do business in hospitality. Improving products, developing exciting new ones for the customers' enjoyment, is the zest of hospitality. It does not mean being zany, although being zany is better than being boring. It means that managements have to think harder about making their places better places for their customers.

A hotel depends on the continuing success of its base products – its room hire, restaurants and bars. If any of these key areas of revenue are not working properly, it affects other products, its market position and profit. This means that management must constantly appraise the performances of its products in search of doing everything better than before while maintaining that sense of excitement and interest.

Product development, either through improvement or modification, is a growth strategy. Its purpose is to retain existing customers and attract new customers. Product development is a continuing concern. Management has to improve sales, if possible, remain competitive and increase or maintain profit levels by improving the products by adding new experiences for the customers.

Product life cycles

Every product (and the hotel itself is included) has a life cycle which involves a series of stages:

- *Development*, which is where the product is conceived, researched and market analysed, target markets selected, the product is tested, given a feasibility study and made ready for sale, provided that it passes all the test criteria.
- *Introduction*, when the product is exposed to the customers and given promotion to provide awareness and assist in the selling process.
- *Growth* occurs if the product is accepted by the customers, and if it is, sales begin to repay the effort of creating the product.
- *Maturation*, when the product has reached the peak of its sales performance and is providing good profits. It is also when there is considerable competition from other organizations.
- *Decline*, when the product becomes a bit boring and sales begin a steady slide downwards.
- *Death or revitalization*, when the management has to decide whether to let the product die a natural death or revitalize it in some way.

Depending on the product, each of these stages can either be drawn out or startlingly brief. Without growth or innovation, a hotel, restaurant or any hospitality establishment faces the problem of looking like a tired facility, a ghost which haunts every establishment after it has been in business for a while. Innovation, glamour and glitz always appeal to the fickle publics of hospitality, and many customers move on when they get the feeling that a place has lost its edge: 'It isn't as good as it used to be'.

Beware of drastic change

Product development can represent a problem for management because change usually has a broad range of effects and unpredictable outcomes. It is a time when disastrous mistakes can occur. Most of them happen as a result of management making changes to increase sales without checking to find out if the changes are what the customers want.

New is not necessarily better. There is no point in changing a winning formula; just keep on improving it. It is not that people do not like change, it is just that they do not like being changed. They hate being told, 'Things are going to be different around here. What we're going to do is . . .'. Therefore before changes are made their outcomes need to be forecasted and assessed.

For example, in order to increase bar sales a hotel may decide to extend its public bar, redecorate it and add two additional bar people to cope with the supposed lift in sales, the presumption being that there is sufficient demand to warrant the expenditure. That is fine, but an examination of all the factors affected by change could alter that decision. For example:

- How will the bar extensions be accepted by the existing patrons? Most people are very funny about change. They even have their favourite positions at the bar, or favourite table, and are quite put out when someone else occupies 'their' area. Will many customers be lost when their 'old haunt' changes from being a cosy, busy bar to a larger, less private and even strange environment?
- How many new customers will be attracted just because the bar is now bigger? Is size enough to get them to change their habits? Perhaps the demand has been assessed on the number of occasions that the bar 'fills' and becomes cramped. Is that really preventing a number of 'new' customers from drinking there? Most customers like to be part of a 'crowd'.
- What will happen to costs if more staff are allocated?
- If the additional customers do not materialize, what will happen to profits?
- How will the staff react to the proposed extension? Are they in favour of it? Maybe the bar is very popular as it is because of their personalities and they do not want new staff members sharing their patch.

It could be that an additional bar would achieve the same objective. Or it may be better to attract customers at other times of the day by offering 'happy hours', with drinks reduced to half price, or 'feeding times', with free snacks on offer. To get more use from the same bar may make sense and achieve the desired objective of increased sales without adding to infrastructure costs and running the risk of losing existing custom.

	INCREASE	DECREASE	NO CHANGE	OUTCOME £
CUSTOMER APPRECIATION				
NO. EXISTING CUSTOMERS				
NO. NEW CUSTOMERS				
PRICES				
SALES				
COSTS – BUILDING				
COSTS – RESOURCE ALLOCATION				
MARKET SHARE				
STAFF GOODWILL				
PROPERTY VALUE				
PROFIT				

Tick whether the outcome will result in an increase, decrease or no
change, and if applicable, express the probable outcome in pound terms.

Figure 31.1 *Outcome assessment table*

Assessing the outcome of change

The starting point for developing a product or improving it involves consultation with the customers and research. Time and time again, this will reveal
some improvement, modification or change that will help to increase sales,
build customer numbers, improve market share or reduce costs. Sometimes
the assessment will reveal that the product or facility should be closed down
because it has exceeded its useful life.

When seeking to improve or change a product there is a host of strategic
options to consider, involving promotion, staff, price offers, change in merchandise, product presentation, infrastructure, decor, product quality, efficiency,
timing quantity, systems, specialization, productivity, expansion, contraction
or diversification. Which strategic option will be best to use?

The 'outcome assessment table' shown in Figure 31.1 is designed for management to use as a tool for evaluating product changes and their probable
outcomes. It is simply a screening process for the ideas and strategic options
put forward. Its purpose is to cover the factors that may be impacted by
change and to forecast the effects over six months. Research should be used to
test the reactions of customers, existing and potential, and establish which
solutions are the least disruptive and promise the best outcome.

After careful screening of all the options using the outcome assessment
table, the concept which indicates the most positive finding is chosen and
it becomes the strategy for product development. Goals are then set for the

product changes and the strategy is implemented. After six months, all the factors are checked and compared with the forecasts. If the outcomes have not met the objectives, further changes may be required and the process is repeated.

The expectations of the customers

The reasons why people choose to use any establishment's facilities provide the key to product development. Whereas accommodation and food are the basic reasons, the added value they seek may be convenience, escape, companionship, an unusual experience, a special occasion, a popular activity, entertainment, fun, comfort or sheer indulgence. Certainly their choice of establishment will be influenced by the friendliness of the staff. There is also class consciousness which influences many people, most preferring to be with their own 'types'. The popularity of a place is a strong draw card for others. There is a sense of security when people are with others like themselves.

The key to product development in most cases is to build on a successful product base and a sound position in the market. Only when there is nothing to lose by drastic change should it be contemplated.

When property owners are faced with a 'death or revitalization' option there is always a tendency to blame the location or the building itself, and they either refurbish or sell. If they sell, what often happens is that the new owners buy a lemon and do no better than the previous owners. Something really different and better in the way of customer experiences may turn around the fortunes of the place. It is not easy. A place which becomes run-down becomes tainted by its reputation.

Opportunities for product development

Managing an establishment in the hospitality industry is like directing a live theatre performance. It is a long-running show that should keep on getting better and better. If it is a good show, people will come from miles around to experience and enjoy the actors' performances. This means developing exciting and interesting new products, which in most cases will simply be innovative ways of doing things that most places do.

The secret of Club Mediterranean, a company which has marketed organized holidays around villages built by the company in attractive, beachside locations, was not the concept of cheap holidays so much as having fun-loving organizer managers. The organizers were carefully chosen for their friendliness, love of fun and the ability to involve people in activities. They were always gracious hosts and the heart and soul of the villages.

Club Med has now been going for forty years, and it too has changed over the years to meet the changes in people's needs. The owners use targeting to pick their markets as a result of focus groups and extensive studies of customer behaviour. Their products are then carefully developed to satisfy new markets while never losing sight of the basics of their successful operation.

The best hospitality establishments have a flair for making people feel relaxed, comfortable and welcome. They provide a busy, sometimes even noisy, environment with lots of things happening and many people coming and going for customers who like that. They also consider those who prefer quietness, privacy and solitude, and make sure there is a special place where people can retreat when they need to be that 'away from the madding crowd'.

Hospitality is about providing customers with a sense of occasion, the feeling of being involved in something special. And, as has been said many times, it's the extras that count, and that means developing the way of doing things which goes beyond the customers' expectations. Be a miser, and you will make people miserable.

Forget new systems as a means of attracting new customers unless the system is perceived by the customers to be of direct benefit to them. Systems are designed for the operation's efficiency. As Michael Hurst says, 'You can go out of business in an organized way.'

Give customers something to talk about. Let them take away a memory of a wonderful occasion. That requires management to develop products which customize the place. It means shaping the products so that they are special and different for individuals and which avoid the pursuit of sameness. There is not a right or wrong way to do things, only ways that customers appreciate.

Products make statements about people. What you offer tells the customers the sort of place yours is. What they expect and will accept from a place tells everyone the sort of person they are. Therefore management should set out to capture markets that have a synergy with each other and, with your customer mix in mind, let them grow with you. Explain the reasons for the improvements so that they appreciate what you are doing for them. Unless a hotel has completely 'lost its soul', management should seldom consider abandoning its core base of customers, but should concentrate on building on the existing base.

Improve before thinking of change

Management would do better to think of improving rather than changing. It makes sense to do what a place is doing better than to try to do what someone else is doing and not do it as well. Products can be developed independently of each other. A place can make gradual changes to each product without exciting the natives, perhaps beginning with a new concept themed bar while retaining the old faithful. When the new one gains acceptance renovate the old one, then move on with the planned improvements to the restaurants, and so on.

Synergy is the relationship between the place's mission, positioning and its distinctive competencies. Hart and Troy (1986) say that synergy is the key criterion used to evaluate growth options and guide investment and new product development decisions. It is especially critical in regard to considerations involving diversification because diversification in this area often involves taking on business that may be new and unfamiliar to current management. Financial troubles may result from over-extended resources when a company fails to evaluate growth opportunities in terms of basic synergies.

There are many effective product development strategies to consider which can be added to existing products. A hotel, for instance, should think about increasing the range and nature of merchandise on offer through shops, bars and reception areas. There may be scope to develop interesting holiday packages, local tours, discount vouchers for shops, ticketing facilities for theatres, sporting events, casinos, etc. If the restaurants and the food are a feature of an establishment, it may consider offering new eating experiences. In this case, it would be best to use the Michael Hurst approach and experiment with different dishes and, when the customers are vocal in their approval, make the dishes a regular item on the menu.

Opportunities could exist for capitalizing on assets by up-grading some sections of the accommodation into different categories, such as self-catering apartments, family suites, temporary offices, display areas. If there is a swimming pool, perhaps add saunas, massage, swimming lessons, water aerobics, etc.

Cycles, fads, fashions and trends

Many establishments offer a wide range of services. Adding more presents a problem when they would rather remove many of the less profitable ones. The retraction of services and facilities which customers have come to expect is difficult. However, the same outcome analysis can be used, this time to test how many customers would be lost by the change.

With all new products, experimentation is important before final commitment. Test marketing saves time and money and avoids the embarrassment of failure.

New concepts take time as a rule before there is market acceptance. This is called the diffusion process. Some people are early adopters and others (called laggards) take time to accept change. The greater the relative advantage of a new concept to the customer the more compatible it will be with his or her status and lifestyle and, as a consequence, the sooner it will be purchased.

One of the barriers to acceptance is complexity. Another barrier is communication. The easier it is to communicate a new idea and the simpler the idea is, the more readily it will be understood.

Timing the introduction of a new product is also vital. Changes can be too soon, too late, or ill-timed. Feeling the mood of the customers is the only way to judge timing.

Three other issues can influence product development strategies:

- *Recycling*. Investigate old ideas that can be reintroduced. In fact, most of today's new concepts are yesterday's old concepts in different clothes. The advantage of copying old ideas that will suit today's markets is that they have a track record, a history of success that can be emulated and examples of failures that can be avoided.
- *Fads and fashions*. These are mostly different ways of doing the same thing. They are often copied by others and then they become 'what everybody does' and lose their point and value. There is no doubt that to ignore them

can be folly, but to slavishly follow them is often economically unsound for establishments building an individual positioning image.
- *Trends*. These are usually decided by economic and technological developments. When times are good, people travel and spend more, and the opposite occurs when the economy tightens. There are usually early indicators of trends. However, many of these indicators seem to be missed by operators who then find themselves reacting to change instead of planning for it.

Hospitality is a person-to-person, customized business, and the volatility of its markets means that situations seldom remain stable. To be successful, management must be thinking all the time about how to make the place better for customers. Product development is not just the key to success, it is also the means of survival.

Questions for discussion or revision

1   Your restaurant has been successful for the last ten years and business has remained steady until now. Do you make changes? If so, explain why. Also, describe the types of changes you would contemplate.
2   Explain how synergy works in a large hotel with many outlets such as restaurants, coffee shops, bars and a variety of room and suite categories.
3   List the various options for growth.

Further reading

Hart, G. and Troy, J. (1986). *Strategic Hotel/Motel Marketing*. Educational Institute, American Motel & Hotel Association, Michigan.

32 Forecasting market demand

Aim of this chapter

To explain the purpose of forecasting market demand, how it can be used and to provide an outline of the methodologies which are available.

The theory and the practice

Owners of hospitality properties and management generally seem to have an optimistic view of the future of their establishments. Their belief is that promotion glamour, glitz and hype will override all other market indicators and return a handsome profit on their investment. This is the classic delusion of McCarthy (1978): 'Build a better mousetrap and the world will beat a path to your door.'

In the UK between 1989 and 1990, hoteliers desperately tried to hold their average room rates as, due to the recession, occupancy began to fall. By 1991 discounting of room rates was widespread and continued to be so until demand started to recover in 1994, but the level of discounting still remained high. Hoteliers were advised by Horwath and Horwath (1993) to capitalize on the increased demand, beginning to restore average room rates by reducing discounts as soon as demand is sufficiently strong to permit it. What the recession taught today's customer is that there are plenty of hotels in the UK, the majority of which are desperate for their business.

It could be said that economically the late 1980s and early 1990s were exceptionally bad around the world, and that being caught in such circumstances was an understandable error. And yet history has a habit of repeating itself. There are still many operators who blithely set sales quotas each year in the belief that markets will grow because the recession will soon go away and boom times will be resumed. Even the most optimistic economists are not saying that.

Accurate forecasting based on a careful assessment of market and economic indicators is one of the most critical aspects of business planning. Massive sums of money and the commitment of human resources depend on good forecasting.

It is not an easy task because there must be an element of risk in every venture. No-one can truly predict the future. However, the purpose of forecasting market demand is to minimize the risks and leave only totally unpredictable events to chance. Even then, good marketers should always allow for the unpredictable by planning for a fall-back position. The reasons for forecasting are:

- to provide a diagnostic tool for setting corporate objectives for sales, profit and asset realization;
- to provide an early warning system to protect the organization's assets in investment capital, knowledge, staff, premises, facilities and equipment, etc.

Market size

The size of a market is assessed by adding up the total sales of each market category affecting the hospitality industry, such as bed-night sales, wine, beer and spirit sales. Most governments produce statistics from which the industry can extract information required to get a historical picture of market size, and from there predict its potential for the forthcoming year after making allowances for known market factors which could affect the result.

Market expansion occurs as a result of demands created by population increases, migration intakes, increased numbers of tourists, new trends in product usage or economic changes which increase the amount of discretionary expenditure available to the population. A market in recession occurs when the demand for travel by holidaymakers or businesses decreases from all sources. These are termed 'market factors'. A market factor is an item, consumer behaviour pattern or set of circumstances which is affecting the market demand for a product and which therefore will affect the market's total sales potential.

The market demand for a product is the anticipated number of customers who, based on previous sales and trends, would buy hospitality products in a given location over a specified period of time. The market potential for a product is the anticipated total number of sales of a product by all sellers in the market over a specified period of time given a defined set of circumstances. When market demand and market potential are roughly calculated, a property can estimate its share of the total market or its share of some segments of that market. It can also decide which share it wants in the future.

Sometimes, despite market factors, it is how the user and the consumer respond to the forces of change which will dictate the expansion or contraction of demand. For instance, it is fair to say that there has been a worldwide trend towards more people eating away from home, and it can be anticipated that this trend will continue and overcome the frailties of the economic situation.

Predicting the future is a guessing game. The majority of economists have been made to look a little foolish in the last twenty years. Some can say with modest justification that they have been proved less wrong than others in their predictions, but which economist will be right next time is still the gamble it ever was. The best that anyone can say is that the demand for hospitality will continue. Four thousand years of history says that it will always be a viable business in which to be involved.

Management often does not heed the fact that in a static market any growth must occur at the expense of other establishments. This means that the property's marketing strategies have to offer an SCA to keep their existing customer base while attempting to get the customers from rival establishments to break with habit, or their loyalty, and shift their business to them.

If investors and new business owners are looking for reassurance on return for their capital, they can do no better than to assess the future of a property on the ability of their marketing strategies to perform competitively. A realistic appraisal of the amount of business that can be captured from the targeted customer groups, together with favourable market factors, is a sound basis for forecasting sales. When coupled with the arithmetic of costs and return on capital, investors can be more certain of their outlay.

A 'market forecast' is the realistic anticipation of market demand for a product provided that the expected circumstances prevail. From the market forecast, a property can make a sales forecast in financial terms or numbers of units upon which it prepares a sales budget. Production and expenditure estimates are then set, based on the sales forecast which will direct the operation's performance over the ensuing budgetary period within prescribed financial guidelines.

Market factor analysis

Forecasting relies on a combination of several or all of the methods which examine market factors. When attempting to measure demand and forecast change, management must specify what it wants measured. For instance, in forecasting luxury hotel accommodation requirements it would be misleading to predict demand merely on the basis of a general increase in travel to the area near the establishment. The travellers may be caravan owners, families in cars or backpackers with limited or no interest in the property.

Forecasting must be measured against demand criteria which predict and segment, such as:

- numbers of people by their demographic and psychographic types and geographic origins;
- numbers of people by their requirements for products, frequency of purchase, duration of stay;
- numbers of people by unit sales and their financial expenditure;
- numbers of competitors after the same market segments.

Using the above criteria, the history of the market measured over several years is an indication of trends which can be projected into the forthcoming year. However, such projections have to be modified by the information acquired from various other forecasting methods. Havoc can be wreaked with a projection which is merely based on trends and fails to consider shifts in market preferences, impending economic change or government intervention.

If a project is so finely balanced that the profit, interest repayments and required capital return on the investment cannot withstand a 25 per cent short-fall in the forecast sales, it becomes a gamble and not a venture, and it would be unwise to proceed. Many properties rely heavily on asset growth and the sale of the property to make their investment worthwhile. It has been accepted practice, for example, to believe that capital recovery requires seven to ten years for completion. That is an arguable proposition. Running costs are variable and can be adjusted to match sales. The fixed costs of rent, interest repayments and capital recovery march on remorselessly despite the sales, often making a mockery of profit projections.

There should not be too much reliance on asset growth because the tangible assets of a hospitality property, such as the real estate (building and land), stock and fittings and goodwill (number of customers, sales and profit), tend to depreciate in real value terms (after the inflationary effect is discounted) when there is a declining market.

What it all means from an investment viewpoint is that the viability of a hospitality venture is more dependent upon strategic marketing than the real estate because the real estate value in most cases relies on the income-earning potential of the business. A high-income-earning property which has a burgeoning customer base is worth money. A tired property with waning customer interest is not.

Market research and market analysis

Market research and market analysis are used to find out whether there is untapped potential for sales in the current market. There may be people who cannot use the facilities because of cost, do not find the facilities attractive enough to use, have been given no reason to use the facilities or cannot travel to the establishment easily. This situation can change when markets from other countries are opened up by increased transport capacity, a new airport or better flight schedules. Market analysis can also indicate whether the total market can be increased, or whether the competition is vulnerable to attack.

Surveys of buyers' intentions

Market research among known users of hospitality can be an effective way of estimating demand. When their responses are graded from 'almost certain' down to 'most unlikely', a mean is taken of their total responses.

Economic indicators

The market factors which affect demand are mainly changes in economic conditions. These are the most useful indicators of future alterations to the market environment, such as significant changes to interest rates, wages, personal taxation, company taxation, investment incentives, availability of credit, tariffs, exchange rates, etc.

Leading indicators

There is a sales lag between some goods which has a pass-on effect to others. In the building industry, for example, architectural activity, finance applications and tenders called indicate the amount of building work in the pipeline which will filter through the whole economy. In the hospitality industry, it is often travel agencies and tourist information centres which first notice changes in interest by the travelling public. Financiers, banks and trade commissioners also are able to note the attitudes of business towards corporate expansion or contraction and therefore the likelihood of there being an increase or decrease in business travel.

Impending events

Along with economic indicators, impending events of considerable interest to people who are known producers of business for industry are reliable indicators of increased demand, such as large festivals, sporting events, big development projects, new industries, better transport facilities, etc.

Extension of demand curve

This is called statistical demand analysis (or correlation analysis), and it is a set of procedures designed to discover and rate the market factors affecting demand, such as prices, incomes, population, market size, promotion, product evolution or innovation.

Measurement of trends

Trends are like contagious diseases which spread from region to region and country to country. Observable changes to the hospitality industry in other countries can be transferred and possibly win acceptance in one's own country or region. Assessment of these is made on:

- the size of the market, its demographics, the cities, regions and countries it has affected, the kinds of outlets used and the rate of rise and fall of the trend;
- cyclicality of market behaviour – who uses, buys or influences, their social class, lifestyle, personality type and the utilitarian, fashion, fun or psychological need it satisfies.

The property's potential

Forecasting is relevant to the property's capacity to meet demand on its premises, facilities, staff and finances. As a result of forecasts, management can plan for change and capitalize on growth opportunities through either market development or product development.

A market is seldom as big as everyone expects. With so much investment in premises, equipment and people involved, it is better to err on the side of caution than optimism. But then, that is unlikely because the industry seems to prosper on the hopes and enthusiasm of its participants, which is why hospitality is arguably the world's most exciting industry.

Questions for discussion or revision

1 List the reasons for forecasting.
2 Explain the terms 'market demand', 'market potential' and 'market factors'.
3 Describe the main methodologies that are applied when forecasting demand.

Further reading

Horwath & Horwath (1993). *Business Review*, Horwath & Horwath Consulting, London.
McCarthy, E. (1978). *Basic Marketing*. USA. Richard D. Irwin Inc.

33 Product strategies: how to provide a better experience for your customers

Aims of this chapter

1   To explain why product strategies should be customized and to provide an experience that attracts and retains customers.
2   To outline some examples of how a property can use product strategies to achieve an SCA.

The theory

Every hospitality property in the world will sell you either a bed, some food or a drink. It is how a place does things which makes the difference between the experience being ordinary and being special. In most cases, the difference is between gaining customers and losing them. You could say that how a place does things is its style. Actually, its style is how the place considers its customers.

The way you do things is a product. If you want more customers, make sure that what you do is distinctively your product, an entity that not only provides a difference, but offers obvious benefits for your customers. When you do that, you have an SCA.

Hospitality is a series of products which have to be customer-orientated to work. The emphasis – therefore – has to be on product strategies – the means by which you provide a better experience for your customers. The only way to succeed in business is to think about strategies all the time; to think about pleasing, appealing in which and the surprising ways you can make being at your place a better experience for customers.

You should always aim to create for customers a sense of ownership or belonging to an establishment. Regulars at a local pub feel this and love it. It is harder to achieve with transients. Even so, some sense of being wanted and being among friends is important to everyone. For the long-distance traveller, a place which offers these sorts of attributes is providing a haven of solace, he or she and will return when the opportunity is presented. If not, he or she will pass on memories of the pleasant experience to others. This is how solid reputations are built, not with crystal, silver, marble and chandeliers.

The enemies of hospitality strategies are apathy, ignorance and arrogance. In any failing establishment, it is always one or more of these shortcomings which are plainly evident, and it is because the owners are in the business only for the money and not the customers. They push for every penny they can get. They cut back on the food portions, reduce the staffing level, minimize the hours they trade and try to sell instead of serving.

'Everyone does it that way. Why change?' That is a typical apathy response. 'That's good enough, it's too hard, why worry, the guests seem to be happy enough,' are other typical comments from people who lack interest or enthusiasm for their customers.

Ignorance is lack of empathy for the customer, an inability to understand his or her needs. It is associated with a person who lacks interest in alternative strategies and is devoid of imagination.

Arrogance is a disdain for any other point of view than the person's own. It is typical of the type who believes that he or she knows what the customer will like. They brook no argument and get furious when the customers reject their plans. It is always someone else's fault.

Some people are so busy being in business that they forget that the customers are the reason why they are in business.

Examples of apathy, ignorance and arrogance outside the hospitality industry abound: doctors and hospitals who turn people into victims instead of customers in need of help. Public servants who do not serve the public. Builders who build to suit their pocket instead of the owner's comfort. Appliances that meet the manufacturer's cost economies instead of the users' needs. Manuals that are not easily understood. Public transport that suits the staff rosters instead of travellers' needs. Many of life's frustrations are simply caused by people who do not consider other people. It is bad enough in ordinary business. In the hospitality sector it is business suicide.

Business is people

Business is people. As Michael Hurst says:

> I realised that the customer was important, but suddenly I saw that the most important people to me were my front of house/guest contact people. All the rest of us were supporters in making them look great. With that in mind, the internal focus had to be first on recruitment and selection, but then more importantly, on making the work exciting and fun. The whole thing couldn't be labour. The guest experience was determined by the staff performance and that was geared the way I directed them. Service was and is the highest level of competition in the hospitality industry. Giving away the gift of friendship is as important or even more so than good food, the decor, etc. The lesson I took so long to learn is that the

greatest compliment I can get is, 'Where do you get the nice people who work here?'

Back to the basics

Hotels seem to have lost the plot in contemporary times. The idea of offering travellers a place of friendship, solace, comfort and warmth has been overcome by the demands of getting a return on investment. The competitive push towards building bigger, better, brighter properties to attract the big-spending corporate customers spiralled in the 1980s to the point where each room was costing investors in excess of £1 million, an impossible figure on which to gain a profitable return. There was an over-supply of high-priced accommodation and, coinciding with an economic recession, property values fell.

As a consequence, hotel marketing resorted to auctioning rooms, getting whatever price the customer would wear for the value offered. Discount clubs, packaged deals, added-value services and price-inclusive special facilities became enticements which put the customer into the unhappy role of either haggling for bargains or accepting offers.

The same situation exists today. It can be argued that the customer has never been better off, but in fact the average customer is missing out on the basics of hospitality unless he or she asks for them and pays for them.

The nice, welcoming, home-from-home touches on arrival, such as a fruit basket or afternoon tea, are more likely to be negotiable than something that hotel people do as a matter of custom. Custom is a habitual or usual practice which is created for the comfort and convenience of the customer. Custom is a product strategy. Once, it was the way a place did things that made the customer feel special and made the place special. It should not be an add-on to be paid for by the customer.

Custom seems to have gone out of the window in many of the big properties. The attitude of some is, 'If you want them, you pay for them.' Other hotels will claim in their defence, 'Nothing has changed. All those niceties we still do, it's just that they are included in the price!' Thus the point is made: in a cost-conscious market, hospitality is price-driven rather than customer-driven.

A random sample of hotel users reveals an entirely different picture of what customers want from the way hotels are marketing. Benefits sought by customers from hotels are: friendliness, compatibility with other guests, helpfulness, knowledge, location, comfort, reputation, cleanliness, value, facilities, minimal noise, personalized service and consideration. Few of the respondents to the survey volunteered that they wanted size, impressiveness, luxurious surroundings, free facilities, discounts, fitness centre, pool, spa, restaurants, bars, shops or valet service and free bottles of champagne. Further probing shows that customers do not assess a hotel by the amount of marble, silver or number of chandeliers. The free bottle of champagne is 'nice', but a cup of tea is just as acceptable.

Of course, there are some customers who want and can afford to stay at the most luxurious place in town, but they are human too. The hotels which concentrate on the basics of hospitality and develop product strategies that offer customers recognition, friendship, help, simple comforts, personalized services and consideration will always be the winners.

Examples of product strategies

It would be quite wrong to believe that copying any one of these product strategies will change the fortunes of an establishment. It is the culmination of customer-concerned product strategies, the sum total of customer experiences, which contribute to success. When product strategies become perfunctory services performed by robotic waiters, the magic dies. Business is people, and people means not just the customers but the people who serve the people.

Here are some examples of product strategies which can provide a better experience for customers. The great thing about most of them is that they do not cost a penny to do.

Food strategies

Food starts dying the moment it comes out of the oven or off the stove. To get the food fast to the customer, and hot, use a runner. Michael Hurst explains:

> We use waiters and waitresses. But food servers never leave their station. Runners bring the food from the kitchen and put it on the sidestands. This way, food comes hot from the kitchen and the server can befriend his customers. By using runners I can serve 30 per cent more people. Serve hot foods hot. Make an art of it, not an empty claim. Every restaurant operator claims he serves hot food, but how many do? Serve cold foods cold. Serve salads ice cold.

Choice seems to be a problem for restaurants. Their ideal is to have a set menu because it avoids wastage. Are they so devoid of kitchen skills and imagination that they cannot develop ways of offering a selection of dishes that can still appeal to the customer without waste?

The 'soup of the day' is a classic example of minimal thought by the chef. One soup? How about offering thirty soups to the customer and making it a product strategy? If waste is a worry, soup can be frozen in portions and thawed in minutes by microwave.

How about desserts? There are hordes of customers who regard the main course as something they have to eat before they get to the best part of the meal. Des Hunt, a well-known educator and public speaker, once said: 'Life's so short I would prefer to eat the dessert first.'

Some places have the same menu for months and even years. Michael Hurst believes that hospitality should be fun, for him and the customers. He believes that creativity keeps customers coming back. 'I perceive us as not selling food and beverage, but as trying to provide a pleasant experience for our guests,' he says. 'That's the rule of hospitality.' Hurst, who teaches restaurant management and merchandising at Florida International University, believes that variety and improvement is the constant challenge of the business. He has devised a unique sampling and market research programme which involves servers with customers. The programmes are charged to the advertising budget. 'When I develop a budget, I set aside a bundle for marketing. We have to do things for people who patronise the restaurant to help them enjoy themselves so that when they leave they talk about and recommend the restaurant.'

First, Hurst tests two or three new food items each week. Anyone in the restaurant can contribute ideas, but the final selection is Hurst's. When an item is good and has a chance to get on the menu, it is taste-tested by the employees. If 85 per cent of them think it is good, it goes into the first phase, which is to do nothing for thirty to sixty days except have servers whet customers' appetites by telling them that something new, different and good is coming up. Then Hurst puts his market research programme into effect. Each day a set amount of the new item is prepared. Hurst hand-picks guests as they enter the restaurant and tells them he would like them to try a new item. He does not tell them what it is, but he does ask them to let him know if they like it, and if it should go on the menu. After they have eaten it, the server explains what the item is.

'I want to do unusual foods; things people haven't had before,' says Hurst, who served shark long before Jaws became famous, and promoted alligator into a saleable item. On his lecture circuit he constantly looks for different items. In Australia he found bugs. After going through his research programme he put 'Bugs' on the menu without explanation and everyone had to ask what they were. Actually, bugs are Moreton Bay Bugs and they are like small, delicious crayfish or lobster. He also found 'barking crayfish', and they are now on the menu. In another part of the world he discovered a fish called 'slugs'. It is innovation, creating product strategies all the time that makes people talk about a place, and talk brings more customers.

Hospitality is personal

At the Grape Vine Restaurant in Bothwell, the operation is run for the customers and not for the convenience of the chef and the staff. From the moment it opens at 9 o'clock in the morning until it closes at midnight customers can get whatever they want, from a cup of coffee to a snack, a four-course meal or a pint of ale. It is open all hours, every day of the week, in the heart of a community.

'Who am I to tell people when they should come and eat?' says proprietor Colin Morrison. 'I am here to fit in with the customers' lifestyles, not them with mine. While we have an extensive menu, we get more and more customers with a wide range of food intolerances, so the kitchen is flexible, creating special dishes on order to meet their needs. They are over-the-moon when you offer this service – it's worth it,' says Colin. That is what hospitality is all about – being flexible and willing to satisfy the personal needs of the individual.

As society evolves, more and more people are choosing to live alone. Why then do many restaurants still treat single diners as second-class citizens? At La Grillade, a friendly, Parisian-style brasserie in Leeds, owner Guy Martin-Laval serves between four and six lone diners each evening, some regulars, some newcomers. 'Whatever they spend, we make sure they don't feel like a rare species,' says Martin-Laval. He recognizes that a single person who spends £10 on his or her meal and gets treated well is good business if he or she comes back every week.

The People's Palace, a breathtaking 200-seat riverfront restaurant located in the Royal Festival Hall, London, has a Central Club Table catering for single diners. It is a friendly touch. In addition, single diners are more likely to eat out during the slow midweek evening when there is plenty of capacity. At weekends, they will eat out with their friends. The message here is that the solo diner is good business – it pays to provide welcoming, personal and individual service.

The Allensbank, in Cardiff, has the biggest play area of all Whitbread's Brewers Fayre pubs in the south-west. Every effort has been made to personalize the area to the children's needs, including tiny toilets for the tots and a separate toddler Fun Factory with its own ball pool and soft objects to clamber over. Outside the pens, some effort has been made to appeal to older children, with a Sega Megadrive game. Since it opened six months ago, the family area has been busy throughout the day, with mothers or fathers meeting for coffee, grandparents bringing their family for a treat, and kids' birthday parties. It pays to personalize the hospitality product for the kids, as a result the family area is a big income generator.

Beverages

For most establishments, a drink is just a drink and served much the same as anywhere. Where is their imagination? The way beverages are served presents an ideal opportunity to excite and enthuse the customer. For example, the Japanese have turned serving tea into a ritual ceremony.

We can go in for a coffee anywhere; however, Costas Coffee Bars, which can be seen at major rail stations and airports, offer an immense selection of coffees for their customers' enjoyment. As a result, 'grabbing a coffee' moves from being a basic necessity to a memorable experience.

We consume beverages mainly out of habit and set routines. Wise restaurateurs rethink the habit to put a sparkle into their customers' day, coming up with innovative, fun, interesting ways of doing the same thing.

Serving alcoholic drinks

At the Bonne Accord real ale pub in Glasgow, customers can taste several ales before making their choice. If they feel uncertain, the barman, who is a recognized expert, recommends one. In many Belgium beer bars, litres of beer are served in the most elegant of glass vessels which require wooden stands in order to keep them upright (the vessels that is, not the drinkers, of course). There are dozens of different ways of serving and drinking the same beer. It is fun for the customers, and there is always the yard or half yard of beer for the enterprising drinker looking for a challenge.

There are many different ways of doing things when it comes to serving drink. Ninety-five per cent of places serve them in the same way as everyone else! Where is the sense of fun and excitement for the customers? Drinking should be fun, and the Whitbread TGIF concept has proven the success of this approach.

Giving to get

The last word on the subject comes from Michael Hurst. He learned from a friend called Win Schuler that dining out was a total experience and that people were buying a pleasant experience. That included recognition and friendliness and helping them to have fun. 'Win was a genius at all of them,' said Hurst. 'From the greeting to the goodbye and the good food in between, he proved over and over again his philosophy of 'giving to get'. It is easy to say those words. They do not mean much until you see all the unexpected things that can be done to make the dining experience more pleasant. I learned that money expended to sell my present customers was worth far more than any spent trying to create a new customer. From remembering names to special tables, from lover salads to special appetisers and desserts, the philosophy of 'giving to get' meant exceeding customers' expectations.'

Turning a failing property around

Turning a property around which has slumped into the doldrums requires a change of culture. It needs a whole new attitude from the management across the whole staff. It means eliminating apathy, ignorance and arrogance.

Usually it is too hard to change people who do not understand that business is people and that hospitality is giving to get. To turn a property around means weeding out the ones who do not have the ability to share the gift of friendship and recruiting those who do. It means making the place an enjoyable experience for the staff as well as the customers by giving them goals, incentives and rewards. An establishment should aim to make service a fun thing to do.

Every business has to make a profit. That is as obvious as saying that in order to live we have to breathe. Fixed costs and overheads dwindle rapidly when sales soar. So do not work for budgets, accountants, rosters and regimented systems. The name of the game is customer numbers, and that means trying at all times to turn the customers into unpaid sales people to get those numbers up. Review the product strategies, the way you do things, and provide excitement and interest. Do not go mad and do things which are different for the sake of being different. Do what is going to make the people you target say, 'It's been wonderful. Thank you. I must tell my friends!'

Questions for discussion or revision

1 What is meant by 'giving to get'?
2 What are the main benefits sought by customers, according to research?

3 What would be the five key strategies you would employ to turn a failing property around?

Further reading

Hurst, M. *Restaurant Hospitality*. USA. Penton/IPC.

Index